T. MACCI PLAVTI

CAPTIVI

MACMILLAN AND CO., LIMITED
LONDON · BOMBAY · CALCUTTA
MELBOURNE

THE MACMILLAN COMPANY
NEW YORK · BOSTON · CHICAGO
ATLANTA · SAN FRANCISCO

THE MACMILLAN CO. OF CANADA, LTD.
TORONTO

INTRODUCTION.

THE PLOT OF THE CAPTIVI.

1 Hegio, a rich old gentleman of Aetolia, had two sons; the younger, when a boy of four, was stolen by one of the slaves, Stalagmus, and neither boy nor slave had since been heard of. Twenty years afterwards war broke out between Aetolia and Elis, and Hegio's remaining son Philopolemus, serving in the army, was taken prisoner by the Eleans. Thereupon Hegio, with a view to negotiating an exchange, began to buy the Elean prisoners-of-war who were from time to time sold into slavery by the Aetolian authorities; among them he bought two young men Philocrates and Tyndarus, the latter of whom had in Elis been the slave of the former. This is the state of affairs when the play opens.

2 The scene is a street in front of Hegio's house in a seaport town of Aetolia, and when the curtain rises (or rather falls, for in a Roman theatre the curtain was fixed at the bottom, not the top, and was raised and lowered by pulleys) the two captives are standing, fettered together, at the back of the stage.

3 In the Prologue we are at once informed that of the two captives the one who appears to be the master is really the slave, Tyndarus; he has changed clothes with

his master Philocrates in the hope of facilitating the latter's escape. We are further told that this Tyndarus is no other than the long-lost younger son of Hegio; the slave Stalagmus had taken him to Elis and there sold him to Theodoromedes the father of Philocrates, who had brought him up with his own son, a boy of about the same age. The two boys had become firm friends, and it is on the devotion of Tyndarus to his young master that the whole play turns.

4 In the first scene of Act I., Ergasilus enters; he wears
I. i. a black or dark grey cloak (*pallium*), the recognised stage-dress of a parasite, but lest the spectators should be in any doubt what he is he begins by discussing the parasite's life and its hardships; he then explains that he is the hanger-on of Hegio's family but that, as he has now lost his particular patron, Philopolemus, he is often in sad straits for a dinner.

5 This soliloquy is interrupted by the entrance of Hegio
I. ii. from his house followed by his slave-overseer, to whom he is giving directions that the two captives are no longer to be fettered together but may be allowed a certain amount of liberty. He is accosted by Ergasilus who feelingly laments the loss of Philopolemus. Hegio consoles him by saying that he hopes to manage an exchange with the Elean prisoner; and on the strength of this Ergasilus, alleging that it is his birthday, invites himself to dinner with Hegio. The old man agrees to give him a frugal meal, if he cannot in the meantime get a better invitation, and they part, Hegio returning to his house and Ergasilus going off to the market-place.

6 In the second Act the captives appear in front of the
II. i. house attended by the slave-overseer and his subordinates. They are allowed to have a private conversation, which serves to impress on the audience that Philocrates who is dressed as the slave is really the master, and vice versâ. Philocrates urges Tyndarus by the memory of past

kindness to be faithful to him although no longer under any obligation to be so, and Tyndarus replies that he has proved his loyalty by agreeing to change clothes and stay behind, in order that Philocrates may escape; he implores Philocrates, when he has effected his own escape, not to abandon him to his fate.

7
II. ii. Hegio coming out to question his new purchases, Philocrates at once assumes the pert manner of the stage-slave, and Hegio takes him apart and questions him about the position of his master's family in Elis; Tyndarus creeps up behind to listen and enjoys the adroitness with which Philocrates acts his assumed character. Hegio is told, in order to induce him to think of a ransom, that Philocrates' father is known as Thensaurochrysonicochrysides on account of his fabulous wealth, but that he is as niggardly as he is rich. Turning to Tyndarus, Hegio questions him too apart, and Tyndarus (who, it must not be forgotten, is Hegio's own son) assumes an air of high-souled resignation such as would become a freeborn man who had fallen into adversity, and assures Hegio that he is the son of a rich father. Only the audience know the real facts and are able to enjoy the spectacle of Tyndarus doing his best to deceive Hegio and yet occasionally telling the truth in spite of himself. Hegio then proposes an exchange for his own son who, he has learnt, has been sold in Elis to a certain doctor called Menarchus. He is informed that this Menarchus is a client of Philocrates' father, and Tyndarus persuades him to send Philocrates (who is, of course, supposed to be the slave Tyndarus) back to Elis to negotiate the exchange.

8
iii. This arrangement being announced to the pretended slave, Philocrates, he conceals his joy but professes his readiness to do anything he is ordered. In a pathetic scene, which moves the feelings of the old man, Tyndarus appeals to Philocrates not to forget him when safe in his own country, and Philocrates in reply assures him that he

will be true to the trust reposed in him. The language of both is designedly ambiguous, as Hegio is standing by, but the whole of the dialogue is very cleverly managed. Hegio then takes Philocrates away to his banker's to provide him with money for the journey and Tyndarus dejectedly reenters the house.

9 The third Act is opened by Ergasilus who is on his
III. i. way from the market-place to the harbour. This is, he says, the most unfortunate day for him, the meanest and most niggardly day that in his long experience he has ever come across, and he would like to punch its head. He has tried to screw an invitation out of the young men in the market-place, but with one accord they have all refused to have anything to do with him. In the harbour he thinks he may possibly meet some new arrival who in the joy of getting home may give him a dinner, so he sets off there intending, if that last resource fail him, to return and claim Hegio's frugal meal.

10 Hegio then enters and in animated language describes
III. ii. how he has provided Philocrates with journey money and a passport and sent him off to Elis. He has been overwhelmed with the congratulations of his fellow-citizens on what now seems the certainty of recovering his son Philopolemus. He has then gone to a suburban farm where several other Elean prisoners whom he had bought were kept, and has discovered that one of them, Aristophontes, used to be an intimate friend of Philocrates in his own country. At this man's earnest entreaty he has brought him back to town to see his old friend and in the highest of spirits now takes him into the house.

11 No sooner have they gone in than Tyndarus comes
III. iii. running out in a state of the greatest alarm. Aristophontes will of course recognise him, and Hegio will then discover how he has been deceived; he tries to hit upon some device to avoid this, but his wits refuse to work and he is interrupted by the appearance of Hegio and Aris-

Classical Series.

THE CAPTIVI OF T. MACCIUS PLAUTUS

WITH INTRODUCTION AND NOTES

BY

ARCHIBALD R. S. HALLIDIE, M.A.

FORMERLY JUNIOR STUDENT OF CHRIST CHURCH, OXFORD.

MACMILLAN AND CO., LIMITED
ST MARTIN'S STREET. LONDON
1909

First Edition 1891.
Reprinted 1895, 1900, 1905, 1909.

PREFACE.

In preparing the text of this edition I have availed myself of the invaluable *apparatus criticus* in Professor Schoell's edition of the play (Leipzig, 1887), as well as of the collation of V which he has included in his preface to the *Casina* (1890). From these two sources I have compiled the short notes of MS. readings which are given at the foot of each page of the text; they include, I think, all the important variations, and will at any rate enable the student to see at once whether any particular reading in the text has MS. authority or not; further than this it is in my opinion inadvisable to go, in a book intended primarily *in usum scholarum.* The insertion of English stage directions in the text is intended to avoid the necessity for longer explanations in the notes and to bring the scene more vividly before the minds of younger students.

In the Introduction I have devoted considerable space to an account of Plautine metre and prosody, in which I have tried to emphasize the fact—not generally realized, at any rate by young students—that the versification of Plautus is not a thing apart, either in its rules or its irregularities. The notes on scansion, which I have added at the foot of each page of text, will I hope serve a double purpose;

they will guide young students in scanning the lines, and they will complete the general account in the Introduction by pointing out the particular illustrations to be found in the text of this play.

In writing the commentary I have made use of all previous editions and have to acknowledge my indebtedness especially to those of Brix and Ussing. I have tried to make the notes illustrate the grammar and phraseology not merely of this play, but of Plautus as a whole, and with that object have quoted more freely than I should otherwise have done from the rest of the plays. Moreover I have attempted in the notes to call attention to as many points as possible—some of them may seem of minor importance—believing that a better knowledge of the language and more valuable habits of mind are acquired by the thorough study of one work, or even of a portion of one work, than by the hasty reading of half-a-dozen.

The grammars to which I have referred are Roby's *Grammar of the Latin Language* and Kennedy's *Revised Latin Primer;* these are referred to as R. and K., and quoted by sections. In the quotations from other Plautine plays the references are to Tyrrell's *Miles*, Benoist's *Cistellaria*, Ussing's *Mostellaria* and *Persa*, and in the case of the remainder to Ritschl's new edition.

LINCOLN'S INN,
July, 1891.

tophontes before he has decided upon any plan of action.

12 Aristophontes of course at once lets the cat out of
iv. the bag by addressing him as Tyndarus and, unable to think of any better plan, Tyndarus boldly asserts that Aristophontes is a dangerous madman and advises Hegio not to go near him. This at first creates a diversion, for Aristophontes flies into such a passion as almost to bear out Tyndarus' statement, but soon the behaviour of Tyndarus, who is trying to make signs to Aristophontes secretly, arouses Hegio's suspicions and he determines to hear what Aristophontes has to say. When, in proof of his assertion that Tyndarus is an impostor, Aristophontes proceeds to describe the real Philocrates, Hegio recognises the description at once, and seeing how he has been deceived summons the slave-overseers and orders them to bind Tyndarus hand and foot.

3 Tyndarus then gives up the game and admits the
v. deception, but justifies his conduct in a much higher strain than is usual in Roman comedy; his first duty, he says, was to his young master with whom he had lived all his life and who had been specially committed to his care, and if he must die he will die in the consciousness of having done what he ought. This lofty tone does not tend to conciliate Hegio, who sends him off to labour in the stone-quarries with orders that his life is to be made a burden to him. Then it is that Aristophontes understands the real state of the case and regrets his previous stupidity, the more so as Hegio, on whose good humour he had founded great anticipations, now takes him back to his work on the farm.

4 The fourth Act opens with the appearance of Erga-
i. silus running from the harbour in a state of intense excitement and joy. He has completely changed his opinion about the day; it is, he says, the most fortunate and the happiest day in all his life; he has wonderful news

for Hegio: no more asking now and then for a frugal meal: Hegio will be only too delighted to offer him perpetual banquets.

15 While he is approaching the house in this frame of
IV. ii. mind, Hegio comes down the street in a state of dejection that serves as a strong contrast; he catches sight of Ergasilus and, supposing him to have come back to dinner, he listens in surprise to the bombastic threats which Ergasilus is pouring forth against all and sundry who may impede his triumphal progress to Hegio's house. When Ergasilus has reached the door he accosts him, and then ensues a game of cross-purposes. Ergasilus proposes the most extravagant preparation for a meal without saying why; Hegio tells him he is raving; Ergasilus insists, Hegio refuses. Then Ergasilus tells his news; he has run all the way from the harbour, where he has just witnessed the return of Philocrates with Hegio's son Philopolemus and the slave Stalagmus who had escaped twenty years before, and whom Philopolemus had recognised and secured in Elis. At first Hegio refuses to believe that this can be true, but when at last he sees that Ergasilus is in earnest he gives him *carte blanche* as to the preparations for a feast and hurries off to the harbour; Ergasilus rushes into the house in an equal hurry to begin his congenial labours.

16 The fifth Act begins with the appearance of a slave
V. i. from the house, who describes the outrageous proceedings of Ergasilus in the kitchen and the pantry. Then Hegio returns with the two young men and the runaway slave, whom he had met at the harbour. He expresses his deep gratitude to Philocrates and wonders how he can ever repay him. 'By restoring Tyndarus,' answers Philocrates, 'to his Elean master, who purposes to emancipate him.' Hegio then relates his discovery of the deception practised upon him and his consequent harshness to Tyndarus, to fetch whom a messenger is despatched at

once. The young men then go in to bathe after their journey.

17 Hegio remains behind to question Stalagmus; with
ii. the greatest indifference and *sang-froid* this rascal tells how he had stolen off with Hegio's younger son and sold him into slavery at Elis. 'To whom?' asks Hegio. 'To Theodoromedes the father of Philocrates.'

18 Hegio summons Philocrates from the house and it
iii. then appears (as the spectators have known all along) that the long-lost son is no other than the faithful Tyndarus.

19 This is no sooner made clear than Tyndarus himself
iv. appears, laden with fetters and carrying the pick which he has been using in the quarries. He begins describing his sufferings there, when he is suddenly overwhelmed with joy in recognising Philocrates; his real identity is then explained to him, but he takes some time to grasp the wonderful news. A blacksmith is sent for to transfer his fetters to Stalagmus, and the play ends with a short epilogue sung by the whole of the company.

THE MANUSCRIPTS OF PLAUTUS.

20 In speaking of the manuscripts of Plautus a distinction is drawn between the first eight plays and the last twelve; by the first eight plays one means the *Amphitruo, Asinaria, Aulularia, Captiui, Casina, Cistellaria, Curculio* and *Epidicus*; the last twelve are the *Bacchides, Menaechmi* and the rest. The alphabetical order which obtains (as far as the initial letters are concerned) among the other plays is departed from in the case of the *Bacchides*, doubtless because it contains an allusion to the *Epidicus*[1], to which it was therefore subsequent in point of time.

[1] Bac. 214 *Etiam Epidicum, quam ego fabulam aeque ac me ipsum amo,*
Nullam aeque inuitus specto, si agit Pellio.

21 At the beginning of the 15th century only the first eight plays, so understood, were known to exist; the last twelve had been lost. But in 1428 a MS. was discovered in Germany which comprised not only the *Am.*, *As.*, *Aul.*, and half the *Captiui* (to 503), but also the missing twelve. This MS. (now known as D) was brought to Rome and passed into the hands of Cardinal Orsini, after whom it is named the Codex Ursinianus; by him it was placed in the Vatican Library, where it now is. It is a cursive MS. of German origin dating from the 11th century, written by the same hand throughout; the lines are generally run together and the words are often wrongly divided.

22 Various transcripts were made of it, but, as every transcriber emended as he went along and aimed at giving an intelligible text rather than an accurate copy, the interpolated MSS. which resulted are of no value. One so-called MS. (F) of this date, now in the University Library at Leipsic, may here be mentioned; it was compiled in the first half of the 15th century, and the scholars who edited it took great liberties with the text and were almost entirely ignorant of Plautine prosody.

23 The *editio princeps* (quoted by Ritschl as Z) was published at Venice in 1472 by Georgius Merula; he was dependent to a great extent upon interpolated copies of D.

24 In the middle of the 16th century Camerarius of Leipsic obtained possession of two other MSS. previously unknown, B and C, upon which he founded his edition (Lips. 1552); after his death they were purchased and placed in the Palatine Library, and subsequently removed to the Vatican. B still remains there, C was transferred in 1797 to Paris, and in 1815 to Heidelberg, where it still is.

25 B, the Codex Vetus Camerarii, is a cursive MS. of the 11th century, containing all the plays and occupying 213 folio sheets. It is irregularly written by different hands, but, speaking generally (for the execution of the different parts varies considerably), the lines and words are

for the most part correctly divided and the contractions are not many or difficult. There is no division into acts; spaces were left by the original copyists for the headings of scenes and the names of speakers, and in most cases these have been subsequently filled in. In many of the plays corrections have been made by various hands.

26 C, the Codex Decurtatus (so called because, although it originally contained the whole twenty plays, the first eight had been torn off before it came into the possession of Camerarius), is a cursive MS. of the 11th century, written in Germany by different hands; it bears a strong resemblance to D, but the writing is not so good and the words are more often wrongly divided. It is also very like B, and it is clear that these three MSS. were derived, though not immediately, from the same source.

27 In 1815 Cardinal Mai discovered that a copy of the Book of Kings in the Ambrosian Library at Milan had been written on parchment which had previously formed part of a MS. of the plays of Plautus, dating probably from the 4th century. This MS. (now known as the Milan Palimpsest and quoted by Ritschl as A) had originally consisted of bundles (*fasciculi*) of four sheets of parchment laid upon one another and doubled down the middle so as to form sixteen pages in each *fasciculus*. In the 9th century these had been taken to pieces and some of them washed and scraped so as to receive the new writing and then re-bound, but not of course in the original order. The remainder of the original MS. has been lost, while of those sheets which we have the original writing is in some totally illegible, in others only a few lines or a few letters are to be deciphered. Its readings however, where legible, are of course of the greatest authority. It is clearly written in capital letters without any division between words. Originally the MS. contained all the 21 Varronian plays, i.e. the 20 now extant and the *Vidularia*; but nothing is now left of the first three plays or the *Cur-*

culio. Of the *Captiui* only a few fragments of two passages remain (905—931, 1008—1029). An elaborate edition of this MS. by Studemund has recently been published (Berlin, 1890).

28 In addition to these four MSS., ABCD, there are three or four others which require notice, although of secondary importance. V is a cursive MS., dating from the beginning of the 12th century, in the University Library at Leyden. Doubtless it originally contained the first eight plays, but its beginning and end have been mutilated and it now comprises the *Aulularia* (190—end), *Captiui*, *Curculio*, *Casina*, *Cistellaria* and *Epidicus* (to 244). An account of it may be found in Schoell's preface to his edition of the *Casina.* E is a cursive MS. of the 13th century, and contains the first eight plays. J, which is preserved in the British Museum, dates from the beginning of the 12th century. It is a MS. of 194 leaves, of which the first 112 contain three treatises of Cicero, the remainder the first eight plays of Pl. It has been damaged by fire, and the beginnings and ends of lines are often illegible.

29 These three MSS. are considered to have had a common archetype, belonging to the same family as B and D and related to both of them in the same way as they are related to each other; to this archetype V corresponds most closely, then E; the authority of J being reckoned lower than that of the other two. These MSS. are obviously of value to supplement B in those plays (including the last half of the *Captiui*) where neither C nor D is available. How they agree in reproducing errors in which their archetype differed from B and D may be seen in the critical notes on lines 35, 90, 151, 174, 390, 436, 466, 469, 508, 516, 573, 615, 777, 864, 917, 935, 951, 962, 1030.

30 A fragment of the *Captiui* (400—555) is contained in a MS. (O) which Loewe considers of the same age as D; it is transcribed in Goetz's Analecta Plautina, p. 86 sqq.

THE METRES OF PLAUTUS.

31 The Greek system of versification, used for the first time in Latin by Livius Andronicus, who began to write about the date of Plautus' birth, was based upon *quantity*, i.e. the length of time during which the voice dwells upon the different syllables in a word. In ordinary speech there is, of course, great variety in this respect, but for metrical purposes the Greeks recognised only two varieties as possible, and classified all syllables as either short or long, the short syllable containing one 'time' (*mora, tempus*), the long syllable being taken as equal to two short and so containing two 'times.'

32 The different combinations of two, three or four syllables belonging to these two classes are called *feet*, and two consecutive feet are sometimes called a *dipodia*.

33 Feet may be classified according to (*a*) the number of syllables, or (*b*) the number of 'times,' which they contain.

(*a*) the Dissyllabic feet are

Pyrrhic (⏑ ⏑)	**Iambus (⏑ –)**
Spondee (– –)	**Trochee (– ⏑)**

the Trisyllabic are

Tribrach (⏑ ⏑ ⏑)	**Cretic (– ⏑ –)**
Dactyl (– ⏑ ⏑)	**Bacchius (⏑ – –)**
Amphibrach (⏑ – ⏑)	**Antibacchius (– – ⏑)**
Anapaest (⏑ ⏑ –)	**Molossus (– – –)**

the Tetrasyllabic are 16 in number, of which we need only notice the

Proceleusmatic (⏑ ⏑ ⏑ ⏑)	**Choriambus (– ⏑ ⏑ –)**
First Paeon (– ⏑ ⏑ ⏑)	**Ionic a majori (– – ⏑ ⏑)**
Fourth Paeon (⏑ ⏑ ⏑ –)	**Ionic a minori (⏑ ⏑ – –)**

34 (*b*) These feet may be tabulated according to the number of 'times' they contain, thus:—

	2	3	4	5	6
Dissyllabic	⏑ ⏑	⏑ – – ⏑	– –		
Trisyllabic		⏑ ⏑ ⏑	⏑ ⏑ – – ⏑ ⏑ ⏑ – ⏑	– ⏑ – ⏑ – – – – ⏑	– – –
Tetrasyllabic			⏑ ⏑ ⏑ ⏑	– ⏑ ⏑ ⏑ ⏑ ⏑ ⏑ –	– ⏑ ⏑ – – – ⏑ ⏑ ⏑ ⏑ – –

35 A combination of not more than eight feet, arranged according to certain rules, is called a *verse* or *line*; this forms a metrical unit and is, in most kinds of verse, to be scanned by itself, independently of the lines which precede and follow; when this is the case, it ends with the end of a word, and the last syllable is 'doubtful,' i.e., is considered long or short according to the requirements of the metre, whatever its real quantity may be.

36 When a verse, instead of ending with a complete foot, has the last syllable wanting, it is called Catalectic; if two syllables are wanting, Brachycatalectic; if the line is complete, Acatalectic; if there be one or two syllables too many, Hypercatalectic.

37 Verses are sometimes named from the number of feet they contain, a senarius containing 6 feet, a septenarius 7, an octonarius 8, &c.

38 'Metre' has two meanings: in the wider and more usual sense it means a kind of verse, as when we speak of Iambic metre, but in the narrower and more technical sense, 'a metre' means either a single foot, or a dipodia; in Iambic, Trochaic and Anapaestic verse, a metre consists of a dipodia, being the first, or any subsequent, pair of feet in a line: e.g.

(1) *Homunculi | quanti sunt, quom | recogito.* (Iambic.)

(2) *Odi ego aurum; | multa multis | saepe suasit | perperam.* (Trochaic.)

(3) *Emi hosce homines; | ubi quisque uident.* (Anapaestic.)

In Dactylic, Cretic and Bacchiac verse a metre consists of a single foot; e.g.

(4) *Tityre, | tu patu|lae recu|bans sub | tegmine | fagi.* (Dactylic.)

(5) *Ne arbitri | dicta nos|tra arbitra|ri queant.* (Cretic.)

(6) *Agundumst. | Ero ut me | uoles es|se. Spero.* (Bacchiac.)

Verses are named according to the number of metres they contain; thus (1) is a trimeter, (2) a tetrameter catalectic, (3) a dimeter, (4) a hexameter, (5) and (6) tetrameters.

39 "Ictus Metricus is the stress which must be laid upon particular syllables in repeating verse, in order that the rhythm of the measure may be made perceptible to the ear[1]." Thus in the lines

Tityre tú patulaé recubáns sub tégmine fági,
Ódi ego aúrum: múlta múltis saépe suásit pérperám,
Homúnculí quantí sunt, quóm recógitó,

some stress must be laid upon the accented syllables in order to mark the rhythm of the respective measures. The ictus falls once in every foot[2], but in those verses in which a metre contains two feet, the accent denoting ictus is generally printed only upon the first foot in each dipodia.

40 The rhythm of verses would naturally be marked by movements of the feet or hands: thus Horace says, Sat. I. x. 42, *Pollio regum Facta canit pede ter percusso*, alluding to the Iambic Trimeter, which was the usual metre of

[1] Ramsay, Lat. Pros. p. 270.

[2] Hor. A. P. 253.

Tragedy. Hence that part of the foot which receives the ictus was originally called the θέσις, for there the reciter put down his hand or his foot, while the part which is free from the ictus was called the ἄρσις, for there he lifted it up. This was the usage of the older grammarians Dionysius and Hephaestio; but later writers, such as Priscian and Martianus Capella (5th century A.D.), thinking that these terms referred to the voice and noticing that stress is laid upon a syllable by raising the voice not by lowering it, reversed the practice of their predecessors and called that part of the foot which received the ictus the ἄρσις and the other the θέσις; and this usage is now so well established that any attempt to return to the ancient practice would only lead to confusion. The words will therefore be used here in the later and less correct way, as referring to the voice, that part of the foot upon which the stress is laid being called the ἄρσις or said to be *in arsi*, while the other part is called the θέσις or said to be *in thesi*.

41 In an iambus, anapaest or bacchius the stress falls upon the final long syllable; in a trochee, cretic or dactyl upon the initial long syllable. And so with the measures of which these are the original feet; in the Iambic Anapaestic and Bacchiac measures the ictus falls on the latter part of the foot whether it be the proper foot of the measure or any other foot which may be substituted therefor, while in Trochaic, Cretic and Dactylic it falls on the first part.

42 Thus there are two distinct and opposite kinds of verse, that in which the feet begin with the *thesis* (rising rhythm), and that in which they begin with the *arsis* (falling rhythm). We will consider first the rising rhythms.

I. IAMBIC.

43 The iambic senarius, or iambic trimeter acat., is the usual vehicle of ordinary stage dialogue. The original foot was the iambus, for which the equivalent tribrach was admissible in every place but the last; but, to give more

steadiness to the verse, the Greeks admitted the spondee in the first foot of each dipodia, i.e. in the 1st, 3rd and 5th feet: cf. Hor. A. P. 255

> *Tardior ut paullo grauiorque ueniret ad aures*
> *Spondeos stabiles in iura paterna recepit* [*iambus*].

The spondee by the resolution of one of its long syllables into two short ones becomes either an anapaest or a dactyl, both of which were admitted by the Greek comic dramatists in the odd feet (the dactyl rarely in 5th), while the anapaest appears also in 2nd and 4th. The anapaest, however, is very rarely permitted in Greek comedy to stand after a tribrach or a dactyl.

Thus the scheme of Greek Comedy is

⏑ –	⏑ –	⏑ –	⏑ –	⏑ –	⏑ ⏓
⏑ ⏑ ⏑	⏑ ⏑ ⏑	⏑ ⏑ ⏑	⏑ ⏑ ⏑	⏑ ⏑ ⏑	
– –		– –		– –	
⏑ ⏑ –	⏑ ⏑ –	⏑ ⏑ –	⏑ ⏑ –	⏑ ⏑ –	
– ⏑ ⏑		– ⏑ ⏑		[– ⏑ ⏑]	

44 As has been already explained, the ictus in iambic measure falls upon the latter part of the foot ⏑ –́, – –́, and when the accented long syllables are resolved into two short, upon the first of these two short: thus ⏑ ⏑́ ⏑, – ⏑́ ⏑; but ⏑ ⏑ –́. It will now be seen why in Greek iambics an anapaest never, or very seldom, follows a tribrach or dactyl (⏑ ⏑́ ⏑ | ⏑ ⏑ –́, or – ⏑́ ⏑ | ⏑ ⏑ –́); for that would give four syllables from ictus to ictus, while the measure admits at most three syllables to a foot.

45 Caesura is a division of the verse caused by the ending of a word in the middle, and not at the end of a foot; in iambic trimeters (and dactylic hexameters) it is found almost invariably in the third or fourth foot; in the former case it is called Penthemimeral, because it occurs after $2\frac{1}{2}$ feet (πενθημιμερής 'of 5 halves'), in the latter Hephthemimeral (ἑφθημιμερής 'of 7 halves'). Both are

considered legitimate but the former is much the commoner:

Classica iamque sonant, || it bello tessera signum. Aen. VII. 637,
Homines captiuos || conmercatur, si queat. Cap. 100,

are instances of the former, while

Quo perii superimponas. || Abolere nefandi. Aen. IV. 497,
Homunculi quanti sunt, || quom recogito. Cap. 51,

are instances of the latter.

The *raison d'être* of a caesura seems to have been that some division of the line was necessary to relieve the monotony of the rhythm, that this division would naturally be wanted about the middle of the line, but that if it occurred exactly at the middle, i.e. at the end of the 3rd foot, the result would have been to make two complete lines of 3 feet each.

46 Such were the chief rules of the Greek comic iambic trimeter; the Plautine usage was different in the following respects:—

(i) he admitted the spondee, and occasionally the dactyl, in the 2nd and 4th.

(ii) he very rarely puts a dactyl in 5th; there are but six instances in the Cap., 5, 53, 103, 514, 745, 747.

(iii) the spondee is almost invariable in 5th; Luchs says that the final iambus is never preceded in Pl. by an iambic word or a cretic word or a word ending in a cretic.

(iv) tribrachs are much less common in all metres than in Greek, three or more short syllables rarely occurring consecutively in Latin.

(v) Pl. occasionally puts anapaest after dactyl or tribrach; chiefly at the beginning of a line, as in Trin. 804 *Continuo operito.* There are three doubtful instances in the Cap., 39, 62, 157.

(vi) another licence, which from what has been said above (§ 44) will be seen to be somewhat similar to the last, is the admission of a proceleusmatic (⏑⏑⏑⏑); although it is only the metrical equivalent of a spondee, it should be excluded by the number of its syllables. Instances are Trin. 806 *Ita faciam*, Per. 318, Mil. 362, 1037 and other lines quoted in § 144. Examples in the Cap. are (in 1st foot) 40, 95, 109, 133, 167, 530, 724, 743, (in 2nd foot) 12, (in 3rd foot) 62, and (in 4th) 697.

In other instances bacchii, cretics and 2nd paeons are apparently found in this and other iambic measures; but these feet could not be regarded as admissible, for the nature of the metre does not admit any foot containing more than the metrical equivalent for two long syllables; and these instances may all be explained in a different way (§§ 136, sqq.).

47 The following are the approximate figures for the senarii in the Captiui:—

	1st	2nd	3rd	4th	5th	6th
iambus	53	108	52	126	37	327
spondee	152	149	194	154	237	
dactyl	30	35	64	22	8	
anapaest	82	20	4	14	45	
tribrach	3	14	12	10		
proceleusmatic	7	1	1	1		

48 The iambic septenarius or tetram. cat. (called *comicus quadratus* by the Romans) contains seven complete feet and a syllable; it is the favourite measure in which to express joyful excitement, and is common in Aristophanes, but unknown to Greek tragedy. The Greek scheme is as follows:—

⏑ –	⏑ –	⏑ –	⏑ –	⏑ –	⏑ –	⏑ –	⏓
⏑⏑⏑	⏑⏑⏑	⏑⏑⏑	[⏑⏑⏑]	⏑⏑⏑	⏑⏑⏑		
– –		– –		– –			
– ⏑⏑		– ⏑⏑		– ⏑⏑			
⏑⏑ –	⏑⏑ –	⏑⏑ –	[⏑⏑ –]	⏑⏑ –	⏑⏑ –		

The anapaest is never put after a tribrach or dactyl and is used less often in the even than in the odd feet, while neither anapaest nor tribrach is frequent in the 4th; indeed trisyllabic feet generally are more sparingly used than in senarii.

At the end of the 4th foot there is a division of the verse, called in this instance diaeresis (*διαίρεσις* 'division'); the 4th foot should consequently end with the end of a word, but the rule is often neglected.

49 The practice of Pl. differs from that of the Greeks in the following points:—

(i) He admits spondee and dactyl in 2nd and 6th; in 7th he admits spondee and occasionally tribrach and dactyl, very rarely anapaest.

(ii) He admits proceleusmatic rarely in 1st and very rarely in the other odd feet[1].

(iii) On the other hand, in observing the diaeresis he is more strict than the Greeks, neglecting it only once in about every seventy lines; indeed this division seems to be regarded almost as the end of a verse, the iambus (which alone, with very rare exceptions, is allowed in 4th) being sometimes replaced by a pyrrhic, while hiatus is frequent (§ 84). Thus the Plautine scheme is

⏑ –	⏑ –	⏑ –	⏑ ⏓	⏑ –	⏑ –	⏑ –
[⏑⏑⏑]	[⏑⏑⏑]	[⏑⏑⏑]		[⏑⏑⏑]	[⏑⏑⏑]	[⏑⏑⏑]
– –	– –	– –		– –	– –	– –
– ⏑⏑	– ⏑⏑	[– ⏑⏑]		[– ⏑⏑]	[– ⏑⏑]	[– ⏑⏑]
⏑⏑ –	[⏑⏑ –]	[⏑⏑ –]		⏑⏑ –	[⏑⏑ –]	
[⏑⏑⏑⏑]						

[1] In 7th, Mil. 927, As. 430.

50 The measure is not common, the only instances in this play being scattered lines, e.g. 231, 510, 515. In the 422 lines, Mil. 354—425, 874—946, 1216—1283, As. 381—503, 545—633, there are approximately

	1st	2nd	3rd	4th	5th	6th	7th
iambus	40	139	65	418	90	119	243
spondee	208	180	289	? 3	166	217	115
anapaest	96	24	25	? 1	106	20	11
dactyl	63	54	29		43	48	27
tribrach	4	24	12		11	18	24
proceleusmatic	11	1	2		6		2

hiatus at diaeresis 30 times, no diaeresis 6 times; of the 418 iambi in 4th foot, 48 are really pyrrhics.

51 The iambic octonarius, or tetram. acat., is the same as the preceding with the final foot completed; thus the verse consists of two distinct dimeters, and the Greeks always wrote it as two separate verses. The Romans however preferred the longer measure, and even neglected the diaeresis more frequently than in septenarii, while the fourth foot is sometimes trisyllabic. Where, however, the diaeresis is neglected there is generally a caesura in the middle of the 5th foot; in the 43 lines in the Captiui there are 24 instances of caesura alone and 7 of diaeresis alone, while in the other 12 there are both. The iambus is alone admissible in the 8th foot, and predominates in the 2nd and 4th, while the spondee is most usual in the other feet, and almost invariable in the 7th, the dactyl, anapaest and tribrach occurring but very rarely: in all other respects the rules as to septenarii apply.

52 This measure is chiefly used to express consternation (as in 516 sqq., 909 sqq.) or hurry (as in 770 sqq.). Sometimes whole scenes are written in it (as 909—921),

but usually, when the excitement with which the scene opened is supposed to be calming down, the metre changes, generally to troch. sept., as in 540, 541.

Shorter iambic lines are sometimes interpolated in a series of octonarii, as 197; and occasionally a series is preceded by a troch. sept., which, being catalectic, runs on in one rhythm with the following iambi; cf. the three short systems 769—771, 772—4, 775—780.

53 Of these shorter iambic lines we need only notice (*a*) the dimeter acat. or quaternarius, the final foot of which must be an iambus; examples are 197 and Merc. 135,

C. Princípium id inimicís dato.
A. At tíbi sortito id óbtigit.
C. Loquere íd negoti quídquid est.
A. Placidé; uolo acquiéscere—

(*b*) the dim. cat., e.g. 212, 508, 784, and (*c*) tripodiae, e.g. 233, and Per. 664 *Abi, árgentum ecfer húc*; lines are sometimes found composed of two catalectic tripodiae, as 216 and Most. 851

Vt adhuc fuit mi | *corium esse oportet,*
Sincerum atque ut uo|*tem uerberari.*
Si huic imperabo | *probe tectum habebo.*

II. ANAPAESTIC.

54 This was a favourite measure with the Greeks, but unsuited to Latin, and little used by Plautus; Terence abstains from it altogether. Its chief forms in Greek were the septenarius and the acatalectic dimeter.

55 The septenarius, called the Aristophanic, was peculiar to comedy; it consists of seven feet and a syllable and its scheme is

⏑⏑–	⏑⏑–	⏑⏑–	⏑⏑–	⏑⏑–	⏑⏑–	⏑⏑–	⏓
––	––	––	––	––	––		
–⏑⏑	[–⏑⏑]	–⏑⏑		–⏑⏑			

In Aristophanes out of over 1200 lines less than 20 have a dactyl in 2nd, and it is never found in the other even places. There is a division of the verse after the first dipodia, where however it is often neglected, as well as after the second, where it is nearly always observed. The ictus metricus falls on the last of the anapaest, ⏑⏑–́; therefore on the last of the spondee, ––́; consequently on the second of the dactyl, –⏑́⏑. Hence in Greek anapaests, dactyl is never or very rarely followed by anapaest; cf. sup. § 44.

56 Plautus uses this metre but rarely and without success; its difficulties and the absence of oxytone words in Latin compelled him to take so many liberties that the anapaestic character is often entirely lost. There is a passage of 82 lines in the Miles (1011—1092), in which there are the following irregularities of structure[1]:—(*a*) dactyls admitted into 2nd, 6th and 7th, and sometimes followed by anapaests, (*b*) occasional proceleusmatics, (*c*) the diaeresis after first dipodia not observed, that after second neglected twice, (*d*) anapaests comparatively rare in 7th, (*e*) many lines which have only one anapaest, several which have none.

But the irregularity of Pl.'s anapaests lies mainly in the prosody; for instance, of the 171 anapaests in these 82 lines, over 40 are really bacchii (see inf. § 136 sqq.).

57 The dimeter was much used in Greek tragedy, its scheme being the same as that of the first half of the

[1] The figures for this passage are approximately

	1st	2nd	3rd	4th	5th	6th	7th
anapaests	39	28	16	26	31	17	14
spondees	33	49	56	56	37	58	53
dactyls	9	5	9		9	5	12
proceleusmatics	1		1		4	2	3

septenarius; the dactyl however was admitted into the 4th. It was usually written in systems, consisting of a number of dimeters with an occasional monometer, the whole ending with a catalectic verse, usually a dimeter, called Paroemiac, because it often contained a proverbial saying (*παροιμία*)[1]. In these systems the scansion was continuous throughout, so that the last syllable of a line was subject to the ordinary rules of prosody except at the end of a sentence or any marked pause in the sense.

58 Two dimeters occur in this play, 498, 500, but the Romans generally preferred to write them, like the iambic and trochaic, in double measure as tetrameters, concluding the set with a septenarius or shorter catalectic line; e.g. Aul. 713 sqq. These octonarii are governed by the same rules as the septenarii.

III. BACCHIAC.

59 This metre, which in Greek is only found in a few scattered lines, is sometimes considered as arising from an iambus being prefixed to cretics, and certainly the catalectic lines may be so scanned (§ 63), but the acatalectic lines, whatever their origin, may be more conveniently taken as consisting of bacchii or equivalent feet, and indeed seem, from the position of the diaeresis and the rules as to substitution of feet, to have been so taken by the Romans.

60 Pl.'s usual form is the tetrameter, which consists properly of 4 bacchii, as in 228

Agundumst. | *Ero ut me* | *uolēs es*|*se. Spero,*

but the molossus is also admitted, more readily in the odd than in the even places. These feet are also found with one

[1] The scheme of the paroimiac was

⏑ ⏑ – – – – ⏑ ⏑	⏑ ⏑ – – –	⏑ ⏑ –	⏓

of their long syllables resolved; thus from the bacchius (⏑––) we get the 4th paeon (⏑⏑⏑–) and the 2nd paeon (⏑–⏑⏑), from the molossus (–––) we get the ionic a minori (⏑⏑––), the choriambus (–⏑⏑–) and the ionic a majori (––⏑⏑).

The ictus is generally marked on the first long of the bacchius (⏑–́–), so it would fall thus in the other feet; ⏑⏑́⏑–, ⏑–́⏑⏑, ––́–, ⏑⏑–́–, –⏑́⏑–, ––́⏑⏑.

There is sometimes a diaeresis after the second bacchius, but it is often neglected, cf. Cap. 782—789; when it is observed, hiatus sometimes occurs, cf. § 84.

61 Dimeters acatalectic are also found (cf. 503); according to Seyffert they do not admit a molossus or resolved molossus in 2nd.

62 Trimeters occur rarely, if at all. 206 is a doubtful example; more certain are

Most. 124 *sibique haud* | *materiae* | *neparcunt*
nec sumptus | *sibi sumptui es*|*se ducunt.*

63 Catalectic bacchiacs have an iambus instead of the last bacchius, and, as above mentioned, may also be scanned as cretics with an iambus prefixed. The form of the tetrameter is thus ⏑–|–|⏑–|–‖⏑–|–|⏑–, while the dimeter is the same as the latter part of the tetrameter. 506, 507 contain four dimeters.

Turning next to falling rhythms we may take first

IV. TROCHAIC.

64 The trochaic septenarius, or catalectic tetrameter, was, like the iambic septenarius, called *uersus quadratus* by the Romans, cf. Gell. II. 29.

It probably arose from a cretic being prefixed to the Iambic Senarius; at any rate the caesura in the latter corresponds to the diaeresis in the former, thus

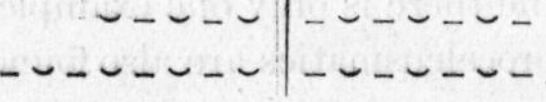

and Luchs maintains that in the early dramatists the same rules regulate the admission of a penultimate iambus as in the iambic senarius, (§ 46, iii.), while in both kinds of verse hiatus is sometimes found before the final cretic (§ 84, 3).

65 The septenarius consists of 7 complete feet and a syllable and in construction it is similar to the iambic septenarius. The proper foot is the trochee which, with its equivalent the tribrach, is admissible in any place; the Greeks also admitted the spondee and anapaest into the even feet, except that a spondee or anapaest in tragedy never, and even in comedy very seldom, precedes a tribrach in 7th. The dactyl was only admissible in the case of proper names, and then not in 4th or 7th; the diaeresis after the second dipodia was occasionally neglected.

Thus the scheme of Greek comedy was

– ⏑	– ⏑	– ⏑	– ⏑	– ⏑	– ⏑	– ⏑	⏓
⏑ ⏑ ⏑	⏑ ⏑ ⏑	⏑ ⏑ ⏑	⏑ ⏑ ⏑	⏑ ⏑ ⏑	⏑ ⏑ ⏑	⏑ ⏑ ⏑	
	– –		– –		– –		
	⏑ ⏑ –		⏑ ⏑ –		⏑ ⏑ –		
[– ⏑ ⏑	– ⏑ ⏑	– ⏑ ⏑		– ⏑ ⏑	– ⏑ ⏑]		

63 By the Roman dramatists this measure was used in dialogue to a greater extent than the iambic trimeter, and seems to have been thought suitable to conversation of a more animated or important character. Plautus uses it with better effect and greater strictness than the senarius, but in common with the other Latin dramatists allows himself certain licences; viz., (i) spondee and anapaest are admitted into all the first six feet, (ii) the dactyl of a common noun is admitted into all feet but the 4th and 7th: out of 567 troch. sept. in this play there are only nine examples of a dactyl in 4th (326, 559, 570, 827, 839, 874, 960, 1005, 1007) while there is only one example of a dactyl in 7th (823), (iii) proceleusmatics are also found, chiefly in 1st,

but also in other feet[1], (iv) either anapaest or spondee may, and a spondee usually does, precede a tribrach in 7th. On the other hand (v) the tribrach is less common than in Greek especially in the 7th foot (there are only about 20 examples in this play), while in the 4th it is exceedingly rare: examples may be found at 267, 393, 411.

The apparent introduction of feet which are foreign to the metre, such as bacchii, cretics, etc., is to be differently explained (inf. § 136 sqq.).

The Plautine scheme, then, is

– ⏑ ⏑ ⏑ ⏑ – – ⏑ ⏑ – – ⏑ ⏑ [⏑ ⏑ ⏑ ⏑]	– ⏑ ⏑ ⏑ ⏑ – – ⏑ ⏑ – – ⏑ ⏑	– ⏑ ⏑ ⏑ ⏑ – – ⏑ ⏑ – – ⏑ ⏑	– ⏑ [⏑ ⏑ ⏑] – – ⏑ ⏑ – [– ⏑ ⏑]	– ⏑ ⏑ ⏑ ⏑ – – ⏑ ⏑ – – ⏑ ⏑	– ⏑ ⏑ ⏑ ⏑ – – ⏑ ⏑ – – ⏑ ⏑	– ⏑ ⏑ ⏑ ⏑	⏓

67 The ictus metricus in trochaic metre falls upon the first syllable of the foot, –́ ⏑, ⏑́ ⏑ ⏑, –́ –, ⏑́ ⏑ –, –́ ⏑ ⏑; consequently the rule in iambics and anapaestics that anapaest must not follow tribrach or dactyl does not apply to trochaics.

68 The octonarius or tetrameter acat. was, like the iambic oct., unknown to the Greeks, who wrote the two halves of the line separately as dimeters.

The same feet were admitted by the Romans as in the septenarius, the trochee and tribrach alone being allowed in the 8th; but as the last syllable of a verse is doubtful, these feet are often replaced by spondees and anapaests. At the end of the 4th foot diaeresis occurs and hiatus is allowed.

[1] Proceleusmatics are rarer and more objectionable in trochaic than in iambic metre; in the latter, unless they are preceded by a dactyl or tribrach or followed by an anapaest, the ictus recurs within three syllables, while in the former it necessarily always requires four.

69 The troch. oct. is rarer than the iambic oct., and is usually confined to occasional lines; but short scenes written in it sometimes occur, e.g. Trin. 820—839. Often a scene opens with it and quickly changes to septenarii; cf. Cap. 240, 928.

V. CRETIC.

70 The cretic tetrameter consists properly and generally of four cretics, but any cretic may have one of its long syllables resolved into two shorts, thus producing a 1st or 4th Paeon, cf. 217, 238; the former is not allowed in the final foot. Moreover the Romans admitted the molossus in the first 3 places, rarely in the 4th, and this also could have one of its long syllables resolved, producing either a choriambus, an Ionic a majori or an Ionic a minori. Sometimes lines occur composed almost entirely of choriambi, as Cap. 224 and

Men. 110 *Ni mala, ni | stulta sies, | ni indomita im|posque animi.*

As. 132 *Perlecebrae | pernicies | adulescen|tum exitium.*

The Ionics occur chiefly in the first place, as in 207, 217, and

Am. 241 *Quisque ut stete|rat iacet | obtinet|que ordinem,*
244 *Equites par|ent citi ab | dextera | maxumo.*

There is diaeresis after the second cretic, where hiatus sometimes occurs and a doubtful final syllable is allowed. The latter is of course admitted at the end of the line, cf. 221. Thus the Plautine scheme is

– ⏑ –	– ⏑ –	– ⏑ –	– ⏑ ⏓
⏑ ⏑ ⏑ –	⏑ ⏑ ⏑ –	⏑ ⏑ ⏑ –	⏑ ⏑ ⏑ –
– ⏑ ⏑ ⏑	– ⏑ ⏑ ⏑	– ⏑ ⏑ ⏑	
– – –	– – –	– – –	[– – –]
⏑ ⏑ – –	⏑ ⏑ – –	⏑ ⏑ – –	⏑ ⏑ – –
– – ⏑ ⏑	– – ⏑ ⏑	– – ⏑ ⏑	?
– ⏑ ⏑ –	– ⏑ ⏑ –	– ⏑ ⏑ –	– ⏑ ⏑ –

COMPOSITE VERSES.

71 Composite verses are those in which two different metres are combined, the metres, however, being of similar nature; thus bacchiacs are combined with iambics (both being rising rhythms) and cretics with trochaics (falling rhythms). The five following combinations are the most usual.

72 (1) Bacchiac dimeter + iambic tripodia catalectic or semiquinarius,

⏑ – – | ⏑ – – || ⏒ – | ⏒ – | ⏒

The second foot of the dimeter must be a bacchius and the tripodia ought to contain one pure iambus. There is diaeresis between the two parts which is sometimes neglected, and hiatus and a doubtful final syllable are sometimes found there. The following are examples of this verse:—

Most. 306 sq. *Aduorsum | uenire || mihi ad | Philola|chem*
Volo tem|peri. audi, hem || tibi im|pera|tumst.

Cas. 694 *Occisis|sumus sum om||nium | qui uiu|ont.*

Cist. 36 *Aquam fri|gidam sub||dole | subfun|dunt.*

73 (2) Iambic tripodia cat. + bacchiac dimeter,

≚ – | ≚ – | ≚ || ⏑ – – | ⏑ – –

this is the preceding line arranged the other way;

Ps. 1275 *Amic|tus hac | in||cessi lud|ibundus.*

74 Lines (1) and (2) are often found together: e.g.

Ps. 1273 sq. *Id ut sal|tem. ad hunc me || modum in|tuli il|li* (bac. iam.)
Satis | face|te; || enim ex dis|ciplina (iam. bac.).

Cas. 664 sq. *Metu mus|sitant. Oc||cidi at|que interi|i* (bac. iam.)
Quid il|li obiec|tumst || mali tam | repente (iam. bac.)

Cas. 695 sq. *Loricam in|duam: hoc mi op||tumum es|se opi|nor* (bac. iam.)
Quid ux|or mea | non || adiit at|que ademit (iam. bac.).

Poen. 242 sq. *Sine omni | lepore et || sine sua|uita|te* (bac. iam.)
Nisi mul|ta aqua us|que et || diu ma|cerantur (iam. bac.).

75 (3) Cretic dimeter + trochaic tripodia cat. or semiquinarius,

_ ⏑ _ | _ ⏑ ⏒ || _ ⏓ | _ ⏓ | ⏓

The second foot of the dimeter must be a cretic, but a doubtful syllable and hiatus are permitted at the division: the semiquinarius generally contains two trochees and must contain one. Examples are

Most. 677 sqq. *Melius an|no hoc mihi || non fu|it do|mi*
Nec quod u|na esca me || iuue|rit ma|gis.
Prandium u|xor mihi || perbo|num de|dit.
Non mihi | forte ui||sum ili|co fu|it,
Melius quom | prandium || quam so|let de|dit.

76 (4) Trochaic tripodia cat. + cretic dimeter

_ ⏓ | _ ⏓ | _ || _ ⏑ _ | _ ⏑ _

This is the last verse put the other way about; examples are 204, 215 and

Most. 111 *Atque haud | est fab|ri || culpa. Sed | magna pars.*
148 *Cursu ar|mis e|quo || uectita|bam uolup.*

77 (5) Cretic dimeter + trochaic dipodia acat.

_ ⏑ _ | _ ⏑ ⏒ || _ ⏑ | _ ⏑

Of this form of verse we have an example in Cap. 214, and

Cas. 643 *Quidquid hoc | est cito || iam ti|bi istuc,*

but more generally an anapaest is found instead of the second trochee, e.g.

Most. 331 sqq. *Ecquis hic | est? Adest. || Eu Phi| lolches!*
Salue ami|cissume || mi omni|um hominum!
Di te ament. | Accuba || Calli|damates.

78 Table of Metres.

1—194	Iam. sen.	501, 502	Bac. tetram.
195, 196	Iam. oct.	503	Bac. dim.
197	Iam. dim. acat.	504, 505	Bac. tetram.
198, 199	Iam. oct.	506, 507	Four Bac. dim. cat.
200	Iam. sen.	508	Iam. dim. cat.
201	Iam. oct.	509	Bac. dim.
202	Iam. sen.	510—513	Iam. sept.
203	Iam. oct.	514	Iam. sen.
204	Tr. trip. cat. + Cret. dim.	515	Iam. sept.
		516—524	Iam. oct.
205	Cret. tetram.	[525	Iam. sen.
206	Bac. trim.	526—528	Tr. sept.]
207 *a*, *b*	Cret. tetram.	529	Iam. oct.
208, 209	Tr. oct.	530	Iam. sen.
210, 211	Cret. tetram.	531	Tr. sept.
212	Iam. dim. cat.	532	Iam. sen.
213	Cret. tetram.	533	Iam. oct.
214	Cret. dim. + Tr. dip. acat.	534	Tr. sept.
		535	Tr. oct.
215	Tr. trip. cat. + Cret. dim.	536—540	Iam. oct.
		541—658	Tr. sept.
216	Two Iam. tripodiae acat.	659—767	Iam. sen.
		768, 769	Tr. sept.
217—224	Cret. tetram.	770, 771	Iam. oct.
225	Iam. oct.	772	Tr. sept.
226—230	Bac. tetram.	773, 774	Iam. oct.
231	Iam. sept.	775	Tr. sept.
232	Cret. tetram.	776—780	Iam. oct.
233	Iam. trip. acat.	781—783	Bac. tetram.
234—239	Cret. tetram.	784	Iam. dim. cat.
240, 241	Tr. oct.	785—787	Bac. tetram.
242—360	Tr. sept.	788	Bac. dim. + Iam. trip. cat.
361—384	Iam. sen.		
385—497	Tr. sept.	789	Bac. tetram.
498	Anap. dim.	790	Bac. dim. + Iam. trip. cat.
499	Bac. tetram.		
500	Anap. dim.	791—832	Tr. sept.

833, 834	Iam. oct.	922—927	Bac. tetram.
837	Iam. sept.	928, 929	Tr. oct.
835—908	Tr. sept.	930—1036	Tr. sept.
909—921	Iam. oct.		

PROSODY.

79 In noticing the points of difference between the prosody of Pl. and that of the Augustan poets, there are two things to be remembered: first, that in accordance with the tendency of all languages to substitute easier sounds for more difficult, many syllables, especially final ones, which were originally long had been shortened by the time of Augustus; and, secondly, that Pl. wrote when the older Saturnian verse, which was based upon cadence or rhythm, had been but recently replaced by the Greek metrical system founded upon quantity. We are therefore prepared to find (1) that so-called 'licences' or departures from the strict rules of this system, which are found even in the Augustan poets, occur much more freely in Pl., (2) that certain terminations and other syllables, short in later writers, are used by Pl. with their original long quantity, and (3) that accent, which had been supreme in the old Saturnian measure, is sometimes allowed by Pl. to override the quantity of a syllable as fixed by the Greek metrical system, in which of course accent has properly no place.

80 The first class of peculiarities, those so-called licences which may be to some extent paralleled in the classical poets, fall under three heads, Hiatus, Apocope and Contraction.

Hiatus.

81 When a word ends with a vowel, diphthong or *m*, and the following word in the same line begins with a vowel,

diphthong or *h*, the final syllable of the former word is said to be elided, i.e. must be omitted in scanning; and the neglect of this elision is called Hiatus.

82 The question when hiatus should be admitted in Pl., and when its occurrence should make us suspect corruption in the text, is one upon which scholars have differed greatly. Some, by alterations and insertions in the text and the introduction of various archaic forms, have succeeded in eradicating it almost entirely; but this method is certainly unscientific, because it is the text of the MSS. which forms the main source of our knowledge of the subject. The proper course is surely to classify all the instances which are found in the MSS., omitting those which occur in lines otherwise suspicious or unmetrical or of which the scansion is doubtful; the probability of each class will depend upon the number of undoubted instances which it contains.

83 The Captiui contains 60 or 70 such instances, which fall into three classes; those which occur (A) at a division of the verse, or (B) at a pause or break in the sense, or which (C) are to be justified by the form of the words themselves.

84 A. Of the first class we may remark that even in the Augustan poets hiatus is sometimes found at the caesura; e.g.

Verg. Ecl. III. 6 *Et succus pecori | et lac subducitur agnis.*

(1) Similarly in Pl. hiatus is generally admitted at the *diaeresis* of tetrameters, e.g.

Mil. 358 *Quid aís tu, Sceledre? S. Hanc rém gero; | habeo aúris, loquere quíduis* (iam. sept.). Cf. Cap. 510.

Cap. 780 *Speróque me ob hunc núntium | aetérnum adepturúm cibum* (iam. oct.).

Men. 968 *Vt ábsente eró rem | erí diligénter* (bac. tetr.). Cf. Cap. 505.

Cap. 331 *Eúm si reddis míhi praeterea | únum nummum né duis* (tr. sept.).

Rud. 930 *Iám ubi liber ero, ígitur demum | ínstruam agrum atque aedís, mancipia* (tr. oct.).

Cas. 190 *Néc mihi iús meum | óbtinendi óptiost* (cret. tetr.).

(2) Hiatus is also admissible at the *caesura* (penthemim. or hephthemim.) of iambic senarii, as

Cap. 709 *Sed málene id factum | árbitrare? HE. Péssume.* Cf. 169, 364, 372, etc.

Cap. 665 *Decet ínnocentem séruom | atque innóxium.*

(3) It is also found in MSS., although not generally accepted by edd., at a similar division of the 5th foot, i.e. before the final cretic, in iambic senarii, as

Trin. 158 *Quae míhi mandatast hábeo dotem | únde dem.*
539 *Nam fúlguritae súnt alternae | árbores.* Cf. Cap. 532, 682.

And Wagner, pref. Trin., 2nd ed., p. vi, defends it also before the final cretic of tr. septenarii (§ 64); e.g. Cap. 337, 426; cf. 481[1].

85 B. Even in Vergil we find hiatus at a marked pause or break in the sense; cf.

Ecl. II. 53 *Addam cerea pruna; | honos erit huic quoque pomo.*
Aen. I. 405 *Et uera incessu patuit Dea. | Ille ubi matrem.*

(4) So in Pl. hiatus after such a pause or break is generally allowed; examples are

Cap. 532 *Nugás! Ineptias íncipisso. | Haéreo.*
1024 *Quási per nebulam, | Hégionem méum patrem uocárier.*

And perhaps 481.

[1] In 201 hiatus is found at the caesura of an iam. oct. (see § 50), and it also occurs in the MSS. somewhat often at the end of the 4th foot of senarii, as in

Trin. 540 *Sués moriuntur ángina | acérrume.* Cf. Cap. 373.

(5) A *change of speakers* causes such a break, and so excuses hiatus.

So 139 *Ne flé.* | *ER. Egone illum nón fleam? Ego non défleam* and 354, etc.

(6) *Interjections* are in their nature interruptions, and hiatus before or after them is common to all poetry. Cf. Cap. 152, etc.

(7) Similarly hiatus is admitted by some edd. after *vocatives*; e.g.

Am. 1081 *Amphítruo,* | *ita mihi ánimus etiam núnc abest.*
AM. Agedum, éxpedi.

C. But there are many instances which do not come under the preceding heads; most edd. take these to be a sign of some corruption in the text and alter the MS. reading; others however justify most of them by considering hiatus to have been admitted by Plautus in the two following cases:—

86 (8) After *monosyllables* ending in a long vowel, diphthong or *-m*, the monosyllable being scanned as short: examples are

Cap. 807 *Túm pistores scrófipasci, quĭ* | *alunt furfuribús sues.*
705 *Quia uéra obessent ílli quoĭ* | *operám dabam.*
841 *Ĭám* | *ego ex corpore éxigam omnis máculas maerorúm tibi.*

87 (9) After *dissyllables* which scan as pyrrhics or iambics, the final long in the latter case being shortened; examples are

Men. 389 *Égon' te iussi cóquere? ER. Certo, tíbĭ* | *et parasitó tuo.*

Am. 280 *Nísi* | *item unam, uérberatus quám pependi pérpetem.*

Cf. Cap. 415, 749, 950, etc.

88 The two last kinds of hiatus, (8) and (9), are far from being universally accepted, but the former may be

paralleled in later poets; e.g.

Verg. Ecl. VIII. 108 *Credimus? An quĭ | amant, ipsi sibi somnia fingunt?*

Aen. VI. 507 *Nomen et arma locum seruant, tĕ | amice nequiui.*

With regard to monosyllables ending in *-m*, it is probable (Corssen Ausspr. II. 790) that final *m* was much more distinctly heard in the time of Pl. than afterwards[1], and therefore, although hiatus would not be allowable after monosyllables ending in a short vowel, for they could not be shortened by it, it might be less objectionable after monosyllables ending with *-m*. Even Lucretius has

III. 1082 *Sed dŭm | abest quod auemus, id exsuperare uidetur.*

89 One other point is remarked by Ussing (Prol., p. 220): that hiatus seemed to be considered an ornament rather than a blemish when the two open vowels were the same[2]; thus

Verg. G. I. 281 *Ter sunt conati | imponere Peliŏ | Ossam.*
Hor. Od. I. 28. 24 *Ossibus et capiti | inhumato.*
II. 20. 13 *Iam Daedaleo | ocior Icaro.*

This is the case in Cap. 139, 152, 263, 354, 364, 374, 426, 823, 850, 866, 1006, 1016.

90 To sum up, hiatus can only be admitted after these monosyllabic and dissyllabic words, unless it can be accounted for under one of the headings (A) or (B): in all other cases it must be attributed to some corruption in the text. Its comparative rareness would seem almost strange in such conversational verse if we did not know on the authority of Cicero that the Romans were given to running their vowels together in ordinary talk: *hoc Latina lingua*

[1] Quintilian, IX. 4. 40, says of final *m* before a word beginning with a vowel, "neque enim eximitur sed obscuratur, et tantum aliqua inter duas uocales uelut nota est, ne ipsae coeant."

[2] Gellius, VII. 20, quotes several instances from Homer.

sic obseruat, nemo ut tam rusticus sit, qui uocales nolit coniungere, Orat. 44. 150.

APOCOPE.

91 This is the neglect in scansion of a final letter, otherwise than by elision. The name is objectionable, as it implies that the poets *metri gratia* cut off a letter which was pronounced in ordinary speech. The contrary is the fact; the early dramatists and poets, in the peculiarities noticed below, merely followed the popular pronunciation, in which sounds were omitted or weakened to a much greater extent than ever appeared in the written language: this was due to the constant tendency, felt in all languages, to reduce the effort of articulation.

92 The effect of this tendency upon final letters and syllables is noticed in § 116; the two instances of it which come under the head of Apocope are:

(1) The interrogative particle *-ne*, when added to a word ending in a vowel, and followed by a word beginning with a consonant, was probably pronounced simply as *n'*, at any rate in short sharp questions, and the early poets frequently, and the later ones sometimes, followed this general usage; e.g. Verg. Aen. XII. 503 *tanton' placuit*, 797 *mortalin' decuit*, Cap. 643 *certon'? Quin...*, etc.

93 (2) A final *s*, in words ending in *ĭs* or *ŭs*, was in early poetry frequently neglected before a consonant, the final syllable thus remaining short. Cicero, in speaking of this usage[1], mentions only the termination *-us*, but cf.

[1] Quod iam subrusticum uidetur, olim autem politius, eorum uerborum, quorum eaedem erant postremae duae litterae quae sunt in *optumus*, postremam litteram detrahebant, nisi uocalis insequebatur. Ita non erat ea offensio in uersibus quam nunc fugiunt poetae noui. Ita enim loquebamur *qui est omnibu' princeps* non *omnibus princeps* et *uita illa dignu' locoque* non *dignus*. Orat. 48. 161.

Enn. 601 (Vahlen) *Tum lateralĭs dolor certissimŭs nuntiŭs mortis.*

Lucr. II. 53 *Quid dubitas quin omnĭs sit haec rationĭs potestas?*

Cat. 116. 8 *At fixus nostris tu dabĭs supplicium,*

as well as Lucr. I. 159 *ex omnibŭs rebus*, 186 *infantibŭs paruis*, Cic. Arat. *lustratŭs nitore.*

So in this play we have *facis* 949, *magis* 290 etc., *satis* 125 etc., as well as *bonus* 956, *erus* 200, *minus* 430, *suauius* 498, *sumus* 120, *tribus* 915, with the final *s* dropped.

94 That this was not regarded as a licence is shewn by its occurrence at the end of a line, where the versification is most careful; e.g. 14 *rupturŭs sum*, Am. 411 *Amphitruonĭs sum*, Bac. 313 *occidistĭs me*, Ter. Hec. 653 *nullŭs sum*, etc. Final *s* after a vowel was in fact very lightly sounded or altogether omitted in common speech, and in some instances disappeared from the written language; cf. *nauta* ναύτης, *amabare amabaris*, *ipse ipsus*, *pote potis*, *mage magis*, *luxuria luxuries*, *familiae* and *pater-familias*, and the old nom. plur. of *o-* stems in *s* (see on 35). The *s* would naturally be less marked when not followed by a vowel, and the early writers availed themselves of this pronunciation; the poets of the Augustan age, however, following the Greek rules, restored to it its full force as a consonant.

95 Both these kinds of apocope are sometimes combined, when *-ne* is added to the second pers. sing. of verbs or to words ending in *-is* or *-us*; that is, both *s* and *e* are omitted. Thus we have *ain audin credin faterin iuben pergin sponden uiden uin satin* in this play, *in* for *isne* (pronoun) Merc. 598, for *isne* (verb) Ter. Eun. 651, *expectatun* Am. 679, *sanun* As. 385, etc. If the final syllable was naturally short it remains short, as in *credĭn satĭn sanŭn*; if long, it is sometimes shortened before a vowel, but not always; thus

Verg. Aen. vi. 780 *Educet. Vidĕn ut geminae stant uertice cristae ?*

Cap. 846 *Iúbĕn an non iubés astitui.*

As. 598 *Audī́n hunc opera ut lárgus est.*

96 Here may be noticed the peculiarity of scansion by which the final syllable of a word ending in *s* sometimes coalesces with a following *es* or *est*; thus we have *sperabilist* (=*sperabilis est*) in 518, *fassust* in 295, *uenturu's* in 183, *uirtust* in Pers. 267, etc.

CONTRACTION.

97 Under this head come peculiarities of scansion which arise (i) by synaeresis, (ii) by syncope, (iii) owing to the double character of the vowel and consonant *i* and (iv) of the vowel and consonant *u*. It must be borne in mind that these were popular pronunciations, not arbitrary changes introduced by the poets *metri gratia*.

98 (i) Synaeresis is the contraction of vowels (consecutive or separated by an *h*), which properly form separate syllables in the same word, so as to form one syllable (cf. Cic. Orat. 44. 150 quoted in § 90); thus we have

99 EA, EHA. Verg. G. iv. 34 *alue̅a̅ria*, Aen. x. 487 and Lucr. i. 306 *e̅a̅dem*, Hor. Od. i. 37. 5 *Ante̅h̅a̅c nefas depromere Caecubum*, etc. So in this play *e̅a̅dem*, *e̅a̅m*, *me̅a̅*, *me̅a̅m* etc., *e̅a̅mus* 1027, *ante̅h̅a̅c* 244, *de̅a̅rtuauisti* 672.

100 EI, EHI. Verg. Aen. vii. 603 *Centum aere̅i̅ claudunt*, i. 131 *uocat, de̅h̅i̅nc talia fertur*, Lucr. iii. 383 *ărāne̅i̅ tenuia fila*, etc. In Pl. *me̅i̅ me̅i̅s e̅i̅ e̅i̅s* often (see R. 377); so *re̅i̅* (Cap. 460, Lucr. iii. 918, etc.), *die̅i̅* (Cap. 464, Verg. G. i. 208, etc.). But *rēi*, *diēi*, *fidēi* are also found, as well as *rĕi*, and, in the time of the Empire, *fidĕī* (see R. 342).

101 EO. Lucr. ii. 205 *est de̅o̅rsum*, Prop. ii. 8. 26 *hoc e̅o̅dem ferro*, etc. So in this play *me̅o̅* 141, *me̅o̅s* 541, *e̅o̅dem* 42, *e̅o̅s* 473, *e̅o̅* (adv.) 70, (verb) 510, *de̅o̅rum* 622, *de̅o̅s* 727.

102 EU. In this play we have *e̅u̅m* 9, *me̅u̅m* 552, as well as *meus deus* which may be instances of apocope.

103 II, IHI. Instances of *i* before another vowel forming one syllable with it are usually to be explained by the *i* being treated as a consonant (§ 109), but where the second vowel is another *i* contraction probably takes place. Thus Hor. Ep. I. 1. 71 *iudiciis fruar i̅i̅sdem,* Verg. Aen. v. 269 *euincti tempora taeni̅i̅s;* so in ordinary speech *gratiis* was contracted to *gratis, audiisse* to *audisse, mihi nihil* to *mi nil,* etc.; *dii, ii* are probably always contracted in the early poets.

104 OI, OHI. Lucr. I. 976 *quod pro̅h̅i̅beat efficiatque,* Verg. Aen. XI. 383 *pro̅i̅nde tono,* and *pro̅i̅nde* probably always in good writers. In this play we have *pro̅h̅i̅bete* 804, *pro̅i̅n* always.

105 Perhaps the scansion of *eius, huius, quoius* as monosyllables is due to synaeresis, the *u* coalescing with the previous diphthong *ei ui oi*; instances are

Lucr. I. 139 *Principium cu̅i̅u̅s hinc nobis exordia sumet.*
Cic. Arat. *Atque e̅i̅u̅s ipse manet religatus corpore torto.*

In this play we have *e̅i̅u̅s* 107, 289, *hu̅i̅u̅s* 39, 641, 800, *quo̅i̅u̅s* 106, as well as other instances which may be explained by apocope of the final *s.*

106 The scansion of *aio* is peculiar: the original form was *ai-io* (so written by Cic., according to Quint. I. 4. 11; in Trin. 428, A has *aiiebas,* in 642 *maiiores,* in 201 *peiiurius*), but the first *i* was usually dropped both in writing and pronunciation, the *a* being either shortened or taken as a diphthong with the following *i*; e.g. either *ăit* (Cap. 592 613) or *a̅i̅t* (Cap. 567, 979); sometimes, however, the original length of the first syllable is preserved, as in *āit* Cap. 365, *āin* Am. 284, As. 901. With regard to the imperfect, the MSS. always have the uncontracted form *aiebam,* etc.; but often the metre shews the scansion to be *a̅i̅bam*; as in Cap. 561,

Merc. 635 *Cíuisne esset án peregrinus. Cíuem esse aibant Átticum.*
804 *Rus ábiisse aibant. Núnc domum renúntio.*

On the other hand, the longer form is required in Cap. 676, Trin. 428, Am. 387, etc.

107 (ii) Syncope is the omission of a short vowel standing between two consonants which may be easily pronounced consecutively; e.g. *dextra aspris caldus saeclum lamnae lardus maniplus puertiae calfecit repostus porgere surpere*; such contractions must have been common in ordinary speech. In this play we have *altrum* 8, *periclum* 740, *uinclis* 413, *surpuit* 760.

108 On the other hand in some cases either the MSS. preserve or the scansion demands the uncontracted form, even when it is one which early went out of use; e.g. Cap. 620 *expurigare*, 655 *nuculeus*, Trin. 70 *obiurigare*, Most. 150 *discipulina*, Bac. 968 *extempulo*.

109 (iii) Another form of contraction is caused by the vowel *i* being pronounced as the consonant *i* (*y*). This method of pronunciation is adopted by the Augustan poets in such words as *ābiĕtĕ* (Verg. Aen. II. 16), *pāriĕtĭbus* (Aen. II. 442), *āriĕtĕ* (Aen. II. 492); cf. also

Verg. G. I. 482 *Flūuiorum rex Eridanus camposque per omnes.*
Hor. Od. III. 4. 41 *Vos lene consīlium et datis et dato.*
Od. III. 6. 6 *Hinc omne princīpium huc refer exitum.*

In Pl. we find *diu die diebus*, as well as *gratiam* (Cap. 721), *gratias* (Trin. 821, 824), *otio* (Trin. 838), etc. *Lien* is always a monosyllable in Pl.; cf. Cas. 414, Curc. 220, 236, 240.

110 In *scio* and *nescio* the *i* probably always remained a vowel, the *o* being often shortened; these verbs alone are found with the *o* short in Lucr., Verg. and Hor. Odes; Catullus has *uolŏ* and Hor. in the Satires *uolŏ eŏ uetŏ dixerŏ*; instances are frequent in Ovid and later poets treated the *o* in all verbs as common. It is possible, of course, to scan *scio nescio* in the scenic poets, but not always in other writers; e.g. in Hor. Od. III. 24. 64 *nēsciŏ quid* must form a choriambus.

111 (iv) The double character of *u*, vowel and consonant, also facilitated contraction; thus

(*a*) a short vowel *u* before another vowel is almost indistinguishable from a consonant *u* (pronounced *w*); *tenuis*, for instance, seems to have been, until after Vergil's time, always dissyllabic (*tenwis*);

G. II. 180 *Tēnuĭs ubi argilla et dumosis calculus aruis.*
Aen. v. 432 *Gēnuă labant, uastos quatit aeger anhelitus artus.*

So in this play *dūellum* 68, *sūī tūī* etc. frequently, *fūisse* 638, *fūisti* 628, *fūistis* 197, and *fuit* (monosyllable) often.

112 On the other hand in the early language *u* was treated as a vowel in many words in which it was afterwards considered a consonant; and this usage was occasionally adopted by later poets as an intentional archaism. Thus in Lucr. we find *sŭemus, sŭadent, reliqŭas, aqŭae, solŭo* etc., in Hor. *silŭae, milŭae*, in Catullus *euolŭam*, etc.

In Pl. *reliquos* is always tetrasyllabic, and *miluos, larua* trisyllabic.

113 (*b*) Consonantal *u* (*w*) between two vowels is apt to drop out and allow the two vowels to coalesce, as in *amasti insuerit norit malo prudens aetas udus iunior mobilis momentum* etc., for *amauisti insueuerit nouerit mauolo prouidens aeuitas* etc.

So *sis* (110) for *si uis*, *sultis* (456) for *si uoltis*, *dīuītiis* (170), and perhaps *iūuentus* (104).

114 (*c*) Sometimes, however, the *u* forms a diphthong with the preceding vowel, and a succeeding short vowel drops out; thus *fautor cautor nauta auceps* are shortened forms of *fauitor cauitor nauita auiceps*; on this depends the pun in Truc. 685, on *cauillator* and *caulis*. To the same effect is the well-known story of Crassus (Cic. Div. II. 40. 84), who, embarking with his army for the ill-fated Parthian expedition, met an itinerant fig-seller crying "*Cauneas!*" (sc. *ficos*, figs from Caunus in Asia). This, says Cicero, might have been taken as a warning; being apparently identical in sound with *caue ne eas*. So perhaps

in this play $\overline{auis}$ 123, and $\overline{caue}$ 431 al.; but see inf. § 136 sqq.

5 Some scholars have maintained that contraction in the writings of Pl. was far from being confined within the above limits. Prof. Ramsay, for instance, considered that most of the difficulties of Plautine scansion were to be explained by a species of contraction, or 'correption,' which consisted in running two syllables into one. Among the examples which he gives[1] are the following:— *tibi ab*, *uocat*, *quid hoc*, *quod omnes*, *quid a*, *ego inter*, *quid tu inter*, which he supposes to have been pronounced *tb' ab*, *wcat*, *qud hoc* or *quid hc*, *quod 'mnes*, *qud a*, *eg' 'nter*, *quid t' 'nter*. But this theory is open to many objections; among others, that it would lead to the confusion of similar words, that when two monosyllables were thus run together, it would leave one of them formless and unrecognisable; and that it would produce collocations of consonants unknown to Latin and, one would think, beyond the power of the human tongue to pronounce. The instances which are given in support of it are susceptible of another and a far more probable explanation (cf. inf. § 136 sqq.).

The remaining points in which Pl. scansion differs from that of the Augustan poets are two: vowels which are scanned short by the latter are sometimes long in Pl., and vowels long by nature or position are sometimes scanned short in Pl.

ARCHAIC LONG VOWELS.

The tendency to reduce the effort of articulation, which has been already mentioned, acts most strongly upon unaccented syllables, and as the final syllable in Latin was always unaccented[2], it naturally suffered most from this

[1] Intr. to Mostellaria, p. c.—cvi.

[2] The accent referred to is not the *ictus metricus* but the accent of ordinary speech, which in Latin did not differ much from the English practice; see R. bk I. ch. 13.

cause. Sometimes the whole syllable was lost, as in *ager(us)*, *puer(us)*; *animal(i)*; *ferunt(i)*, cf. φέρουσι, Dor. φέροντι; *sum(i)*, *inquam(i)*, cf. Gr. verbs in -μι; *ut* and *uti*; and *fac(e) dic(e) hic(e) sin(e)*, etc.; but with these instances Prosody has nothing to do. Sometimes the final consonant was lost (e.g. ablatival *d*, see on 405) or weakened in pronunciation, as with *m* and *s* (§§ 88, 93); and sometimes the final vowel, originally long, came to be pronounced short. In the following instances this change had not been completed before the time of Pl.

117 *a* is sometimes long in nom. sing. of proper names and masc. nouns of 1st declension; e.g. *Sosiā*, Am. 439. The case originally end in *ās*, cf. Gr. -ης, and ποιητής, ναύτης with *poeta*, *nauta*. The XII. Tables have *paricidas* for *paricida*.

Ita probably had the *a* long originally; see Corssen Musspr. II. p. 454 and cf. Cap. 502.

118 *e* final was originally long in the inf. and is occasionally found so in Pl.; e.g. Truc. 425 *darē*, Ps. 355, Mil. 848 *promerē*.

119 *e* is sometimes found long in abl. of 3rd declension; the original form was *īd* (cf. *couentinoid* for *couentionid* in S. C. de Bacch.), but the *d* disappeared early (see on 405); the *ī* was retained throughout the classical period in adjectives in -*is* (to prevent confusion with the neuter) and in some substantives, but was shortened to *ĕ* in most substantives from about 150 B.C. onwards. Pl. wrote in the transitional time, and so we find in his plays many ablatives in *i* which later ended in *ĕ* (e.g. *sorti parti luci*, etc.) as well as ablatives which are written with *e* in the MSS. but which the metre shews to have the last syllable long. Such are 914 *carnē*, Cas. 140 *prietē*, Ps. 616 *militē*, Mil. 699 *uxorē*, 707 *mortē*, Pers. 42 *pumicē*, and probably Cap. 229 *capitē*; and we have in

Lucr. I. 806 *Imbribus ut tabē nimborum arbusta uacillent.*
III. 734 *Et mala multa animus contagē fungitur eius.*

20 *o* final is long in Pl. always in *immo* and sometimes in *modo* and *ego*.

Immo was originally an ablative (=*imo?*) but it is usually said to have the *o* short. It is doubtful if there are any such instances before the time of Martial; Catullus has it long, and out of about 180 examples in Pl. it is long in 10 instances (Bac. 146, Men. 546, Merc. 297, 388, 708, 737, 1015, Ps. 934, Poen. 151, Trin. 427) and doubtful in the remainder.

In *modo*, another abl., the final *o* had been shortened by Vergil's time, but in earlier writers it is occasionally found long: e.g.

Lucil. *Vnu' modo de multis qui ingenio sit.*
Ter. Hec. 830 *Eum haéc cognouit Mýrrhina in digitó modo me habénte.*
Lucr. II. 941 *Nec congressa mọdo uitalis conuenienti.*
1135 *Plura modo dispargit et a se corpora mittit.*
IV. 1181 *Vna modo, causas abeundi quaerat honestas.*
Cat. 10. 7 *Iam Bithynia quomodō se haberet.*
Cic. Arat. frag. *Huic non una modo caput.*

In Pl. it is long in Cap. 458 and other passages, such as As. 5, 869, 876, Aul. 239, etc.

Ego in classical Latin has the *o* short, but it is long in several passages in Pl.; e.g.

As. 810 *Sequere hác; egone haec pátiar aut taceam? émori.*
Aul. 457 *Cóctum ego non uápulatum dúdum conductús fui.*
Cas. 781 *Cena úbi erit cocta egó ruri cenáuero.*

For *o* final in verbs, see § 110.

1 *āt, ēt, īt.* In verbs of the 1st, 2nd and 4th conjugation the bases ended in a long vowel, *amā monē audī*, and as this vowel is always long in the 2nd person *amās* etc., and in the 3rd person of the passive *amātur* etc., it was

no doubt originally long in the 3rd person of the active *amāt* etc.[1] So in Pl. we find *arāt* As. 874, *habēt* Am. 652, *īt* Curc. 489, Poen. 683, and in the Cap., 11 *negāt*, 196 *decēt*, 25 *fīt*, 350 *scīt*. In the 3rd pers. of the perfect also, the *-it* seems to have been originally long (= *-ist*, Papillon, Gr. and Lat. Term. p. 182) and is occasionally spelt *-eit* in inscriptions; in Merc. 530 A has *redieit*. In Am. 643 we find *uicīt*, Mil. 214 *astitīt*, Ps. 311 *vixīt*, etc., and in this play, 9 *vendidīt*, 34 *emīt*, 746 *obtigīt*.

122 *-ār* is often long in Pl., as Am. 559 *loquār*, Am. 1056 *opprimār*. The *-r* of the passive represents the reflexive pronoun *se*, *opprimam-se*, *opprimase*, *opprimar* (Papillon 167).

123 *-ōr* in verbs was originally long for the same reason (*amor* = *amō-se*), and is sometimes found so in Pl., e.g. Mil. 633 *experiōr*, Cap. 1023 *regrediōr*.

124 *-ōr* in the nom. sing. of substantives is sometimes long. The nom. sing. of all nouns was originally formed by adding *-s* to the stem; thus when the stem ended in *ŏr* the nom. would end in *-ors*, and when the *-s* dropped off, as it did in all *-r* stems, the *o* would be lengthened in compensation; cf. πατήρ (for πατερς) *pār* (gen. *păris*). When the stem was *ōr*, the *o* would remain long in nom. after the *s* had dropped off. In both these cases the final *or* was afterwards shortened, but the original length is sometimes preserved in Pl., e.g. Am. 223 *Deinde uterque imperatōr in medium exeunt* (cret. tetr.); so also *sorōr uxōr amōr*, etc.

125 Similarly the original termination of the comparative in Latin was *-iōs* (R. 174), and in Pl. the *-ōr* of comparative is sometimes long; e.g. 782 *auctiōr est*, Am. 548 *longiōr hac*, Bac. 123 *stultiōr es*, etc.

[1] Peile, p. 324.

26 *-būs* in the dative plural is sometimes long in Pl. (see Peile p. 325), e.g. Merc. 900 *aédibūs. aedís probat*, Rud. 975 *ómnibūs adséntio.*

27 *-ĕs* in nom. of 3rd decl., with gen. in *ĕtis, ĭtis, ĭdis*, is short in Augustan poets; but even they make exceptions, e.g. *ariēs, abiēs, pariēs.* In the early language it was long, in compensation for the loss of the stem dental, and the original quantity is perhaps found in Pl., e.g. Aul. 519 *milés impransus*, As. 330 *tum ígitur tu diués es factus.*

28 *ēs* from *sum* is always long in Pl. and Ter. (R. 260); e.g. lines 333, 412, 427, 837, 860 of this play. Being an unemphatic word, it was afterwards shortened contrary to the general rule with monosyllables, and in the Augustan poets is always short.

29 The above are instances in which the general tendency to shorten long unaccented syllables, especially final ones, had not in the time of Pl. entirely obscured their original quantity. In the following three instances syllables originally long were afterwards shortened in accordance with the general rule in Latin that a vowel, standing before another vowel or diphthong and forming a separate syllable, is short.

30 *fio* : here the *i* was long by nature, and is found so in the Augustan poets except in *fit* (supra § 121), in the imperfect subjunctive *fierem* etc., and in the infinitive *fieri.* Some of these forms could not have been used at all in Dactylic verse, others not without elision, if the *i* had been kept long, and the Dactylic poets consequently shortened it in accordance with the general rule. Pl. and Ter., however, to whose metres this would not apply, sometimes kept it long; thus 998 *fīerent*, 843 *fīeri*, but in 587, 965, 996 *fĭeri.*

31 *fui* : the *u* in *fui* and its persons, as well as in other perfects in *-ui*, was long in the oldest writers, according

to Priscian. Probably these perfects were formed, like so many others, by the addition of *-u-* to the stem. Ennius has *fuui* (*fu-u-i*) *annuui genuui*, and *pluuit* occurs often. The consonantal *u* (=*w*) was then absorbed in the preceding vowel *u*, which was thus lengthened, but was subsequently shortened again according to the general rule. In Pl. we sometimes find it long; thus in 262 *fūimus*, 555 and 633 *fūit*, in Mil. 1364 *fūerim*, Men. 63 *plūerat*.

132 *rei*: the *e* in datives of this declension was invariably long (when it did not form a diphthong with the *i*, § 100) except in *rei*; *rĕī* is found in Pl. Ter. and Hor. Od. III. 24. 64; *rēī* in Pl. and Lucr., and *rēi* in Pl. Ter. and Lucr.

133 Finally, under Archaic Long Vowels may be mentioned *Acheruns*, which in Lucr. and Verg. always has the first syllable short (e.g. Lucr. I. 120, III. 37; Verg. Aen. VII. 312), while in Pl. it is long in nearly 20 passages, including lines 689, 998, 999 of this play), short in two, Poen. 831, Most. 498. These two instances are explained (§§ 137, 140) by the peculiarity of Pl. scansion which is noticed next.

LONG VOWELS SHORTENED.

134 We now come to the chief difficulty in Plautine scansion; numerous Iambic, Trochaic and Anapaestic lines occur in which a long syllable stands after a short one and forms with it (as is evident from the scansion of the rest of the line) either the *arsis* or the *thesis* of a foot. Now in these measures neither *arsis* nor *thesis* can contain an iambus; the most that either of them can contain is one long syllable or two short ones. The question therefore arises, are we to scan this iambus as one long syllable or as two short ones? The first alternative is that which is adopted by the advocates of the 'correption' theory, who hold that the two syllables are to be run together and pronounced as one; some of the objections to this theory have

been already pointed out in § 115. The other and better view is that the *long syllable is to be shortened* and the iambus scanned as a pyrrhic. Two explanations of this shortening have been given.

135 (i) The first is that the early dramatists sometimes neglected the law of position. Now in the first place this fails to explain the shortening of vowels long by *nature*, a large proportion of the instances; and in the second place, even with regard to vowels long by position it is no explanation at all, but simply restates the difficulty. These vowels are shewn by the metre to be short, whereas by the law of position they should be long; it is no explanation, but only a paraphrase, to say that in such cases the law of position is neglected. What is wanted is an explanation *why* it is so, and why the *natural* length of other syllables is neglected also.

136 (ii) The second explanation refers this shortening to the influence of the *ictus metricus* (§ 39); an influence which the early drama inherited from the old Saturnian Rhythm, but which disappeared with the complete adoption of the Greek method of versification (cf. § 79). Now the metrical *ictus*, although a different thing from the natural *accent* of a word, very generally coincides with it, and indeed takes its place in the rhythmical recitation of verse, and it is therefore not unnatural to attribute to the *ictus* in verse an effect similar to that produced by the *accent* in ordinary pronunciation. And the effect of accenting a syllable in ordinary speech is to throw the unaccented syllables on each side of it into the shade, as it were; with the common result of weakening or shortening them if long, and often causing them to disappear if short. The following words[1] illustrate this effect of the accent, both backwards and forwards:—*c*(*a*)*lámor*, *discip*(*u*)*lína*, *pur*(*i*)-

[1] Peile, Gr. and Lat. Etym. p. 331. As to final syllables, which were never accented in Latin, see §§ 116 sqq.

gáre, teg(u)méntum, nó(ue)ram, quaés(i)tor, uínc(u)lum, uól(i)tis, íllĭus, hómĭnes, plátĕa, etc.

137 The second explanation, then, attributes to the *ictus metricus* a similar influence, forwards and backwards. For it has been already stated that the iambus which has to be shortened to a pyrrhic always forms the *arsis* or *thesis* of a foot, and a moment's consideration will shew that if it forms the *arsis* the *ictus* must fall on its first syllable (⏑́ –), and if it forms the *thesis* the *ictus* must fall on the first syllable of the following *arsis* (⏑ – ⏑́). Consequently the long syllable which is to be scanned as short stands either just after or just before the syllable receiving the *ictus* and (according to this theory) is thereby shortened. This will be made clearer by the following instances, taken mainly from Brix Trin. p. 15—18. The syllables forming the iambus which has to be shortened to a pyrrhic are printed in ordinary type.

138 (1) Forward influence of the *ictus*:

Trin. 60 *Namque* énĭm *tu, credo, me ínprudentem obrépseris.*

Trin. 80 *Non* pótĕst *utrumque fíeri. M. Quaproptér? C. Rogas?*

902 Áb ĭpson *istas áccepisti? S. E mánibus* dédĭt *mi ipse ín manus.*

Ps. 154 *Numquam édepol uostrum dúrius tergum* érĭt *quam terginum hóc meumst.*

Mil. 696 *Tum óbstetrix expóstulauit mécum,* párŭm *missúm sibi.*

Most. 572 *Immo* ábĭ *domum! Verum hércle dico, abí domum.*

Trin. 763 *Sed* uídĕ *consilium, sí placet. C. Quid cónsilist?*

Most. 256 Nóuă *pictura intérpolare uís opus lepidíssumum.*

Trin. 728 Dédĭ, *reposcam, ut hábeam mecum quód feram uiáticum.*

Sti. 98 Vírŏs *nostros, quibus tú nos uoluisti ésse matres fámilias?*

99 Bónăs *ut aequomst fácere facitis, quóm tamen absentés uiros.*

139 Trin. 851 Pól hĭc *quidem fungíno generest: cápite se totúm tegit.*

Bac. 187 *Salútem* tíbi ăb *sodáli solidam núntio.*

Trin. 630 Quód ĕst *facillumúm facis. LY. Quid id ést? LE. Amico iniúriam.*

Mil. 1138 *Néminem pol uídeo* nísi hŭnc *quem uólumus conuentum. P. Ét ego uos.*

Curc. 698 Béne ĕt *pudice mé domi habuit. T. Haúd uoluntate íd sua.*

Ter. Heaut. 505 *Quam súa? An eo fit* quía ĭn *re nostra aut gaúdio.*

Trin. 969 Quód ă *me te accepísse fassu's. S. Ábs te accepisse? C. Íta loquor.*

Poen. 619 *Sed* quíd hŭc *tantum hominum incédunt? Ecquidnam ádferunt.*

Sti. 237 *Adíbo ad hominem. G.* Quís haĕc *est quae aduorsúm uenit.*

140 Trin. 664 Ín ŏcculto *iacébis, quom te máxume clarúm uoles.*

Trin. 318 Quíd ĕx*probras, bene quód fecisti? Tíbi fecisti, nón mihi.*

Pers. 109 *Sapis múltum ad Genium. T.* Séd ĕc*quid id meminísti, ere.*

Ter. Heaut. 551 *Si* quíd hŭ*ius simile fórte aliquando euénerit.*

[1]Poen. 831 *Quóduis genus ibi hóminum uideas,* quási Ăche*runtem uéneris.*

[1]Most. 498 *Viuóm me accersunt* ád Ăche*runtem mórtui.*

141 Am. 761 Dédĭsse *dono hodié, qua te illi dónatum esse díxeras?*

Sti. 532 *Nós potius onerémus nosmet* uícĭssatim *uoluptátibus.*

142 (2) Backward influence of the *ictus*:—

Mil. 1061 *Dabitúr, quantum ipsus pretí poscet. P.* Talĕntúm Philĭp*pum huic opus aúrist.*

Rud. 895 Sed ŭx*ór scelesta me ómnibus seruát modis.*

143 Trin. 456 Ferĕn*tárium esse amícum inuentum intéllego.*

Mil. 1091 *Lepidé factumst: iam ex sérmone hoc* gubĕr*nábunt doctius pórro.*

[1] V. sup. § 133.

144 Ter. Phor. 902 *Quid ád me ibatis? Rídiculum:* uerĕbámini.

Mil. 1137 *Séquimini:* simŭl *círcumspicite, né quis adsit árbiter.*

Sti. 179 Per ănn*ónam caram dixit me natúm pater.*

Am. 504 *Séd ubi summus ímperator nón adest* ad ĕx*ércitum.*

Aul. 165 *Núnc* ego ĭ*stúm, soror, laborem démam et deminuám tibi.*

Pers. 318 Enĭm *métuo, ut possim reícere in bubílem, ne uagéntur.*

Trin. 1052 *Sí* mage ĕx*ígere occípias, duarum rérum exoritur óptio.*

Ter. Phor. 352 Negăt *Phánium esse hanc síbi cognatam Démipho.*

557 *Quántum opus est* tibi ăr*génti, loquere. P. Sólae trigintá minae.*

Ter. And. 261 Amŏr, *místericordia húius, nuptiárum sollicitátio.*

Ter. Hec. 42 Ego ĭn*térea meum non pótui tutarí locum.*

Ter. Phor. 787 *Factúm uolo: ac pol mínus queo* uirĭ *cúlpa, quam me dígnumst.*

Mil. 362 Erĭ *cóncubina est haéc quidem. P. Mihi quóque pol ita uidétur.*

1037 *Adeát, si quid uolt. P. Sí quid uis,* adĭ, *múlier. M. Pulcer, sálue.*

Poen. 416 Dedĭ *dúdum, prius quam me éuocauistí foras.*

145 Ter. Phor. 648 Vt ăd *paúca redeam ac míttam illius inéptias.*

Poen. 1171 Vt haĕc *ínueniantur hódie esse huius filiae.*

Sti. 107 *Quíd istuc est* quod hŭc *éxquaesitum múlierum morés uenis?*

146 Ep. 418 *Quae hic ád*minĭ*stráret ád rem diuinám tibi.*

Sti. 716 *Haúd tuom istuc ést uereri te. Eripe* ĕx *óre tíbias.*

Mil. 1043 *Heus dí*gniŏr *fuít quisquam hómo qui esset? P. Non hércle humanust érgo.*

1024 *Age age, út tibi maxumĕ cóncinnumst. P. Nullúmst hoc stolidius sáxum.*

1031 *Adsum;* ĭmperă, *si quid uís. PY. Quid illaec narrát tibi? PA. Lamentári.*

147 From the above instances it appears (1) that the forward influence of the *ictus* is not confined to iambic *words*;

the iambus always *begins* with the beginning of a word, but it may be made up of two words, with or without elision, or of a monosyllable and the first syllable of a succeeding word, or of the two first syllables of a polysyllabic word; (2) that the backward influence is exercised whether the *ictus* falls on a long syllable (⏑ – ⏑́) or on the first of two equivalent short ones (⏑ – ⏑́ ⏑), and whether the syllables concerned form one or two complete words or part only of a word or words.

148 The matter, then, may be summed up thus:—

When the arsis or thesis of a foot in an Iambic, Trochaic or Anapaestic line consists of two syllables which in ordinary Prosody would form an iambus, the long syllable (whether long by nature or position) is shortened by reason of the *ictus* falling upon either the preceding or the following syllable; when this happens *in arsi*, i.e. when the influence of the *ictus* is forward, the iambus always begins with the beginning of a word; but when it happens *in thesi* this is not always the case[1].

[1] Prof. Tyrrell in his edition of the Miles states the matter thus:—"(1) In words, or combinations of words, forming in ordinary Prosody an iambus, if the accent (or *ictus metricus*) be on the first syll., the long unaccented syll. is shortened. (2) In words or combinations of words similarly forming a bacchius (⏑ – –), if the accent (or *ictus metricus*) be on the third syll., the second is shortened." To the wording of the first rule no exception can be taken, for the *ictus* can never fall on a short syllable unless the following syllable is intended to be also short, the two together representing the long syllable which in the original or proper foot of the measure would receive the *ictus*. But the wording of the second rule is open to objection; the case, as so stated, is for instance invariable in cretics, without of course the second syllable being shortened; e.g. in 239 *Nám secundúm patrem*, the word *secundum* forms a bacchius with the *ictus* on

149 The following are the most certain instances in the Captiui; other cases, in which either the scansion or the reading is uncertain, or in which independent ground exists for suspicion, are noticed in the metrical notes.

(1) Forward influence of the *ictus* (i.e. in a resolved *arsis*):—

a. Vowels long by nature.

152 *hábĕ*, 196 *lábŏs*, 250 *ín hăc*, 286 *uidĕlicet*, 607 *iúbĕ*, 609 *tácĕ*, 883 *uídĕ*.

b. Vowels long by position.

70 *quía ĭnuocatus*, 193 *ápŭd trapezitam*, 246 *quód hŏstica*, 261 *ápŭd uos*, 279 *quíd ĭpsus*, 330 *ápŭd uos*, 334 *séd ĭs priuatam*, 335 *pól ĭs quidem*, 363 *quód ĭs uelit*, 426 *íd ŭt scias*, 441 *tíbi ĭn perpetuom*, 541 *quíd ĭstuc*, 551 *prócŭl recedas*, 557 *uídĕn tu*, 568 *énĭm repertus*, 571 *négo ĭnquam*, 595 *uídĕn tu*, 597 *ápŭd carnificem*, 620 *séd hŏc primum*, 626 *ápŭd te*, 698 *sít hŏc negoti*, 877 *ábi ĭn malam*, 972 *quía ĕcfugi*, 997 *séd ĕccum*, 1021 *pátĕr meus*.

150 (2) Backward influence of the *ictus* (i.e. in a resolved *thesis*):—

a. Vowels long by nature.

18 *domŏ quém*, 21 *domĭ séruit*, 60 *forĭs íllic*, 90 *uel ĭre éxtra*, 133 *quis hĭc lóquitur*, 167 *habĕ módo*, 197 *domĭ fŭístis*, 343 *uelĭs pérferat*, 364 *dedĭ uíginti*, 642 *uidĕ sís*, 870 *abĭ stúltus*.

b. Vowels long by position.

22 *enĭm uéro*, 49 *ut ĭn séruitute*, 71 *scio ăbsúrde*, 83 *in ŏccúlto*, 124 *ita ŭt dícis*, 246 *perque cŏnséruitium*, 498 *quid ĕst suáuius*, 534 *enĭm uéro*, 572 *quidĕm quám*, 597 *atra pĭx ágitet*, 617 *ego ĭntér*, 657 *quidĕm mé*, 913 *nimĭsque hércle*, 917 *cocŭm pérconta-batur*, 999 *enĭm uéro*.

the last, yet the second is of course long. Again, suppose a trochaic line beginning *Séd amicós* or an iambic line beginning *Sed ís amicós*; the word *amicos* would come under the rule as worded above, yet surely its second syllable would not be shortened.

151 Moreover there are a few words of very common occurrence in which vowels long by position are generally considered to be shortened in Pl. independently of the metrical *ictus.* These are *ille inde unde nempe esse*, and perhaps one or two others. The following examples, among others, shew, if the text be genuine, that Pl. occasionally used these words with the first syllable short, in positions where the *ictus* would not affect it.

Men. 57 *Epidámniensis ílle quem dudum díxeram.*
Most. 205 *Tu íam quod quaerebás habes; ĭlle té nisi amabit últro.*
Trin. 137 *Ĭlle quí mandauit eum éxturbasti ex aédibus.*
853 *Ĭlle qui me condúxit ubi condúxit abduxít domum.*
Am. 156 *Ĭnde crás e promptuária cellá depromar ád flagrum.*
Aul. 366 *Ĭnde cóctam sursum súbducemus córbulis.*
Poen. 2 *Ĭnde mí principium cápiam ex ea tragoédia.*
1153 *Ĭnde pórro ad puteum atque ád robustum códicem.*
109 *Ŭnde sít, quoiatis, cáptane an surrúpta sit.*
Trin. 218 *Ŭnde quídque auditum dícant: nisi id adpáreat.*
Mil. 906 *Nĕmpe lúdificari mílitem tuum erúm uis? P. Exlocúta es.*
922 *Nĕmpe tú nouisti mílitem, meum erúm? A. Rogare mírumst.*
As. 837 *Credam ístuc, si esse te hílarum uidero. Án tu ĕsse me tristém putas?*
Mil. 1118 *Dicás uxorem tíbi necessum ĕsse dúcere.*

152 There are two other words in which Pl. scans as short a syllable which later poets treat as long, viz. *frustră* and *neŭtiquam.*

Frustra with the *a* short occurs six times in Pl., always in the phrase *ne frustră sis*: viz. Cap. 854 and

Men. 692 *Tu húc post hunc diém pedem intro nón feres, ńe frústra sis.*
Merc. 528 *Nunc múlier, ne tu frústra sis, mea nón es; ne arbitrére.*

Rud. 969 *Nón ferat si dóminus ueniat? G. Dóminus huic, ne frústra sis.*
1255 *Ego tíbi daturus níl sum, ne tu frústra sis.*
Pers. 141 *Numquam hércle hodie hic príus edis, ne frústra sis.*

Everywhere else in Pl. and Ter. the *a* is elided or doubtful; in other authors it is always long. Probably in these passages Pl. reproduces the common pronunciation of a colloquial expression.

Neutiquam always has the first short in Pl. and Ter., and was probably written in two words, *ne utiquam*; see Comm. on 586. For the scansion, cf.

Poen. 199 *Sine dámno magno quae élui ne utiquám potest.*
Ter. Heaut. 357 *Quaprópter haec res ne útiquam neglectúst mihi.*
And. 330 *Égo, Charine, ne útiquam offícium liberi esse hominís puto.*

153 *Dierectus* occurs 13 times in Pl., viz. Cap. 636,

Bac. 579 *Recéde hinc dierécte. Vt pulsat própudium.*
[1] Cas. 103 *Abi rús, abi dieréctus tuam in prouínciam.*
[2] Curc. 240 *Lien díerectust. Ámbula; id lieni óptumumst.*
Men. 442 *Dúcit lembum díerectum náuis praedatória.*
[3] Merc. 183 *Ín hinc dieréctus? Nugare ín re capitalí mea.*
[1] 756 *Abin díerectus? Haúd malast. At tú malu's.*
[1] Most. 8 *Abi rús; abi dierécte; abscede ab iánua.*
[1] 834 *St, ábi, canis. St, abi díerecta. St, ábin hinc in malám crucem.*
[1] Poen. 160 *Abi díerectus. Díc mihi uero sério.*
347 *Béllua hercle. I díerecte in máxumam malám crucem.*
Rud. 1170 *Súcula. Quin tu i díerecta cúm sucula et cum pórculis.*
[1] Trin. 457 *Abi[n] hinc díerecte? Si hércle ire occipiám, uotes.*

[1] § 137. [2] § 109. [3] § 95.

and once in Varro ap. Non. p. 49 and 122, *apage ín dierectum á domo nostra ístam insanitátem* (iam. sept.). Palmer, Hermath. v. 65, shews that ī is the only scansion which suits all the lines (including Trin. 457, if one reads *abi*). The ictus always in Pl. falls *díeréctus.* See Comm. on 636.

T. MACCI PLAVTI

CAPTIVI.

PERSONAE.

ERGASILVS, a dependent of Hegio.
HEGIO, an old gentleman of Aetolia.
LORARII, slaves of Hegio.
PHILOCRATES, an Elean prisoner-of-war, purchased by Hegio.
TYNDARVS, slave of Philocrates.
ARISTOPHONTES, another Elean prisoner, previously purchased by Hegio.
PVER, slave of Hegio.
PHILOPOLEMVS, son of Hegio, taken prisoner by the Eleans.
STALAGMVS, runaway slave of Hegio.

The Scene throughout the play is a street in a city of Aetolia, before the house of Hegio. On the spectators' left the street leads to the harbour, on the right through the market-place into the country.

ARGVMENTVM.

Captúst pugna alter Hégionis fílius,
Alium quadrimum fúgiens seruos uéndidit.
Patér capteiuos cónmercatur Áleos
Tantúm studens ut nátum *captum* récuperet,
Et in íbus emit ólim amissum fílium.
Is suó cum domino uéste uersa ac nómine
Vt ámittatur fécit; ipsus pléctitur.
Et ís reduxit cáptum et fugitiuóm simul,
Indício quoius álium agnoscit fílium.

---

v. inibi *M* (ibi B^1).

PROLOGVS.

[*The two Captives,* PHILOCRATES *and* TYNDARUS, *stand chained together in front of the house;* TYNDARUS *is dressed as the master,* PHILOCRATES *as the slave. Enter the* PROLOGUE.]

Hos quós uidetis stáre hic captiuos duos,
Illí qui adstant,—í stant ambo, nón sedent;
Hoc uós mihi testes éstis me uerúm loqui.
Senéx qui hic habitat, Hégio, est huiús pater.
(*pointing to* TYND.)
Sed ís quo pacto séruiat suo síbi patri,
Id ego híc apud uos próloquar, si operám datis.
Seni huíc fuerunt fílii natí duo:
Altrúm quadrimum púerum seruos surrupuit
Eumque hínc profugiens uéndidit in Álide
Patri húius (*pointing to* PHIL.); *cette,* iam hóc tenetis? óptumumst.

(*In these notes of* MSS *readings M stands for all the* MSS *BDVEJ* (*D, of course, being only available up to l.* 503). *See Introduction,* §§ 20—30.) 10 huiusce iam *M.*

(*In these metrical notes reference to the Introduction is by paragraphs, thus* § 101.)

Prologue. This and Act I. are written throughout in Iambic Senarii, §§ 43—47. **2 qui adstant,** hiatus § 86. **5 suō,** § 111; for the dactyl in 5th foot see § 46, ii. **8 Altrum,** § 107. **surrupuit** scanned *surpuit,* as it is sometimes written, § 107. **9 eūm,** § 102. **uendidīt,** § 121. **10 cette** Sch. *met. gr.*

Negát hercle illic últumus; accédito (*to someone in back seats*).
Si nón ubi sedeas lócus est, est ubi ámbules,
Quando hístrionem cógis mendicárier.
Ego mé tua causa, ne érres, non ruptúrus sum.
Vos quí potestis ópe uostra censérier
Accípite relicuom: álieno uti níl moror.
Fugitíuos ille, ut díxeram ante, huiús (*pointing to* PHIL.) patri,
Domo quém profugiens dóminum abstulerat, uéndidit.
Is póstquam hunc (*pointing to* TYND.) emit, dédit eum huic gnató suo (*pointing to* PHIL.)
Pecúliarem, quía quasi una aetás erat.
Hic (*pointing to* TYND.) núnc domi seruit suó patri nec scít pater:
Enim uéro di nos quási pilas hominés habent.
Ratiónem habetis quómodo unum amíserit.
Postquám belligerant Aétoli cum Áleis,
Vt fít in bello, cápitur alter fílius.
Medicús Menarchus émit ibidem in Álide.
Coepít captiuos cónmercari hic Áleos,
Si quém reperire pósset, quo mutét suom

11* ille *M*. 19 Hic postquam *M*. 22 Est uero *M*. 27 alios *M*. 28 cum quo *M*.

11 scarcely scans; **negāt** may be paralleled, § 121, but not *ultumūs*. **12** For the proceleusmatic in 2nd foot see § 46, vi. **14 tūā**, § 111. **rupturus** scanned *rupturŭ'* § 94. **16 relicuom**, tetrasyllable, § 112. Notice the dactyl followed by two tribrachs. **18 Domŏ**, § 142. **21 domĭ**, § 142; **sūō**, § 111. **22 Enĭm uero**, § 142. **24 cum Aleis**, hiatus, §§ 84 (3), 86. Hiatus before this word occurs several times (31, 93, 169) but not always (cf. 59, 881); Bx. writes *Valeis* etc. throughout; Sch. emends, inserting *illi* here after *Aetoli*. **25 fĭt**, § 121. **29 suom esse** scanned either *sŭ' ĕssĕ* (§ 138

—Illúm captiuom ; hunc (*pointing to* TYND.) súom esse nescit quí domist—
Et quóniam heri indaudíuit de summó loco
Summóque genere cáptum esse equitem Áleum,
Nil prétio parsit fílio dum párceret :
Recónciliare ut fácilius possét domum
Emít hosce e praeda ámbos de quaestóribus.
Hisce aútem inter sese húnc confinxerúnt dolum,
Quo pácto hic seruos súom erum hinc amittát domum :
Itaque ínter se conmútant uestem et nómina :
Illíc (*pointing to* TYND.) uocatur Phílocrates, hic (*pointing to* PHIL.) Týndarus,
Huius ílle, hic illius hódie fert imáginem.
Et hic (*pointing to* TYND.) hódie expediet hánc docte falláciam
Et súom erum faciet líbertatis cónpotem :
Eodémque pacto frátrem seruabít suom,
Reducémque faciet líberum in patriam ád patrem
Inprúdens, itidem ut saépe iam in multís locis
Plus ínsciens quis fécit quam prudéns boni.
Sed ínscientes suá sibi fallácia
Ita cónpararunt ét confinxerúnt dolum
[Itaque hí conmenti dé sua senténtia],

---

30 inde audiuit *M* (audiunt *J*). 34 de praeda *M*. 35 hunc *om. VEJ.* 36 his B^1DV, hic B^2E, is *J*. 39 illic hic *M*. 44 ut *BD*, et *VEJ*.

---

or 151) or *sw' ēssĕ* (§ 111). **31 equitem Aleum,** hiatus, cf. 24; Sch. inserts *unum* before *esse*. **34 Emīt,** § 121. **39 Huius ille, hic illius,** the MS. *illic* necessitates dactyl followed by anapaest (§§ 44, 46, v.), for according to Ritschl, Opusc. ii. 687, *illius* has the penult. long. For **hūius** see § 105; for **īllius** § 151. **40** Proceleusmatic in 1st foot, § 46, vi. **42 ēodem,** § 101. **46 sūā,** § 111; **sibī** as often.

Vt in séruitute hic (*pointing to* TYND.) ád suom maneát patrem.
Ita núnc ignorans suó sibi seruít patri:
Homúnculi quantí sunt, quom recógito!
Haec rés agetur nóbis, uobis fábula.
Sed étiamst paucis uós quod monitos uóluerim.
Profécto expediet fábulae huic operám dare:
Non pértractate fáctast neque item ut céterae,
Neque spúrcidici insunt uérsus inmemorábiles:
Hic néque periurus lénost nec meretríx mala
Neque míles gloriósus. ne uereámini
Quia béllum Aetolis ésse dixi cum Áleis;
Foris íllic extra scaénam fient proélia.
Nam hoc paéne iniquomst, cómico chorágio
Conári desubito ágere nos tragoédiam.
Proin sí quis pugnam exspéctat litis cóntrahat;
Valéntiorem náctus aduorsárium
Si erít, ego faciam ut púgnam inspectet nón bonam,
Adeo út spectare póstea òmnis óderit.
Abeó. ualete, iúdices iustíssumi
Domí, duellique duéllatores óptumi. [*Exit.*

---

58 gloriosus esse ne *M* (esse *erased B*²). 59 esse *omitted in M*, ẽẽ *inserted by B*². 62 desubitontos agere *B*¹*DVE*, desubito neos agere *J*. 68 bellique *M*.

---

49 Vt ĭn séruitute, § 142. **50 sŭō**, § 111; **sibĭ**. **53** Dactyl in 5th foot, § 46, ii. **56 Neque spurcidici**; Augustan poets avoid putting a word ending in a short vowel before another beginning with *sc*, *sp*, *sq*, *st*. **60 Forĭs íllic**, § 142. **62** Proceleusmatic in 3rd foot, § 46, vi.; *nos agere* would necessitate dactyl and anapaest in 4th and 5th feet. **63 Prōin**, § 104. **68 dūellique dūellatores**, § 111.

ACTVS I.

[*Enter* Ergasilus *looking hungry and miserable; he addresses the Audience.*]

ERGASILVS.

Iuuéntus nomen índidit Scortó mihi,
Eo quía inuocatus sóleo esse in conuíuio.
Scio absúrde dictum hoc dérisores dícere,
At ego áio recte; nám certo in conuíuio
Sibi amátor talos quóm iacit scortum ínuocat.
Estne ínuocatum scórtum an non? planíssume.
Verum hércle uero nós parasiti plánius,
Quos númquam quisquam néque uocat neque ínuocat.
Quasi múres semper édimus alienúm cibum.
Vbi rés prolatae súnt, quom rus hominés eunt,
Simúl prolatae rés sunt nostris déntibus.
Quasi quóm caletur cócleae in occultó latent,
Suó sibi suco uíuont, ros si nón cadit,
Itém parasiti rébus prolatís latent
In occúlto miseri, uíctitant sucó suo,
Dum rúri rurant hómines quos ligúrriant.
Prolátis rebus párasiti uenátici
Sumús: quando res rédierunt, Molóssici

72 nam scortum *M*. 80 coccleo B^1, occleo *DVEJ*. 85 uenatici canes *M*.

Act I. Sc. 1. **70 ēō quĭa ĭnuocatus**, see §§ 101, 138. **71 Scio ăbsúrde**, § 142. **81 Sŭō sĭbĭ**; cf. 50. **83 In ŏccúlto**, § 142. **86** Sch. inserts *tum* before *Mol.* to improve rhythm.

Odióssicique et múltum incommodéstici.
Et híc quidem hercle nísi qui colaphos pérpeti
Potís parasitus frángique aulas ín caput,
Vel ire éxtra portam trígeminam ad saccúm licet.
Quod míhi ne eueniat nón nullum perículumst,
Postquám meus rex ést potitus hóstium.
Ita núnc belligerant Aétoli cum Áleis.
Nam Aetólia haec est; illic est cáptus in Álide,
Philopólemus, huius Hégionis fílius,
Senís qui hic (*pointing to the house*) habitat; quae aédes lamentáriae
Mihi súnt, quas quotiensquómque conspició, fleo.
Nunc híc occepit quaéstum hunc fili grátia
Inhonéstum, maxume álienum ingenió suo:
Hominés captiuos cónmercatur, sí queat
Aliquem ínuenire suóm qui mutet fílium.
Quod quídem ego nimis quam *cúpide* cupio ut ínpetret:
Nam ni íllum recipit, níhil est quo me récipiam.
Nullást spes *in* iuuentúti: sese omnís amant.
Ille démum antiquis ést adulescens móribus,

---

89 Potes *BDVE*, Potest *J*. 90 sacculum *VEJ*. 92 Nam postquam *M*. 101 qui cūmutet *M* (cum mutet *EJ*). 102—107 *stand in M after v.* 125. 104 spes iuuentutis *M*.

---

90 Vel īre éxtra, § 142. **93 cum Aleis,** hiatus, cf. on 24. Sch. inserts *illi* after *Aetoli*. **94 illĭc** (pronoun), § 151; cf. 39. **95** Proceleusmatic in 1st foot, § 46, vi. **98 hīc;** the pronoun is usually short, whence Sch. reads *hic homo*, but is sometimes found long; cf. 547, 805. **102 nimis** scanned *nimĭ'*, § 94, otherwise a dactyl would be followed by an anapaest. **cupide** inserted by Spengel, *metri gr.*; see comm. on 250. **103** Dactyl in 5th foot, § 46, ii. **104 in iuuentuti** (for MS. *iuuentutis*, which will not scan) must be scanned *in iŭuĕntúti*, § 142, or *iūuentuti*, § 113. **105 ĭlle,** § 151.

Quoius númquam uoltum tránquillaui grátiis.
Condígne pater est eíus moratus móribus.
Nunc ád eum pergam. (*As he turns to the house, the inner door is heard opening*) séd aperitur óstium,
Vnde sáturitate saépe ego exi*ui* ébrius.

HEGIO. LORARIVS. ERGASILVS.

[*Enter* HEGIO *from the house followed by a* LORARIUS, *to whom he speaks without seeing* ERGASILUS.]

HE. Aduórte animum sis tu: ístos captiuós duos
Herí quos emi dé praeda a quaestóribus,
His índito caténas singulárias,
Istás maiores quíbus sunt iuncti démito.
Sinito ámbulare, sí foris si intús uolent,
Sed uti ádseruentur mágna diligéntia.
Libér captiuos auís ferae consímilis est:
Semél fugiundi sí datast occásio,
Satis ést—numquam postílla possis préndere.
LO. Omnés profecto líberi lubéntius
Sumus quám seruimus. HE. Nón uidere ita tú quidem.
LO. Si nón est quod dem, méne uis dem ipse ín pedes?
HE. Si déderis, erit extémplo mihi quod dém tibi.

---

111 depreda dequestoribus *M*. 113 uincti *EJ*. 118 post illa *DVE*, postillā *B*, post illam *J*. 119 *continued to Hegio in M*. 120 LOR. non *M*. 121 *continued to Lor. in M*.

---

106 Quoius, § 105. **107 eius**, § 105. **109 Vnde**: probably the first syllable is short (§ 151) and the first foot a proceleusmatic (§ 46, vi.); for otherwise anapaest would follow dactyl, and the *ictus* would fall unnaturally *undé*. Cf. Cist. II. 3. 19 *ŭndĕ tĭbĭ talenta mágna uigintí, pater?* Poen. 1055 *ŭndĕ sum ŏrĭundus. Di dént tibi omnes quaé uelis.*

Act I. Sc. 2. **113 quibus** scanned *quibŭ'*, § 93. **116** Dactyl in 5th foot, § 46, ii. **120 Sumus** scanned *sumŭ'*, § 93.

LO. Auis mé ferae consímilem faciam ut praédicas.
HE. Ita ut dícis: nam si fáxis, te in caueám dabo.
Sed sátis uerborumst; cúra quae iussi átque abi.
[*Exit* LOR. *into house.*
Ego íbo ad fratrem ad álios captiuós meos;
Visám ne nocte hac quíppiam turbáuerint.
Inde mé continuo récipiam rursúm domum.
[*Moves off.*
ER. (*speaking aloud to attract his attention*) Aegrést
mi hunc facere quaéstum carcerárium
Proptér sui gnati míseriam miserúm senem.
Sed si úllo pacto ille húc conciliarí potest
Vel cárnuficinam hunc fácere possum pérpeti.
HE. (*stopping and turning round*) Quis hic lóquitur?
ER. Ego, qui tuó maerore máceror,
Macésco, consenésco et tabescó miser.
Ossa átque pellis súm misera macritúdine,
Neque úmquam quicquam mé iuuat quod edó—
(*aside*) domi;
Forís aliquantillum étiam quod gusto íd beat.
HE. Ergásile, salue. ER. (*weeping*) Dí te bene
ament, Hégio.
HE. Ne flé. ER. Egone illum nón fleam? egon
non défleam
Talem ádulescentem? HE. Sémper sensi fílio

---

123 pdicisti *B*, predicisti *DVE*, predixisti *J*. 127 quipiam *BDV*. 135 miseri amacritudine B^1, miser amacritudine B^2DVE. 139 egone *BD*, ego me *VEJ*.

---

123 Auis scanned *aui'*, § 93, or *aūis*, § 114. **124 Ita ŭt dícis**, § 142. **125 satis** scanned *satĭ'*, § 93. **128 ĭnde**, § 151. **130 sūī**, § 111. **133 Quĭs hĭc lŏquĭtur**; proceleusmatic in 1st foot (§ 46, vi.), *hic* being shortened by the *ictus*, § 142. **tūō**, § 111. **139** Hiatus after *fle*, § 85 (5).

Meo te ésse amicum et íllum intellexí tibi.
ER. Tum dénique homines nóstra intellegimús bona,
Quom, quae ín potestate hábuimus, ea amísimus:
Ego póstquam gnatus tuós potitust hóstium
Expértus quanti fúerit nunc desídero.
HE. Aliénus quom eius incómmodum tam aegré feras,
Quid mé patrem par fácerest quoi illest únicus?
ER. Aliénus ego? aliénus illi? ah, Hégio,
Numquam ístuc dixis néque animum induxís tuom;
Tibi ille únicust, mi etiam único magis únicus.
HE. Laudó malum quom amíci tuom ducís malum.
Nunc hábe bonum animum.—ER. Éheu! HE. (*to the Audience*) Huic illúd dolet,
Quia núnc remissus ést edundi exércitus.
(*to* ER.) Nullúmne interea náctu's, qui possét tibi
Remíssum quem dixi ímperare exércitum?
ER. Quid crédis? fugitant ómnes hanc prouínciam
[Quoi obtigerat postquam captus est Philopolemus tuus.]
HE. Non pól mirandumst fúgitare hanc prouínciam.
Multís et multigéneribus opus ést tibi
Milítibus: primum dum ópus est Pistorénsibus,
[Eorúm sunt aliquot génera Pistorénsium,]
Opus Pániceis est, ópus Placentinís quoque,

142, 143 *continued to Heg. in M.* 148 *Erg.'s speech begins at* ah *in M.* ille *M.* 151 dicis *VEJ.* 154—157 *given to Erg. in M.* 155 dixit *BDVE*, dixti *J.* 157 Quod *M.* 159—166 *given to Erg. in M.*

---

141 Mēō, § 101. **144 tuos** scanned *tūōs*, § 111, or *tŭŏ'*, § 93. **146 eius incommodum** scanned either *eīūs īncommodum*, § 105, or *ēīŭs ĭncómmodum*, § 142; the former way gives no caesura. **150 ĭlle**, § 151. **151 tūōm**, § 111. **152 hábĕ**, § 138; hiatus before and after *eheu*, § 85 (5). **161 ēōrum**, § 101. **162 Opus** scanned *opŭ'*, twice, § 93; **Pānĭcēīs.**

Opus Túrdetanis, ópus est Ficedulénsibus,
Iam máritumi omnes mílites opus súnt tibi.
ER. Vt saépe summa ingénia in occultó latent!
Hic quális imperátor nunc priuátus est.
HE. Habe módo bonum animum. nam íllum confidó domum
In hís diebus mé reconciliássere.
Nam eccum híc captiuom adulèscentem Áleum
Prognátum genere súmmo et summis diuitiis;
Hoc íllum me mutáre confidó pote.
ER. Ita dí deaeque fáxint! Sed num quó foras
Vocátu's *hodie* ad cénam? HE. Nusquam, quód sciam.
Sed quíd tu id quaeris? ER. Quía mist natalís dies;
Proptérea *a* te uocári ad te ad *ce*nám uolo.
HE. Facéte dictum; séd si pauxilló potes
Conténtus esse. ER. Né perpauxilló modo;
Nam istóc me adsiduo uíctu delectó domi.
Age sís, roga emptum, nísi qui meliorem ádferet
Quae mi átque amicis pláceat condició magis.
Quasi fúndum uendam, meís me addicam légibus.

---

171 confido fore *M.* 172 sed...cenam *given to Heg. in M.* 173 Nusquam...quaeris *given to Erg. in M.* 174 quid diu *VEJ.* Quia...uolo *given to Heg. in M.* 175 ad te ad nam *B*, adte nam *DVE*, ad cenam *J.* 176 Facete...esse *given to Erg. in BD.* pauxillum *M.* 177 perpauxillum *BVEJ.* 179—184 *no names of speakers in M.*

---

163 Opus scanned *opŭ'*, § 93. **Fīcēdŭlensibus**: cf. Juv. XIV. 9, *Mergere ficedulas didicit.* Martial, XIII. 5 and 49, makes the *e* long. **164 opus** scanned *opŭ'*, § 93. **167** Proceleusmatic in 1st foot, followed by tribrach; for **habĕ módo** see § 142. **169** Hiatus both before and after *adulescentem*; for the former see § 84 (2), for the latter § 84 (3) and cf. 24. Sch. inserts *intus* before *Aleum.* **170 dīuĭtiis,** § 113. **181 meīs,** § 100.

HE. Profúndum uendis tú quidem, haud fundúm mihi.
Sed sí uenturu's, témperi. ER. Em, uel iam ótiumst.
HE. I módo, uenare léporem; nunc ictím tenes.
Nam méus scruposam uíctus conmetát uiam.
ER. Numquam ístoc uinces me, Hégio; ne póstules.
Cum cálceatis déntibus ueniám tamen.
HE. Aspér meus uictus sánest. ER. Sentisne éssitas?
HE. Terréstris cenast— ER. Sús terrestris béstiast.
HE. Multís holeribus. ER. Cúrato aegrotós domi.
Numquíd uis? HE. Venias témperi. ER. Memorém mones. [*Exit* ER., *R.*
HE. (*dolefully*) Ibo íntro atque intus súbducam ratiúnculam,
Quantíllum argenti mi ápud trapezitám siet.
Ad frátrem, quo ire díxeram, mox *iu*ero.
[*Exit into house.*

185 Non *M*. 191 tempori *EJ*.

185, 188 meus scanned *mēūs*, § 102, or *mĕŭ'*, § 93. **193 ăpŭd trap.**, § 138.

ACTVS II.

LORARII. CAPTIVI (PHILOCRATES. TYNDARVS).

[*Enter, from the house, the* LORARIUS *and some subordinates with* PHIL. *and* TYND., *still dressed in each other's clothes and looking very dejected. Some house-slaves loiter about the door.*]

LO. Si di ínmortales íd uoluere, uós hanc aerumnam éxsequi,
Decét id pati animo aéquo; si id faciétis, leuior lábos erit.
Domi fuístis, credo, líberi;
Nunc séruitus si euénit, ei uos mórigerari mós bonust;
Eam queít erili império, ingeniis uóstris lenem réddere.
Indígna digna habénda sunt, erus quaé facit.
CA. (*groaning*) Oh Oh Oh!

---

199 Eamque et *M* (Eam que et *B*).

Act II. Sc. 1. This Canticum falls into four parts; the first (to 203) is iambic; the second (to 224) is cretic with trochaic and short iambic lines intermixed; the third (to 231) is bacchiac introduced and concluded by iambics, and the fourth (to 241) is mainly cretic but ends with troch. octonarii introducing the septenarii 241 sqq., with which the scene closes. **195** Iam. oct. with caesura but no diaeresis, § 51. **196** Iam. oct.; **decĕt**, § 121; **lábŏs**, § 138. **197** Iam. dim., § 53; **Domĭ fŭístis**, see §§ 142, 111. **198** Iam. oct.; **euĕnit.** **199** Iam. oct. with caesura, but no diaeresis, § 51. **200** Iam. sen. followed by 'eiulatio'; **erus** scanned *erŭ'*, § 93.

LO. Eiulátione haud ópus est multa; óculis multam iram éditis.
In ré mala animo sí bono utare, ádiuuat.
TY. At nós pudet quia cúm catenis súmus. LO. At pigeat póstea
Nóstrum erum, si uos éximat uínculis
Aút solutós sinat quós argento émerit.
TY. Quid á nobis métuit? Scimús nos
Nóstrum officiúm quod est, sí solutós sinat. 207a
LO. Át fugam fíngitis; séntio quám rem agitis. 207b
TY. Nós fugiamus? quó fugiamus? LO. Ín patriam. TY. Apage, haud nós id deceat
Fúgitiuos imitári. LO. Immo edepol, si érit occasio, haúd dehortor.
TY. V́num exoráre uos sínite nos. LO. Quíd-nam id est?
TY. V́t sine hisce árbitris (*pointing to house-slaves*) átque uobís nobis
Detís locum loquéndi.

201 oculis multa miraclitis *M* (mira clitis *or* ditis *D*).
203—207 CA. *in M instead of* TY. 208 dideceat *DVEJ*.

---

201 Iam. oct. with no diaeresis, but caesura with hiatus in 5th foot, § 51; **eiulatione**, cf. **eius** § 105. **202** Iam. sen. **203** Iam. oct. with caesura but no diaeresis. **204** Troch. trip. cat. + cret. dim., see § 76. Spengel suggests, and Bx. and Sch. read, *suos* for *uos*, making the line a cret. tetr. **205** Cretic tetrameter with molossus in 3rd foot, § 70. **206** may perhaps be a bac. trimeter with choriambus in 2nd foot. Single bacchiac lines sometimes (but rarely) occur with cretics, e.g. Trin. 278, 279 (Bx.). **207 a** Cret. tetr. with Ionic a maiori in 1st foot, § 70. **207 b** Cret. tetr. with choriambus in 4th foot, § 70. **208** Tr. oct. with tribrach in 8th foot, § 68. **209** Tr. oct. **dehortor** usually contracted, but uncontracted here and in Poen. 677 *neque nós hortari néque dehortarí decet.* **210, 211** Cret. tetr. **212** Iam. dim. cat., § 53.

LO. Fíat. Abscédite hinc (*to the house-slaves*); nós (*to his men*) concedámus huc.
Séd breuem orátionem íncipisse.
TY. Ém, istuc mihi cértum erat; (*to* PHIL.) cóncede huc.
LO. (*to the slaves*) Abíte ab istis. TY. Obnóxii ambo
Vóbis sumus própter hanc rém quom, quae uólumus nos,
Cópiae istae *ádfatim* fácitis nos cónpotes.
[*The* LORARII *go apart.*
PH. (*to* TYND. *crossing the stage*) Sécede huc núnciam, sí uidetúr, procul,
Ne árbitri dícta nostra árbitrarí queant,
Neú permanét palam haec nóstra fallácia.
Nám doli nón doli súnt, ni*si* astú colas,
Séd malum máxumum, si íd palam próuenit.
Nám si erus mi es tu átque ego me tuom ésse seruom ádsimulo,
Tamen uíso opust, cautóst opus, ut hoc sóbrie sineque árbitris
Adcúrate agátur, docte ét diligénter.

---

218 Copia est ea facitis *M.* 221 Neue *M.*

---

214 § 77. **215** § 76. **216** consists of two catalectic iam. tripodiae, see § 53. **217** Resolved cret. tetr., consisting of Ionic a mai., cretic, molossus and 4th paeon; see § 70. **sumus, uolumus** scanned *sumŭ'*, *uolumŭ'*, § 93. **221** The last foot, really a dactyl, is considered a cretic, the final syllable being doubtful; §§ 35, 70. **224** A resolved cretic tetr., concluding the series, as 217 began it: § 70; all the feet but the third are choriambi. **erus** scanned *erŭ'*, **tuom** entirely elided. **225** Iam. oct., § 51. **Tamĕn uíso,** § 142. **226—230** Bacchiac tetr., § 60.

Tanta íncepta rés est: haud sómniculóse hoc
Agúndumst. TY. Ero út me uolés esse. PH.
Spéro.
TY. Nam tú nunc uidés pro tuó caro cápite
Carum ófferre *mé* meum capút uilitáti.
PH. Scio. TY. Át memento scíre, quando id quód
uoles habébis.
Nám fere [maxuma pars] mórem hunc hominés
habent: quód sibi
Volúnt, dum id inpetránt,
Súnt boni; séd id ubi iám penes sése habent,
Éx bonis péssumi et fraúdulentíssumi
Fíunt. Nunc út mihi tē uolo esse aútumo.
Quód tibi suádeo, suádeam meó patri.
PH. Pól ego, si te aúdeam, meúm patrem nómi-
nem;
Nám secundúm patrem tu és pater próxumus.
TY. Aúdio. PH. Et proptérea saepiús te*d* ut me-
míneris moneo:
Nón ego erus tibí sed seruos súm. Nunc obsecró te
hoc unum:

229 TY. *om. M.* 231 TY. Scio. PH. *M.* scire memento *M.* 236 Sunt *M.* 237 suadeam suadeam *M.* 238 PH. *om. M.*

229 capitē probably, as a 1st paeon is not considered legitimate in this position. **230 me** inserted *metri gratia*: it might easily have fallen out before *meum*. **meūm**, § 102. **231** Iam. sept., § 48. **memento scire** transposed by Fl. *met. gr.* **232** Cret. tetr. with Ionic a mai. in 2nd foot, omitting the bracketed words; see Comm. **233** Iam. trip. acat., § 53. **234—239** Cret. tetr., § 70. **236 mihī** as often. **237 tibī** as often. **meō**, § 101. **238** Fourth paeon in 1st foot; **meūm**, § 102. **240** Tr. oct., § 68, with caesura but no diaeresis; the final anapaest is reckoned as a tribrach. On the two tr. oct. 240, 241 preceding the tr. sept., see § 69. **241 tibī** as often.

Quóniam nobis di ínmortales ánimum ostenderúnt suom,
Ýtqui erum me tíbi fuisse atque ésse [nunc] conseruóm uelint,
Quom ántehac pro iure ímperitabam meó, nunc te oro pér precem:
Pér fortunam incértam et per mei te érga bonitatém patris,
Pérque conseruitiúm commune quód hostica euenít manu,
Né me secus honóre honestes quám quom seruibás mihi,
Átque ut, qui fuerís et qui nunc sís, meminisse ut mémineris.
TY. Scío equidem me te ésse nunc et te ésse me. PH. Em, istuc sí potes
Mémoriter meminísse, inest spes nóbis in hac astútia.

HEGIO. PHILOCRATES. TYNDARVS.

[*Enter* HEGIO *from house, addressing someone within.*]
HE. Iam égo reuortar íntro, si ex his quaé uolo exquisíuero.
Ýbi sunt isti (*looking round*) quós ante aedis iússi huc producí foras?

---

244 Quod *M*. 247 seruiebas *M*.

---

242 sqq. Trochaic septenarii, §§ 64—66. **243 nunc** was probably inserted from next line; if retained, we must scan *ĕsse*, § 151. **244 antēhac**, § 99; **meō**, § 101. **245 meī**, § 100. **246 Perque cŏnséruitium**, § 142. Sch. omits *-que*, which is often inserted in MSS. Cf. 468, 470. **quód hŏstica**, § 138. **249 Sciŏ**, § 110. **250 ín hăc**, § 138.

Sc. 2. Tr. sept. (§ 64 sqq.) throughout, with the exception of 361—384.

PH. (*coming forward*) Édepol tibi ne in quaéstione essémus cautum intéllego;
Íta uinclis custódiisque círcummoenití sumus.
HE. Quí cauet ne décipiatur, uíx cauet quom etiám cauet;
Étiam quom cauísse ratus est, saépe is cautor cáptus est.
Án uero non iústa causast, út uos seruem sédulo,
Quós tam grandi sím mercatus praésenti pecúnia?
PH. Néque pol tibi nos, quía nos seruas, aéquomst uitio uórtere
Néque te nobis, sí abeamus hínc, si fuat occásio.
HE. V́t uos hic, itidem íllic apud uos méus seruatur fílius.
PH. Cáptus est? HE. Ita. PH. Nón igitur nos sóli ignaui fúimus.
HE. (*taking* PHIL. *apart*) Sécede huc; nam súnt, quae ex te sólo scitarí uolo,
Quárum rerum té falsilocum míhi esse nolo. PH. Nón ero,
Quód sciam; si quíd nescibo, id néscium tradám tibi.
TY. (*watching them*) Núnc senex est ín tostrina; núnc iam cultros ádtinet.
Ne íd quidem inuolúcri inicere uóluit, uestem ut ne ínquinet.

---

259 equō stulcio *B*, equō stul cio *D*, equō stultio *VEJ*. 262 ignari B^1DE, igitari *J*, ingnaui B^2 *in marg.* 265 quid nesciui *M*. 267 inuolucre *M*.

---

253 No diaeresis. **260 sĭ ăbĕamus**, hiatus, § 86. **261 ápŭd uos**, § 138. **meus** monosyllable, § 102, or *mĕŭ'*, § 93. **262 fŭimus**, § 131. **263 quaĕ ex**, hiatus, § 86; Sch. reads *huc tu*, Bx. *ego ex*. **264 mihi esse** scanned *mi ĕssĕ*, or *mĭhi ĕssĕ*, § 151.

Séd utrum strictimne ádtonsurum dícam esse an per péctinem,
Néscio; uerúm si frugist, úsque admutilabít probe.
[*Approaches them softly.*
HE. Quíd tu? seruosne ésse an liber máuelis, memorá mihi.
PH. Próxumum quod sít bono, quodque á malo longíssume,
Íd uolo; quamquám non multum fúit molesta séruitus
Néc mihi secus erát quam si essem fámiliaris fílius.
TY. (*overhearing, to the Audience*) Eúgepae! Thalém talento nón emam Milésium;
Nam ád sapientiam húius *nimiam* nímius nugatór fuit.
Vt facete orátionem ad séruitutem cóntulit!
HE. Quó de genere gnátust illic Phílocrates? PH. Polyplúsio,
Quód genus illist únum pollens átque honoratíssumum.
HE. Quíd ipsus hic? quo honórest illic? PH. Súmmo atque ab summís uiris.
HE. [Tum ígitur ei quom in Áleis tanta grátiast ut praédicas,]
Quíd diuitiae? súntne opimae? PH. Vnde éxcoquat sebúm senex.

---

269 PH. Nescio *M.* admutila labit *BVE*, admutalabit *D.* 278 illic est *M.* 281 optume *BDVE*, optumae *J.* seuum *M.*

---

269 Nesciō. **272 fuĭt**, § 111. **275 nimiam** Sch. *met. gr.* **278 illi** Böthe, *met. gr.*; *illic* (adv.) has last long. **279 Quíd ĭpsus**, § 138. **280** If the line be genuine, we must scan **Alēis**, dissyl., the only example in the play; see Comm.

HE. Quíd pater? uiuítne? PH. Viuom quom índe abimus líquimus;
Núnc uiuat*ne* nécne, id Orcum scíre oportet scílicet.
TY. (*to the Audience*) Sálua res est; phílosophatur quóque iam, non mendáx modost.
HE. Quíd erat ei nomén? PH. Thensaurochrýsonicochrýsides.
HE. Vídelicet proptér diuitias índitum id nomén quasist?
PH. Ímmo edepol proptér auaritiam ipsíus atque audáciam.
(*Aside*) Nam ílle quidem Theodóromedes fúit germano nómine.
HE. Quíd tu ais? tenáxne pater est eíus? PH. Immo edepol pértinax.
Quín etiam ut magis nóscas, genio súo ubi quando sácruficat,
Ád rem diuinám quibus opus est Sámiis uasis útitur—
Ne ípse Genius súbrupiat; proinde áliis ut credát uide.
HE. (*crossing to* TYND.) Séquere hac me igitur. (*Aside*) eádem ego ex hoc quaé uolo exquaesíuero.—
(*To* TYND.) Phílocrates, hic fécit, hominem frúgi ut facere opórtuit.
Nám ego ex hoc, quo génere gnatus sís, scio; hic fassúst mihi.

---

282 abiimus *M*. 288 illic *BD*, illi *VEJ*.

---

285 ēī, § 100. **286 Vídĕlicet**, § 138. **287 ipsīus**; no diaeresis. **288 Thĕŏdōrŏmēdēs. fūīt**, § 111. **289 ēīūs**, § 105. **290 magis** scanned *magĭ'*, § 93. **suo** dissyl. with last elided. **292 proinde**, § 104. **293 ēādem**, § 99. **295 Năm ĕgo ēx**, hiatus, § 86.

Haéc tu eadem si cónfiteri uís, tua *ex* re féceris,
Quaé tamen scis scíre me ex hoc. TY. Fécit officium híc suom,
Quóm tibist conféssus uerum, quám*quam* uolui sédulo
Meám nobilitatem óccultare et génus et diuitiás meas,
Hégio; nunc quándo patriam et líbertatem pérdidi,
Nón ego istunc me pótius quam te métuere aequom cénseo.
Vís hostilis cum ístoc fecit meás opes aequábiles.
Mémini quom dicto haúd audebat, fácto nunc laedát licet.
Séd uiden? Fortúna humana fíngit artatque út lubet;
Mé qui liber fúeram, seruom fécit, e summo ínfumum;
Qui ímperare insuéram nunc altérius imperio óbsequor.
Ét quidem si proínde ut ipse fui ímperator fámiliae
Hábeam dominum, nón uerear ne iniúste aut grauiter mi ímperet.
Hégio, hoc te mónitum, nisi forte ípse non uis, uóluerim.
HE. Lóquere audacter. TY. Tam égo fui ante líber quam gnatús tuos;
Tám mihi quam illi líbertatem hostílis eripuít manus;
Tam ílle apud nos séruit quam ego nunc híc apud te séruio.

---

297 scio scire *M*. 309 uolueram *M*.

---

299 Mēam, § 99. **301 istunc,** § 142. **302 mēas,** § 99. **306** No diaeresis. **alterius,** Ritschl, Opusc. i. 346, scans and spells *altrīus*; so Sch. Bx. **307 prōinde,** § 104. **fui,** probably a monosyllable elided, § 111 (*fw' īmperator*), otherwise dactyl in 4th; see § 66 (ii.). **308** No diaeresis, § 66. **311** No diaeresis, § 66. **312 hīc** (adv.) as always.

Ést profecto déus qui, quae nos gérimus, auditque ét uidet;
Ís, uti tu me hic hábueris, proinde íllum illic curáuerit:
Béne merenti béne profuerit, mále merenti pár erit.
Quám tu filiúm tuom tam patér me meus desíderat.
HE. Mémini ego istuc: séd faterin éadem quae hic fassúst mihi?
TY. Égo patri meo ésse fateor súmmas diuitiás domi
Méque summo génere gnatum; séd te optestor, Hégio,
Né tuom animum auáriorem fáxint diuitiaé meae,
Né patri tam etsi únicus sum decére uideatúr magis
Mé saturum seruíre apud te súmptu et uestitú tuo
Pótius quam illi, ubi mínume honestumst, méndicantem uíuere.
HE. [Égo uirtute deum ét maiorum nóstrum diues súm satis.]
Nón ego omninó lucrum omne esse útile homini exístumo;
Scío ego, multos iám lucrum lutuléntos homines réddidit.
Ést etiam ubi profécto damnum praéstet facere quám lucrum.
Ódi ego aurum; múlta multis saépe suasit pérperam.
Núnc hoc animum aduórte, ut ea quae séntio paritér scias.
Fílius meus íllic apud uos séruit captus Álide;
Eúm si reddis míhi, praeterea únum nummum né duis,

---

313 **deus** scanned *dēūs*, § 102, or *dĕŭ'*, § 93. **314** **prōinde**, § 104. **316** No diaeresis, § 66. **tūōm**, § 111. **meus**=*mēūs*, § 102, or *mĕŭ'*, § 93. **321** **unicus**=*unicu'*, § 93; no diaeresis. **326** No diaeresis, and dactyl in 4th foot, § 66. **330** **ăpŭd uos**, § 138. **331** **ēūm**, § 102. Hiatus at diaeresis, § 84 (1).

Ét te et hunc amíttam hinc; alio pácto abire nón potes.
TY. Óptumum atque aequíssumum oras óptumusque hominum és homo.
Séd is priuatam séruitutem séruit illi an públicam?
HE. Príuatam medicí Menarchi. PH. (*pointing to* TYND.) Pól is quidem huius ést cluens;
Tám hoc quidem tibi ín procliui quam ímber est quandó pluit.
HE. Fác is homo ut redimátur. TY. Faciam, séd ted oro, Hégio— (*taking him aside*)
HE. Quíd uis? dum ab re né quid ores, fáciam. TY. Ausculta, túm scies.
Égo me amitti, dónicum ille huc rédierit, non póstulo;
Vérum, te quaeso, aéstumatum hunc míhi des, quem mittam ád patrem,
V́t is homo redimátur illi. HE. Immo álium potius mísero
Hínc, ubi erunt indútiae, illuc, tuóm qui conueniát patrem,
Quí tua quae tu iússeris mandáta ita ut uelis pérferat.
TY. Át nihil est ignótum ad illum míttere; operam lúseris.
Húnc mitte, hic *rem* omné*m* transactam réddet, si illuc uénerit.

---

335 Pol...cluens *given to Heg. in M* (*D omits speaker*). Pol hic *M*. 337 te id *M*. 340 quaeso ut *M*. 342 conuenit *M*. 345 hic omne transactum *M*.

---

333 ēs, § 128. **334 Séd ĭs pr.,** § 138. **335 Pól ĭs qu.,** § 138. **337 oro Hegio,** hiatus, § 84 (3). **342 tŭŏm,** § 111. **343 uelĭs pérferat,** § 142; no diaeresis, § 66.

Néque quemquám fidéliorem néque quoi plus credát potes
Míttere ad eum néque qui magis sit séruos ex senténtia,
Néque adeo quoi tuóm concredas fílium hodie audácius.
Né uereare; meó periculo húius ego experiár fidem
Frétus ingenio eíus, quod me esse scít erga se béniuolum.
HE. Míttam equidem istunc aéstumatum tuá fide si uís. TY. Volo.
Quám citissumé potest, tam hoc cédere ad factúm uolo.
HE. Núm quae causast quín, si ille huc non rédeat, uigintí minas
Míhi des pro illo? TY. Óptuma immo. HE. (*to the* LORARII) Sóluite istum núnciam,
Átque utrumque. TY. Dí tibi omnes ómnia optata *óf*ferant,
Quóm me tanto honóre honestas quómque ex uinclis éximis.
(*Aside*) Hóc quidem haud moléstumst, iam quod cóllus collarí caret.
HE. Quód bonis benefít beneficium grátia ea grauidást bonis.

---

346 Ne *BDVE*, nec *J*. 347 nequi *BDVE*, nec qui *J*. 348 suum concredat *M*. 349 uice fidem *BDVE*, fidem uel uicem *J*. 357 collaria *M*. 358 *given to Tynd. in M.*

---

347 magis scanned *magĭ'*, § 93. **348 tuom**, § 111. **350 eius**, § 105. **scit**, § 121. **351 tua**, § 111. **354** Hiatus after *illo*, § 85 (5). **nunciam**, trisyllable.

Núnc tu illum (*pointing to* PHIL.) si illó's missurus, díce monstra praécipe,
Quae ád patrem uis núntiari. uín uocem huc ad té? TY. Voca.
HE. (*crossing to* PHIL.) Quae rés bene uortat míhi meoque fílio
Vobísque, uolt te nóuos erus operám dare
Tuo uéteri domino, quód is uelit, fidéliter.
Nam ego te aéstumatum huíc dedi uigintí minis;
Hic aútem te ait míttere hinc uelle ád patrem,
Meum ut íllic redimat fílium, mutátio
Intér me atque illum ut nóstris fiat fíliis.
PH. Vtróque uorsum réctumst ingeniúm meum,
Ad te átque ad illum; pró rota me utí licet.
Vel ego húc uel illuc uórtar quo imperábitis.
HE. Tuté tibi tuopte ingénio prodes plúrumum,
Quom séruitutem íta fers, ut ferrí decet.
Sequere. (*Crosses to* TYND. *and addresses him*) ém tibi hominem. TY. Grátiam habeó tibi,
Quom cópiam istam mi ét potestatém facis,
Vt ego ád parentis húnc remittam núntium,

---

359 dice demonstra *M*. HEGIO, SENEX, PHILOCRATES, ADOLESCENS, TYNDARVS, SERVVS, *M between* 361 *and* 362. 369 ad *om. BDJ*. 371 tibi ea *M*.

---

359 monstra, so most edd., *metri gr.*, as in Mil. 256 (A), but *dice dĕmónstra* is possible, § 142. **361—384.** Iam. senarii, § 43 sqq. **363 Tu͡o**, § 111. **quód ĭs**, § 138. **364** Hiatus before *huic*, § 84 (2). **dedĭ uíginti**, § 142. Most edd. transpose, *dedi aes. huic*. **365 āit**, § 106. **371 tu͡opte**, § 111, otherwise anapaest after dactyl, § 46 (v.). **372 itā**, § 117, or hiatus in caesura, § 84 (2), to avoid which Bx. reads *fers ita*, Uss. suggests *uti*. **373 Gratiam habeo**, hiatus, § 89. Cf. Mil. 1425 *óbsecro uos*. PE. *Sóluite istunc*. PY. *Grátiam habeó tibi.*

Qui mé quid rerum hic ágitem et quid fierí uelim
Patrí meo ordine ómnem rem illuc pérferat.
(*Turning to* PHIL.) Nunc íta conuenit ínter me atque hunc, Týndare,
Vt te aéstumatum in Álidem mittam ád patrem;
Si nón rebitas húc, ut uigintí minas
Dem pró te. PH. Recte cónuenisse séntio;
Nam páter exspectat aút me aut aliquem núntium,
Qui hinc ád se ueniat. TY. Érgo animum aduortás uolo,
Quae núntiare hinc té uolo in patriam ád patrem.
PH. Phílocrates, ut adhúc locorum féci, faciam sédulo
V́t potissumúm, quod in rem récte conducát tuam,
Íd petam idque pérsequar corde ét animo atque uíribus.
TY. Fácis ita ut te fácere oportet; núnc animum aduortás uolo.
Ómnium primúm salutem dícito matri ét patri
Ét cognatis ét si quem alium béneuolentem uíderis;
Me híc ualere et séruitutem séruire huic homini óptumo,
Quí me Honore honéstiorem sémper fecit ét facit.
PH. Ístuc ne praecípias; facile mémoria meminí tamen.
TY. Nam *é*quidem nisi quod cústodem habeo líberum me esse árbitror.

---

387 petam id persequarque *M*. auribus *BDVE*. 390 et quem *VEJ*.

---

376 fĭĕrī, § 130. 378 conuenit, what tense? **385 sqq.** Tr. septenarii resumed.

Dícito patrí quo pacto míhi cum hoc conuénerit
De húius filió—PH. Quae memini móra merast monérier.
TY. Vt eum redimat ét remittat nóstrum huc ambórum uicem—
PH. Méminero. HE. At quam prímum pote; istuc ín rem utriquest máxume.
PH. Nón tuom tu mágis uidere quam ílle suom gnatúm cupit.
HE. Méus mihi, suos quoíquest carus. PH. (*to* TYND.) Núm quid aliud uís patri
Núntiari? TY. Me híc ualere et—túte audacter dícito,
Týndare—inter nós fuisse ingénio haud discordábili,
Néque te conmeruísse culpam néque te aduorsatúm mihi
Béneque ero gessísse morem in tántis aerumnís tamen,
Néque med umquam déseruisse té neque factis néque fide
Rébus in dubiís, egenis, haéc pater quandó sciet,
Týndare, ut fuerís animatus érga suom gnatum átque se,
Númquam erit tam auárus, quin te grátus emittát manu;
Ét mea opera, si hínc rebito, fáciam ut faciat fácilius.

---

398 poteris istuc *M.* 400 *O begins.* 400—406 *in MO form six v. ending* nuntiari, fuisse, culpam, morem, deseruisse te, sciet. 403 me aduorsatum tibi *M.* 405 me umquam *VEJ.* 408 gratis *OJ.*

---

395 cum hoc, hiatus, § 86. **398 pote; istuc,** Spengel's emend. for MSS. *poteris istuc*, which makes the line too long; *póte ĭstuc*, § 138. **399** we must scan either *tu͞om*, § 111, or *magĭ'*, § 93. **400 Meus**=either *me͞us*, § 102, or *mĕŭ'*, § 93. **402** No diaeresis. **407 su͞om,** § 111.

Nám tua opera et cómitate et uírtute et sapiéntia
Fécisti ut redíre liceat ád parentis dénuo;
Quóm apud hunc conféssus es et génus et diuitiás meás;
Quó pacto emisísti e uinclis túom erum tua sapiéntia.
PH. Féci ego ista ut conmémoras et te méminisse id gratúmst mihi.
Séd merito tibi ea éuenerunt á me; nam nunc, Phílocrates,
Sí ego item memorém quae me erga múlta fecistí bene,
Nóx diem adimat; nám si seruos mi ésses, nihilo sétius
Mi óbsequiosus sémper, *ere*, fuísti. HE. (*aside*) Di uostrám fidem,
Hóminum ingenium líberale! ut lácrumas excutiúnt mihi!
Vídeas corde amáre inter se; *quíbus et* quantis laúdibus
Súom erum seruos cónlaudauit. TY. Pól istic me haud centénsumam

---

417 seruus meus esses *MO*. 418—421 *end in MO at* ingenium, corde, seruus, partem. 420 se quantis laudauit *MO* (se quantis laudibus *B*, *but* ibus *by* B^2 *over erasure*). 421 Pol...laudibus *given to Phil. in MO.*

---

412 Quom apud, hiatus, § 86. **ēs,** § 128. **413 uinclis,** § 107. **tŭā,** § 111. **414 ĭsta,** § 142. Böthe reads *ita*. **415** Hiatus, before or after *ea*, § 87. **416** Hiatus after *Si*, probably, § 86. **417 mi** for *meus*, Bosscha and Bentley, *metri gr.* **418 ere** Speijer, *met. gr.*, following Sch.; *obs. m. f. s.* Böthe, *mi obs. s. tu f.* Uss., *mi obsecüe obs. s. f.* Lachm. Lucr. p. 303. **420 quibus et** added by Goetz to fill up the line; see Comm. **421 Pól ĭstic,** § 138.

Pártem laudat quam ípse meritust út laudetur laúdibus.
HE. (*to* PHIL.) Érgo quom optumé fecisti, núnc adest occásio
Bénefacta cumuláre, ut erga hunc (*pointing to* TYND.) rém geras fidéliter.
PH. Mágis non factum póssum uelle quam ópera experiar pérsequi.
Íd ut scias, Iouém supremum téstem *lau*do, Hégio,
Me ínfidelem nón futurum Phílocrati—HE. Probus és homo.
PH. Néc me secus umquam eí facturum quícquam quam memét mihi.
TY. Ístaec dicta te éxpedire et óperis et factís uolo;
Ét quo minus dixí quam uolui dé te animum aduortás uolo—
Átque horunc uerbórum causa cáue tu mi iratús fuas,
Séd, te quaeso, cógitato hinc meá fide mittí domum
Te aéstumatum et méam esse uitam hic pró te positam pígneri;
Né tu me ignorés, quom extemplo meo é conspectu abscésseris,
Quóm me seruom in séruitute pró te hic relíqueris,

428 quicquam quam *BE*, quicquam *D*, quam *OJ*. 429 experire B^1, experiri B^2*DOJ*, experi *VE*. opera *DEOJ*. 431 caueto mihi *MO*. 433—444 *om. in O.*

425 Magis=*magĭ'*, § 93. **426 Íd ŭt**, § 138; hiatus before *Hegio*, § 84 (3). **427 ēs**, § 128. **428 eī**, § 100. **429** Hiatus at diaeresis, to prevent which Sch. inserts *re*. **430 minus**=*minŭ'*, § 93. **431 cauĕ**, § 138; but see also § 114. **432 meā**, § 99. **433 meam esse** forms one foot; we must scan either *m' ēssĕ*, § 99, or *mĕam ĕssĕ*, § 151. **434 meo**, monosyllable elided, § 101. **435 tĕ hic**, hiatus, § 86.

Túque te pro líbero esse dúcas, pignus déseras,
Néque des operam pró me ut huius réducem facias fílium.
[Scíto te hinc minís uiginti aéstumatum míttier.]
Fác fidelis sís fideli, cáue fidem fluxám geras;
Sérua tibi in perpétuom amicum me átque hunc inuentu ínueni;
Nám pater scio fáciet quae illum fácere oportet ómnia.
Haéc per dexterám tuam te déxtera retinéns manu
Ópsecro, infidélior mi né fuas quam ego súm tibi.
Hóc age tu; tu míhi erus nunc es, tú patronus, tú pater;
Tíbi commendo spés opesque meás. PH. Mandauistí satis.
Sátin habes, mandáta quae sunt, fácta si referó? TY. Satis.
PH. (*bowing to* HEG. *and* TYND.) Ét tua et tua húc ornatus réueniam ex senténtia.
Númquid aliud? TY. Vt quam primum póssis redeas. PH. Rés monet.
HE. Séquere me, uiáticum ut dem á trapezitá tibi;
Eádem opera a praetóre sumam sýngraphum. TY Quem sýngraphum?

436 ducas *om. VEJ.* desideras *M* (deseras B^2). 437 huius huius *BDV.* 441 inuentum *M.* 444 Tu hoc age tu *M.*

438 Hiatus at diaeresis, § 84 (1). **439 cáuĕ,** § 138 or § 114. **441 tíbi ĭn,** § 138. **440 sciŏ,** § 110. **444 Hoc age tu,** so Sch. to avoid hiatus after *tū*: cf. § 88. **445 mēās,** § 99. **446 Satĭn,** § 95. **449** Hiatus at diaeresis, § 84 (1). **450 ēādem,** § 99.

HE. Quem híc ferat secum ád legionem, hinc íre huic ut liceát domum.
Tu íntro abi. TY. (*to* PHIL.) Bene ámbulato. PH. Béne uale (*exit* TYND. *into house*). HE. (*to himself*) Edepol rém meam
Cónstabiliui quóm illos emi dé praeda a quaestóribus:
Éxpediui ex séruitute fílium, si dís placet.
Át etiam dubitáui hosce homines émerem an non emerém diu!
(*To the* LORARII) Séruate istum súltis intus, sérui, ne quoquám pedem
Écferat sine cústode*la; iám* ego adparebó domi.
Ád fratrem modó captiuos álios inuisó meos;
Eádem percontábor ecquis hunc ádulescentem nóuerit.
(*To* PHIL.) Séquere tu, te ut ámittam; ei rei prímum praeuortí uolo.
[*Exeunt* HEG. *and* PHIL., *R., the* LORARII *into house.*]

---

458 inuisu *D.*

---

457 is incomplete in MSS.; most edd. read as in text (with hiatus after *iam*, § 86), Sch. has *ego desubito.* **458 modō**, § 120. **459 ēădem**, § 99. **ecquis hŭnc ádulescentem** may be scanned under § 142, but most edd. scan *ĕcquis*: see Ribbeck Fragm. Trag. Rom. p. li. **460 ēī rēī**, § 100.

ACTVS III.

ERGASILVS.

[*Enter* ERGASILUS, *R.; he soliloquises.*]

Míser homost, qui ipsús sibi quod edit quaérit et id aegre ínuenit.
Séd illest miseriór, qui et aegre quaérit et nihil ínuenit.
Ílle miserrumúst, qui quom se rúpit, quod edit nón habet.
Nam hércle ego huic dieí si liceat óculos ecfodiám lubens;
Íta malignitáte onerauit ómnis mortalís mihi.
Néque ieiuniósiorem néc magis ecfertúm fame
Vídi nec quoi mínus procedat quídquid facere occéperit;
Íta uenter guttúrque resident ésurialis férias.
Ílicet parasíticae arti máxumam malám crucem:
Íta iuuentus iám ridiculos ínopes ab se ségregat.
Níl morantur iám Lacones ími subsellí uiros,
Plágipatidas, quíbus sunt uerba síne penu et pecúnia;

PARASITVS DV *BVE*, PARASITVS *OJ*, *no heading in D*.
463 quom esse cupit *M*. 466 ecfr. tū *VE*, effractum *JO*. 467 nec qui *BDVE*. 468 Itaque *MO*. 469 Licet *VEOJ*. 470 inopesque ab sese *MO*. 471 uni *MO*. 472—479 *om. in O*.

Act III. Sc. 1. Tr. sept. throughout. **461 ipsus** Böthe, Bx., Sch., to avoid *ipsé*. **462 Ille**, § 151. **464 dieī**, § 100. **467 minus** = *minŭ'*, § 93. **472 quibus** = *quibŭ'*, § 93.

Eós requirunt, quí lubenter quom éderint reddánt domi.
Ípsi obsonant, quaé parasitorum ánte erat prouíncia;
Ípsi de foró tam aperto cápite ad lenonís eunt
Quam ín tribu *ante* apérto capite sóntis condemnánt reos.
Néque ridiculos iám terrunci fáciunt; sese omnés amant.
Nám *ego* ut dudum hinc ábii, accessi ad ádulescentis ín foro;
'Sáluete,' inquam, 'quo ímus una ad prándium?' atque illí tacent.
'Quís ait "hoc," aut quís profitetur?' ínquam; quasi mutí silent,
Néque me rident. 'úbi cenamus?' ínquam; atque illi—ábnuont.
Díco unum ridículum dictum dé dictis melióribus,
Quíbus solebam ménstrualis épulas ante adipíscier;
Némo ridet. scíui extemplo rém de conpectó geri.
Né canem quidem ínritatam uóluit quisquam imitárier,
Sáltem, si non ádriderent, déntis ut restríngerent.
Ábeo ab illis, póstquam uideo mé sic ludificárier;
Pérgo ad alios, uénio ad alios, deínde ad alios—úna res!

---

479 una inquam ad *MO*. 480 agit hoc *O*.

---

473 ēōs, § 101. **476 ante** Sch., *met. gr.* **478** Hiatus after *Nam*, § 86: *ego*, Seyffert Stud. Pl. p. 20. **481 illi abnuont**, hiatus, § 84 (3) or, more probably, § 85 (4). Bx. reads *illisce*. **483 Quibus**=*quibŭ'*, § 93.

Ómnes conpectó rem agunt quasi ín Velabro oleárii.
[Núnc redeo inde, quóniam me ibi uídeo ludificárier.]
Item alii parasíti frustra obámbulabant ín foro.
Núnc barbarica lége certumst iús meum omne pérsequi;
Quí consilium iniére, quo nos uíctu et uita próhibeant,
Ís diem dicam, ínrogabo múltam, ut mihi cenás decem
Meo árbitratu dént quom cara annóna sit; sic égero!
Núnc ibo ad portum hínc; est illic mi úna spes cenática;
Si éa decolabít, redibo huc ád senem ad cenam ásperam. [*Exit, L.*

HEGIO. (ARISTOPHONTES.)

[*Enter* HEGIO, *R., in high spirits, followed by* ARISTOPHONTES.]

Quid est suáuius quam bene rém gerere
Bonó publicó, sicut égo feci herí, quom
Emi hósce homines? ubi quísque uident,

---

493 concilium *MO.* 494 His *B²JO.* 498—503 *four lines in MO, ending* heri, obuiam, restitando, reddiderunt.

---

490 If genuine we must scan *mĕ ĭbĭ* with hiatus, § 86. **491** No diaeresis. **493** Proceleusmatic in 2nd foot; Fl. transposes *cons. qui*, Loewe Anal. p. 210 scans *iniĕre*. **494 mihī,** as often. **495 Meo** monosyllable (§ 101) elided. No diaeresis.

Sc. 2. The first part of this Canticum (to 507) is bacchiac, with two anapaestic lines (498, 500); as Hegio's excitement diminishes the metre changes to iambics, 508 sqq. **498** Anapaestic dimeter, § 57. **Quid ĕst suauiŭs quam**; for *ĕst* see § 142, for *suauiŭ'*, § 93. **499** Bacchiac tetrameter, with fourth paeon in third foot, § 60. **500** Anap. dim., § 57.

Eúnt obuiám gratulánturque eám rem.
Itá me miserúm restitándo, retinéndo,
Lassúm reddidérunt:
Vix éx gratulándo misér iam eminébam.
Tandem ábii ad praetórem; ibí uix requiéui,
Rogó syngraphum; datúr mi ilico;
Dedí Tyndaro; ille ábiit domum.
Inde ílico reuórtor
Domúm, postquam id áctumst.
Eo prótinus ad fratrém, [inde abii] mei ubi súnt alii captíui;
Rogó, Philocratem ex Álide ecquis hóminum norit; tándem hic (*pointing to* AR.)
Exclámat eum sibi ésse sodalem; díco eum esse apúd me;
Hic éxtemplo orat óbsecratque eum [sibi] út liceat uidére;
Iussi ílico hunc exsólui. (*To* AR.) nunc tu séquere me,
Vt quód me orauisti ímpetres, eum hóminem uti conuénias. [*Exeunt into house.*

---

502 retinendoque *MO* (q. *O*). 503 *D ends.* 506, 507 *form one v. in MO, as do* 508, 509. 508 praeuortor *VEOJ.* 511—514 *end at* omnium, sodalem, obsecratque, me *in MO.* 511 omnium nouerit *MO.*

---

501 Bac. tetr., § 60. **502** Probably bac. tetr. with ionic a min. in 2nd and 4th feet, § 60. **Itā**, § 117. **503** Bac. dimeter, § 61. **504** Bac. tetr. **505** Probably bac. tetr. with choriambus in 1st foot and ionic a min. in 4th, § 60. Hiatus at diaeresis, § 84 (1). **ibī.** **506**, **507** consist of four catalectic bac. dimeters, § 63; the last has a choriambus in 1st foot. **508** Iam. dim. cat., § 53. **509** Bac. dim., § 61. **510** Iam. septenarius, §§ 48, 49, with hiatus at diaeresis, § 84 (1). **ēō**, § 101. **511—513** Iam. sept. **514** Iam. sen. with hepthem. caesura and dactyl in 5th foot. **515** Iam. sept., with dactyl in 7th foot, § 49.

TYNDARVS.

[*After a short interval, enter* TYNDARUS *hurriedly from the house.*]

Nunc íllud est quom mé fuisse quam ésse nimio máuelim;
Nunc spés opes auxíliaque a me ségregant spernúntque se.
Hic illést dies quom núlla uitae meaé salus sperábilist,
Neque éxitium exitióst neque adeo spés, quae hunc mi aspellát metum;
[Nec mendaciis subdolis mihi usquam mantellumst meis,]
Nec sýcophantiís nec fucis úllum mantellum óbuiamst,
Neque déprecatió perfidiis meís nec malefactís fugast,
Nec cónfidentiae úsquam hospitiumst néc deuorticulúm dolis;
Opérta quae fuére aperta súnt, patent praestígiae.
[Omnis res palamst, neque de hac re negotiumst,

---

516 nemo *VEJ*. 517 spernuntque me *MO*. 519 Neque exilium *MO*.

Sc. 3 written, with the exception of the suspected lines 525—528, in iam. oct., § 51. **516** Caesura, not diaeresis, § 50; so in 518, 519, 521, 522, 524. **518** **ĭlle**, § 151. **meăē**, § 99. **522** **meīs**, § 100. **525** Here, if the lines be genuine (see comm.), the octonarii are interrupted; Bx. scans this line as iam. sen. transposing *palamst res*, Sch. as tr. sept. reading *res palamst nec latitat.*

Quin male occidam oppetamque pestem eri uicem meamque.
Perdidit me Aristophontes hic, qui uenit modo intro;
Is me nouit; is sodalis Philocrati et cognatus est.]
Neque iám Salus seruáre, si uolt, mé potest, nec cópiast,
Nisi si áliquam corde máchinor astútiam.
Quám, malum? quid máchiner? quid cónminiscar? máxumas
Nugás! ineptias íncipisso. haéreo.

HEGIO. ARISTOPHONTES. TYNDARVS.

[*Re-enter* HEGIO *from house, followed by* ARISTOPHONTES.]

HE. (*looking round*) Quo illúm nunc hominem prórípuisse forás se dicam ex aédibus?
TY. (*aside*) Núnc enimuero óccidi; eunt ad te hóstes, Tyndare. *eí mihi,*

---

532 incipisse *BVE*, incepisse *OJ*.

526—528. Tr. sept., § 66, reading *malam* for *meamque* in 526 with Bosscha. **527** If the line were genuine, we must transpose *intro uenit modo*, with Camer. **529** Iam. oct. **530** Iam. sen. with proceleusmatic in 1st foot, § 46, vi. Sch. makes it a tr. sept. by inserting *nimis scitam* after *si*. **531** Tr. sept. Uss. brackets this line and the next. **532** Iam. sen. with hiatus before *haereo*, § 85 (4). **ineptias** scanned either *ineptĭās*, § 109, or *ineptiăs*, § 142. Sch. reads *núgas, insidiás ineptas íncipisso; em, haéreo*.

Sc. 4. The scene opens with iam. oct. § 51, interrupted by two trochaic lines, 534, 535; in 541 the metre changes to tr. sept. which are continued to the entrance of Lorarii, 658. **534** Tr. sept. **enimuéro**, § 142. **ei mihi** added by Lindem., *met. gr.*; *mihi* is found in MSS. at end of next line.

Quíd loquar? quid fábulabor? quíd negabo aut quíd fatebor?
Res ómnis in incertó sitast; quid rébus confidám meis?
Vtinám te di prius pérderent quam pér*i*isti e patriá tua,
Arístophontes, qui éx parata re ínparatam omném facis!
Occísast haec res, nísi reperio atrócem mi aliquam astútiam.
HE. (*seeing* Tynd., *to* Ar.) Sequere; ém tibi hominem, adi átque adloquere. TY. (*aside*) Quís homost me hominum míserior?
AR. Quíd istuc est quod meós te dicam fúgitare oculos, Týndare,
Próque ignoto me áspernari, quási me numquam nóueris?
Équidem tam sum séruos quam tu, etsi égo domi libér fui,
Tu úsque a puero séruitutem séruiuisti in Álide.
HE. Édepol minume míror, si te fúgitat aut oculós tuos
Aút si te odit, qui ístum appelles Týndarum pro Phílocrate.
TY. Hégio, hic homó rabiosus hábitus est in Álide;

535 fatebor mihi *MO.*

535 Tr. oct., § 68. **537 prius**=*priŭ'*, § 93. **540** contains two iambi (3, 8), the remaining feet being all trisyllabic; this renders the iambic rhythm less marked and so makes the transition to the tr. sept. (541 sqq.) easier. **541 sqq.** Tr. sept., § 66. **Quíd ĭstuc**, § 138. **mē̆os**, § 101. **547 hĭc** pron., cf. 98. Sch. reads *istíc.*

Né tu quod istic fábuletur aúris inmittás tuas.
Nam ístic hastis ínsectatus ést domi matrem ét patrem,
Ét illic isti qui *ín*sputatur mórbus interdúm uenit.
Proín tu ab istoc procul recedas. HE. (*recoiling*) Vltro istum a me. AR. (*enraged*) Ain, uérbero?
Mé rabiosum atque ínsectatum esse hástis meum memorás patrem,
Ét eum morbum mi ésse, utqui me ópus sit insputárier?
HE. (*soothingly*) Né uerere, múltos iste mórbus homines mácerat,
Quíbus insputarí saluti fúit atque is prófuit.
AR. Quíd tu autem? etiam huic crédis? HE. Quid ego crédam huic? AR. Insanum ésse me.
TY. Víden tu hunc, quam inimíco uoltu intúitur? concedi óptumumst,
Hégio; fit quód [tibi] ego dixi—glíscit rabies; cáue tibi.
HE. Crédidi esse insánum extemplo, ubi te áppellauit Týndarum.
TY. Quín suom ipse intérdum ignorat nómen neque scit quí siet.

---

551 abstoc *J.* 554 *O ends.* 555 iis (*corr. to* his) *BV*, his *J.* 557 intuetur *M.* 560 Quia *M* (*J illeg.*).

---

548 quód ĭstic, § 138. **550 ĭllic**, § 151. **551 Proīn**, § 104. We must scan either **ab ĭstóc**, § 142, or **prócŭl**, § 138. **aīn**, §§ 95, 106. **552 meūm**, § 102. **553** Hiatus at diaeresis, § 84 (1). **opus**=*opŭ'*, § 93. **555 fūit**, § 131. **557 Vídĕn**, § 138. No diaeresis. Hiatus after *quam*, § 86. **558 caue** scanned *cáuĕ*, § 138, or $\overline{caue}$, § 114. **559** Dactyl in 4th foot, § 66.

HE. Át etiam te suóm sodalem esse aíbat. TY. (*ironically*) Haud uidí magis;
Ét quidem Alcumeus átque Orestes ét Lycurgus póstea
Vna opera mihi súnt sodales qua íste. AR. At etiam, fúrcifer,
Mále loqui mi audés? non ego te nóui? HE. Pol planum íd quidemst,
Nón nouisse, qui ístum appelles Týndarum pro Phílocrate.
Quém uides eum ignóras; illum nóminas quem nón uides.
AR. Ímmo iste eum sese aít, qui non est, ésse et, qui uerόst, negat.
TY. Tu énim repertu's, Phílocratem qui súperes ueriuérbio.
AR. Pól, ego ut rem uideó, tu inuentu's, uéra uanitúdine
Quí conuincas. séd quaeso hercle agedum áspice ad me. TY. (*facing him*) Em. AR. Díc modo,
Tén negas *tu* Týndarum esse? TY. Négo inquam. AR. Tun te Phílocratem
Ésse ais? TY. *Aio* ego ínquam. AR. (*to Heg.*) Tune huic crédis? HE. Plus quidem quám tibi;
Nam ílle quidem, quem tu húnc memoras esse, hódie hinc abiit Álidem

561 aiebat *M* (agiebat *E*). audiui di *VEJ*. 572 tibi aut mihi *M*. 573 hunc *om*. *VEJ*.

561 su͞om, § 111. **a͞ibat**, § 106. **562 Ălcúmeus**, § 142. **566 eum**, monosyllable (§ 102) elided. **567 e͞um**, § 102. **a͞it**, § 106. **568 énĭm**, § 138. **570** Dactyl in 4th foot, § 66. **571 tu** Uss., *met. gr.* **Négo ĭnquam**, § 138. **572 Aio** Langen, Bx., Uss.; see Comm. **quidĕm quám**, § 142.

Ád patrem huius. AR. Quém patrem, qui séruos est? TY. Et tú quidem
Séruos es, libér fuisti; et égo me confidó fore,
Si húius huc recónciliasso in líbertatem fílium.
AR. Quíd ais, furcifér? tun te *esse* gnátum memoras líberum?
TY. Nón equidem me Líberum, sed Phílocratem esse aió. AR. Quid est?
Ýt scelestus, Hégio, nunc íste *te* ludós facit.
Nám is est seruos ípse, neque praetér se umquam ei seruós fuit.
TY. Quía tute ipse egés in patria néc tibi, qui uiuás, domist,
Ómnis inueníri similis tíbi uis. non mirúm facis;
Ést miserorum, ut máleuolentes sínt atque inuideánt bonis.
AR. Hégio, uide sís, ne quid tu huic témere insistas crédere;
Átque ut perspició, profecto iám aliquid pugnae édidit.
Fílium tuom quód redimere se aít id ne utiquam míhi placet.
TY. Scío te id nolle fíeri; ecficiam támen ego id, si di ádiuuant.
Íllum restituam huíc, hic autem in Álidem me meó patri;

575 Seruus et liber *M*. 582 inuenire *M*.

577 **ăis**, § 106. **esse**, *met. gr.* **579** **te** inserted by Lindem., *met. gr.* **580** No diaeresis; hiatus after *Nam*, § 86. **ēī**, § 100. **585** Hiatus after *iam*, § 86. **586** **tūōm**, § 111. **ne ŭtiquam**, § 152. **587** **Sciŏ**, § 110. **fīĕrī**, § 130. **588** **mēō**, § 101.

Própterea ad patrem hínc amisi Týndarum. AR. Quin túte is es,
Néque praeter te in Álide ullus séruos istoc nóminest.
TY. Pérgin seruom me éxprobrare esse, íd quod ui hostili óptigit?
AR. Énim iam nequeo cóntineri. TY. (*to* Heg.) Heus, aúdin quid ait? quín fugis?
Iam íllic hic nos ínsectabit lápidibus, nisi illúnc iubes
Cónprehendi. AR. Crúcior. TY. Ardent óculi; fune opus, Hégio.
Víden tu illi maculári corpus tótum maculis lúridis?
Átra bilis ágitat hominem. AR. At pól te, si hic sapiát senex,
Átra pix agitet ápud carnuficem tuóque capiti inlúceat.
TY. Iám deliraménta loquitur; láruae stimulánt uirum.
HE. Quíd *ais*? quid si hunc cónprehendi iússerim? TY. Sapiás magis.
AR. Crúcior lapidem nón habere mé, ut illi mastígiae
Cérebrum excutiam, quí me insanum uérbis concinnát suis.

---

592 Enim uero iam *M*. 594 oculi fit opus *M*. 599 Quid quid *B*, Hercle quid *VEJ*.

---

592 ĕnĭm iam, § 138. **ăit**, § 106. **593 Illunc**, § 151, probably. **595 Vídĕn**, § 138. **597 pĭx ágitet**, § 142, most edd. transpose. **ápŭd carn.**, § 138. **tŭŏque**, § 111. **598 lārŭae**, always in Pl., § 112. Cf. Am. 777, Aul. 642, Cas. 592, Men. 890, Merc. 982, etc. **599 ais**, Seyffert, *met. gr.* **600 mĕ ut**, hiatus, § 86.

TY. Aúdin lapidem quaéritare? AR. Sólus te solúm uolo,
Hégio. HE. Istinc lóquere, si quid uís; procul tamen aúdiam.
TY. Námque edepol si adbítes propius, ós denasabít tibi
Mórdicus. AR. Neque pól me insanum, Hégio, esse créduis
Néque fuisse umquám neque esse mórbum quem istic aútumat.
Vérum si quid métuis a me, iúbe me uincirí; uolo,
Dum ístic itidem uínciatur. TY. Ímmo enim uero, Hégio,
Ístic qui uolt uínciatur. AR. Táce modo; ego te, Phílocrates
Fálse, faciam ut uérus hodie réperiare Týndarus. (TYND. *makes signs to him*)
Quíd mi abnutas? TY. Tíbi ego abnuto? AR. (*to* HEG.) Quíd agat, si absis lóngius?
HE. (*to* TYND.) Quíd ais? quid si adeam húnc insanum? TY. Núgas! ludificábitur,
Gárriet quoi néque pes umquam néque caput conpáreat.
Órnamenta absunt: Aiácem, hunc quóm uides, ipsúm uides.
HE. Níhili facio, támen adibo. (*Crosses to* AR.) TY. (*aside*) Núnc ego omnino óccidi;

607 uincire *B*, uincinri *J*. 611 Quid...longius *continued to Tynd. in M.* 614 quod *M.* 615 Ortamenta *VEJ* (Hort. *J*).

605 Hiatus at diaeresis, § 84 (1). 607 iŭbe, § 138. 609 Tácĕ, § 138. 613 ăis, § 106.

Núnc ego inter sacrúm saxumque stó nec quid faciám scio.
HE. Dó tibi operam, Arístophontes, sí quid est quod mé uelis.
AR. Éx me audibis uéra quae nunc fálsa opinare, Hégio.
Séd hoc primum me expúr*i*gare tíbi uolo, me insániam
Néque tenere néque mi esse ullum mórbum,—nisi quod séruio.
Át ita me rex deórum atque hominum fáxit patriae cónpotem,
V́t istic Philocratés non magis est quam aút ego aut tu. HE. Eho, díc mihi,
Quís illic igitur ést? AR. Quem dudum díxi a principió tibi;
Hóc si secus repéries, nullam caúsam dico, quín mihi
Ét parentum et líbertatis ápud te deliquió siet.
HE. (*to* TYND.) Quíd tu ais? TY. Me tuom ésse seruom et té meum erum. HE. Haud istúc rogo.
Fuístin liber? TY. Fúi. AR. (*to* HEG.) Enim uero nón fuit; nugás agit.
TY. Quí tu scis? an tú fortasse fuísti meae matri óbstitrix,

---

617 ego ĭntér, § 142. **620 Séd hŏc,** § 138. **expur*i*gare,** Ritschl, *met. gr.*, § 108. **622 deōrum,** § 101. **623 út ĭstic,** § 138. **Eho** monosyllable, § 101. **624 ĭllic,** § 151. **625 secus**=*secŭ'*, § 93. **626 ápŭd,** § 138. **627** Either *āīs*, § 106, or *tuom* monosyllable elided, § 111. **628 fuĭstin,** §§ 111, 92. **629 fuĭsti,** § 111. **mēāē,** § 99.

Qui íd tam audacter dícere audes? AR. Púerum te uidí puer.
TY. Át ego te uideó maiorem máior; em rursúm tibi!
Meám rem non curés, si recte fácias; num ego curó tuam?
HE. (*to* AR.) Fúitne huic patér Thensaurochrýsonicochrýsides?
AR. Nón fuit, neque ego ístuc nomen úmquam audiui ante húnc diem.
Phílocrati Theodóromedes fuít pater. TY. (*aside*) Pereó probe.
Quín quiescis? *i* díerectum, cór meum, ac suspénde te;
Tú subsultas, égo miser uix ádsto prae formídine.
HE. Sátin istuc mihi éxquisitumst, fuísse hunc seruom in Álide
Néque esse hunc Philocratém? AR. Tam satis, quam númquam hoc inueniés secus.
HE. Tum ígitur ego derúncinatus, deártuatus súm miser
Huíus scelesti téchinis, qui me ut lúbitumst ductauít dolis.
Séd uide sis. AR. Quin éxploratum díco et prouisum hóc tibi.

---

631 maior maiorem hem *M.* 640 *preceded by* 645 *in M.* ego aerumnatus *M.*

---

631 maiorem maior, Bentl. transp., *met. gr.* **632 Mĕām,** § 99. **633 Fŭitne,** § 131. **635 fuĭt,** § 111. **636 ĭ díerectum,** §§ 142, 153. **638 Satĭn,** § 95. **fuĭsse,** § 111. **639 ĕsse,** § 151. **satis**=*satĭ'*, § 93. **640 dēartuatus,** § 99. **641 Huĭus,** § 105. **642 uidĕ sís,** § 142.

HE. Cérton? AR. Quin nihil, ínquam, inuenies mágis hoc certo cértius;
Phílocrates iam inde úsque amicus fuít mihi a pueró puer.
Séd ubi is nunc est? HE. Vbi ego minume atque ípsus se uolt máxume.
Séd qua faciest túos sodalis Phílocrates? AR. Dicám tibi:
Mácilento ore, náso acuto, córpore albo, oculís nigris,
Súbrufus aliquántum, crispus, cíncinnatus. HE. Cónuenit.
TY. (*aside*)—Vt quidem hercle in médium ego hodie péssume procésserim.
Vae íllis uirgis míseris, quae hodie in térgo morientúr meo.
HE. Vérba mihi data ésse uideo. TY. (*aside*) Quíd cessatis, cónpedes,
Cúrrere ad me méaque amplecti crúra, ut uos custódiam?
HE. Sátine me illi hodié scelesti cápti ceperúnt dolo?
Íllic seruom se ádsimulabat, híc sese autem líberum.
Núculeum amisí, retinui pígneri putámina;
Íta mi stolido súrsum uorsum os súbleuere offúciis.
Híc quidem me numquam ínridebit. (*Calling into house*) Cólaphe, Cordalió, Corax,
Íte istinc, ecférte lora.

---

647 et oculis *M*. 655 reliqui *M*. 656 uersus *VEJ*. officiis *B*. 658 istinc atque *M*.

---

644 fuĭt, § 111. **646 tūos**, § 111, or *tŭŏ'*, § 93. **653 Satine** Ritschl, *met. gr.* Cf. Most. 1109, Poen. 919, Trin. 1177. **657 quidĕm mé**, § 142.

HEGIO. LORARII. TYNDARVS. ARISTOPHONTES.

[*Enter from the house* COLAPHUS *and the other* LORARII *with leather thongs in their hands.*]

CO. Núm lignatum míttimur?
HE. Inícite huic manicas *máxumas* mastígiae.
TY. Quid hoc ést negoti? quíd ego deliquí? HE.
Rogas,
Satór sartorque scélerum et messor máxume?
TY. Non óccatorem dícere audebás prius?
Nam sémper occant príus quam sariunt rústici.
HE. At út mihi contra cónfidenter ádstitit!
TY. Decet ínnocentem séruom atque innóxium
Confídentem esse suom ápud erum potíssumum.
HE. (*to* LOR.) Adstríngite isti, súltis, uehementér
manus.
TY. Tuós sum; tu has quidém (*holding out his hands*)
uel praecidí iube.
Sed quíd negotist, quam ób rem suscensés mihi?
HE. Quia mé meamque rém, quod in te unó fuit,
Tuís scelestis fálsidicis falláciis

---

664 confidenter mihi contra *M*. 668 tuas *BVE*[1].

Sc. 5. Iambic senarii; for the commencement of a scene in the middle of a line cf. Ter. And. 580, Eun. 1049, Heaut. 953, Phor. 795, Ad. 80, 635, 958. The change of metre is easy as the ends of tr. sept. and iam. sen. are the same, § 64. **659 maxumas** Spengel, to fill up the line. **663 prius**=*prĭŭ'*, § 93. **664 confidenter** transposed by Spengel, *met. gr.* **665 seruom atque**, hiatus, § 84 (2). **666** Either *ĕsse*, § 151, or *sŭom* monosyll. elided, § 111.

Delácerauisti deártuauistíque opes,
Confécisti omnis rés ac rationés meas;
Ita mi éxemisti Phílocratem falláciis.
Illum ésse seruom crédidi, te líberum;
Ita uósmet aiebátis itaque nómina
Intér uos permutástis. TY. Fateor ómnia
Facta ésse ita ut *tu* dícis, et falláciis
Ab*í*ísse eum abs te méa opera atque astútia;
An, óbsecro hercle te, íd nunc suscensés mihi?
HE. At cúm cruciatu máxumo id factúmst tuo.
TY. Dum ne ób malefacta péream, parui aéstumo.
Si ego híc peribo, ast ílle ut dixit nón redit,
At erít mi hoc factum mórtuo memorábile
Me méum erum captum ex séruitute atque hóstibus
Reducém fecisse líberum in patriam ád patrem,
Meúmque potius mé caput perí*cu*lo
Praeóptauisse, quam ís periret, pónere.
HE. Facito érgo ut Acherúnti clueas glória.
TY. Qui pér uirtutem *périt*, perit at non ínterit.
HE. Quando égo te exemplis péssumis cruciáuero
Atque ób sutelas tuás te Morti mísero,

---

690 uirtutem peritat *M*. 691 excruciauero *M*.

---

672 dēārtuauisti, § 99. **678 tu** add. Camer., *met. gr.* **682 parui aestumo,** hiatus, § 84 (3). Sch. reads *existumo.* **685 Me** add. Fl. Bent., *met. gr.* **687 peri*cu*lo** *met. gr.*, see § 108. **688 Prăeōptauisse** according to the rule of Ovid and Vergil (cf. Ov. Met. VII. 131 *prăeăcutae*, Verg. Aen. VII. 524 *sudibusue prăeustis*); in Trin. 648, Ter. Hec. 532 it is contracted *prāeōpt.* **689 Ācherunti,** § 133. **690** See Comm. **691 excruciauero** of MSS. might be scanned under § 142, *pessumĭs éxcr.*; but cf. Bac. 1092, where B has *excrucior* against the metre. **692 tūās,** § 111.

Vel te ínteriisse uél periisse praédicent;
Dum péreas, nihil intérdico aiant uíuere.
TY. Pol si ístuc faxis, haúd sine poena féceris,
Si ille húc rebitet, sícut confido ádfore.
AR. (*aside*) Pro di ínmortales, núnc ego teneo, núnc
scio
Quid sít hoc negoti; méus sodalis Phílocrates
In líbertatest ád patrem in patriá. benest,
Nec quísquam *homo*st mihi aéque melius quoí uelim.
Sed hóc mihi aegrest me huíc dedisse operám malam,
Qui núnc propter me méaque uerba uínctus est.
HE. Votuín te quicquam mi hódie falsum próloqui?
TY. Votuísti. HE. Quor es aúsus mentirí mihi?
TY. Quia uéra obessent ílli quoi operám dabam;
Nunc fálsa prosunt. HE. Át tibi oberunt. TY.
Óptumest;
At erúm seruaui, quém seruatum gaúdeo,
Quoi mé custodem addíderat erus maiór meus.
Sed málene id factum árbitrare? HE. Péssume.
TY. At ego áio recte, qui ábs te sorsum séntio.
Nam cógitato, sí quis hoc gnató tuo
Tuos séruos faxit, quálem haberes grátiam?
Emítteresne nécne eum seruóm manu?
Essétne apud te is séruos acceptíssumus?

---

694 interdico dicant *M.* 696 huc redibit et *M.* afforet *M.* 700 quisquam est *M.* 704 Votauisti *M.*

---

697 Proceleusmatic, *ego tene-*, in fourth foot, § 46, vi. **698 sít hŏc**, § 138. **meus** = *mēūs*, § 102 or *mĕŭ'*, § 93. **sodalĭ'**, § 93. **700 homo** inserted *met. gr.* **705 quŏi operam**, hiatus, § 86. **709** Hiatus in caesura, § 84 (2), to avoid which most edd. insert *tu.* **712 Tuos** = *tūōs*, § 111, or *tŭŏ'*, § 93.

Respónde. HE. Opinor. TY. Quór ergo iratús mihi's?
HE. Quia illí fuisti quám mihi fidélior.
TY. Quid tu? úna nocte póstulauisti ét die
Recéns captum hominem, núperum et nouícium
Te pérdocere, ut mélius consulerém tibi
Quam illí quicum una *a* púero aetatem exégeram?
HE. Ergo áb eo petito ístam gratiam. dúcite, (*to* Lor.)
Vbi pónderosas, crássas capiat cónpedis.
(*To* Tynd.) Inde íbis porro in látomias lapidárias;
Ibi quom álii octonos lápides ecfodiúnt, nisi
Cottídiano sésquiopus conféceris,
Sescéntoplago nómen indetúr tibi.
AR. Per deós atque homines égo te obtestor, Hégio,
Ne tu ístunc hominem pérduis. HE. Curábitur;
Nam nóctu neruo uínctus custodíbitur,
Intérdius sub térra lapides éximet.
Diu ego húnc cruciabo, nón uno absoluám die.
AR. Certúmnest tíbi istuc? HE. Nón moriri cértius.
(*To* Lor.) Abdúcite istum actútum ad Hippolytúm fabrum,

---

718 nuper *B*, *om. VE*. 725 Cotidianos *BJ*. 731 hunc ego *BVE*, hunc ergo *J*.

---

716 ĭlli, § 151, or **fŭĭstĭ**, § 111. **mĭhĭ**, iambus, as often; see Brix, crit. not. ad Trin. 761. **721 gratĭām**, § 109; hiatus in caesura, § 84 (2). Most edd. transpose, *gratiam istam*. **724** Proceleusmatic in 1st foot, or *alii* scanned *aly'*, § 109. **727 dĕōs**, § 101. **731 ego hunc** transposed *met. gr.*; *dĭu hŭnc ego* would scan as a proceleusmatic under § 142, but that is to be avoided, as an anapaest follows, § 66, note. **732 tíbi ĭstuc**, § 138.

Iubéte huic crassas cónpedis inpíngier;
Inde éxtra portam ad meúm libertum Córdalum
In lápicidinas fácite deductús siet,
Atque húnc me uelle dícite ita curárier,
Ne quí deterius huíc sit—quam quoi péssumest.
TY. Quor égo te inuito me ésse saluom póstulem?
Períclum uitae meaé tuo stat perículo.
Post mórtem in morte níhil est, quod metuám, mali.
Et sí peruiuo usque ád summam aetatém, tamen
Breue spátiumst perferúndi quae minitás míhi.
Vale átque salue, etsi áliter ut dicám meres.
Tu, Arístophontes, dé me ut meruisti, íta uale;
Nam míhi propter te hoc óptigit. HE. (*to* LOR.) Abdúcite.
TY. At únum hoc quaeso, si húc rebitet Phílocrates,
Vt mi éius facias cónueniundi cópiam.
HE. (*furiously, to* LOR.) Periístis, nisi hunc iam é conspectu abdúcitis.
TY. Vis haéc quidem herclest ét trahi et trudí simul.— [*Exit, R., hustled by* LOR.
HE. Illic ést abductus récta in phylacam, ut dígnus est.
Ego illís captiuis áliis documentúm dabo,

---

737 ita *follows* hunc *in M.* 742 Etsi super uiuo *B*, & si p uiuo *E.* 747 Atque *B*, Aut *J.*

---

735 meūm, § 102. **737 ita** placed here by Fl., *met. gr.* **740 Periclum**, § 107. **meae**, § 99. **tuo**, § 111. **743** Probably proceleusmatic in 1st foot, § 46, vi. **745** Dactyl in 5th foot, § 46, ii. **746 obtigīt**, § 121. **747** Dactyl in 5th foot, § 46, ii. **749 nisi hunc**, hiatus, § 87; most edd. transpose, *iam hunc.* **751 illic**, § 151. **752 illis**, § 151. **docŭmentum** as *monŭmentum, integŭm.*, but *argūm.*, *instrūm.*, etc., where the *u* is radical.

Ne tále quisquam fácinus incipere aúdeat.
Quod ábsque hoc esset, quí mihi hoc fecít palam,
Vsque óffrenatum suís me ductarént dolis.
Nunc cértumst nulli pósthac quicquam crédere;
Satis súm semel decéptus; sperauí miser
Ex séruitute me éxemisse fílium—
Ea spés elapsast. pérdidi unum fílium,
Puerúm quadrimum quém mihi seruos súrpuit,
Neque eúm seruom umquam répperi neque fílium;
Maiór potitus hóstiumst. quod hoc ést scelus?
Quasi in órbitatem líberos prodúxerim.
(*To* Ar.) Sequere hác; re*d*ducam te úbi fuisti. néminis
Miseréri certumst, quía mei miseret néminem.
AR. (*sadly*) Exaúspicaui ex uínclis; nunc intéllego
Redaúspicandum esse ín catenas dénuo.
[*Exeunt, R.*

755 ofere natum *B*, offerre natum *VEJ* (gnatū *V*). 756 post haec *M*. 766 *M om.* AR. *B om.* Exausp. ex u.

755 sūīs, § 111. **757 Satis**=*sati'*, § 93. **760 surpuit**, § 107. **765 meī**, § 100.

ACTVS IV.

ERGASILVS.

[*Enter* ERGASILUS, *L., in great excitement; he soliloquises.*]

Iúppiter supréme, seruas mé measque augés opes;
Máxumas opímitatis ópiparasque offérs mihi,
Laudém lucrum, ludúm iocum, festíuitatem férias,
Pompám penum, potátionis sáturitatem, gaúdium.
Néc quoiquam homini súpplicare núnc*iam* certúmst mihi;
Nam uél prodesse amíco possum uél inimicum pérdere.
Ita híc me amoenitáte amoena amoénus onerauít dies:
Síne sacris heréditatem sum áptus ecfertíssumam.
Nunc ád senem cursúm capessam hunc Hégionem, quoí boni

---

774 onerauit mihi *BJ*.

Act IV. Sc. 1, mainly in iambic octonarii, expressive of joyful excitement, § 51. It opens with a tr. sept., then follow three sets or systems, consisting of a troch. sept. followed in the first two systems (769—771, 772—774) by two, and in the last (775—780) by five, iambic octonarii: cf. § 52. **772 nuncïam,** for *nunc*, Gepp., *met. gr.* **773** Caesura, but no diaeresis, § 50.

Tantum ádfero, quantum ípsus a dis óptat atque etiam ámplius.
Nunc cérta res est, eódem pacto ut cómici seruí solent,
Coníciam in collum pállium, primo éx me hanc rem ut aúdiat;
Speróque me ob hunc núntium aetérnum adepturúm cibum.

HEGIO. ERGASILVS.

[*Enter* HEGIO, *R.*, *unobserved by* ERGASILUS.]

HE. Quanto ín pectore hánc rem meó magis uolúto,
Tantó mi aegritúdo auctiór est in ánimo.
Ad íllum modúm sublitum ós esse hodiē mi!
Neque íd perspicere quíui.
Quod quóm scibitúr, *tum* per úrbem inridébor.
Quom extémplo ad forum áduenero, ómnes loquéntur
'Hic íllest senéx doctus, quoí uerba dáta sunt'.—

---

777 offero *VEJ.* ipse *M.* 783 subitum *M.*

---

777 ipsus Reiz., *met. gr.* **778 eōdem**, § 101. **779** Hiatus after either *mĕ* or *rĕm*, § 86. **780** Hiatus after *mĕ*, § 86, also at diaeresis, § 84 (1).

Sc. 2 opens with a short *canticum* (781—790) consisting of bacchiac tetrameters, § 60, with a short iambic line (784) and two composite bac.-iam. lines (788, 790). The following duologue is written in trochaic septenarii, § 65, which are interrupted at the beginning of the dialogue (833), but immediately resumed. **781 magis** = *magĭ*', § 93, the third foot being a 2nd paeon. **782 auctiōr**, § 125. **733** Choriambus in 4th foot. **784** Iam. dim. cat., § 53. **785 tum** Lindem., *met. gr.* **787** Fourth paeon in fourth foot.

Sed (*recognising* Erg.) Érgasilus éstne hic procúl quem uideo ?
Conlécto quidémst pallió ; quidnam actúrust ?
ER. Moue ábs te moram átque, Ergásile, age hanc rem.
Éminor intérminor, ne quís mi obstiterit óbuiam,
Nísi qui satis diú uixisse sése homo arbitrábitur ;
Nám qui obstiterit, óre sistet. HE. (*aside*) Híc homo pugilatum íncipit.
ER. Fácere certumst. proínde ita omnes ítinera insistánt sua,
Né quis in ha*n*c plateá*m* negoti cónferat quicquám sui ;
Nám meus est ballísta pugnus, cúbitus catapultást mihi,
V́merus aries ; túm genu ut quemque ícero, ad terrám dabo.
Déntilegos omnís mortalis fáciam, quemque offéndero.
HE. (*aside*) Quae íllaec eminátiost nam ? néqueo mirarí satis.
ER. Fáciam ut huius dieí locique meíque semper méminerit,

---

791 interminorque *M.* 792 quis *M.* 794 proinde ut *BVE*, proinde ut ut *J.* 797 adquemque iecero *M.*

---

788 Bac. dim. + iam. trip. cat., § 72; second paeon in first foot. **790** Same as 788, with hiatus and doubtful syllable at end of second bacchius, § 72. Sch. makes a bac. tetr. by reading *moram mōram* (adj., cf. Trin. 669). **791 Eminŏr,** § 123; see Comm. **792 satis** = *satĭ'*, § 93. **794 prōinde,** § 104. **795 plătĕa,** always. **800 hūīus,** § 105, **diēī, mēīque,** § 100.

Quí mi in cursu opstíterit; faxo uítae is opstiterít suae.
HE. (*aside*) Quíd hic homo tantum íncipissit fácere cum tantís minis?
ER. Príus edico, né quis propter cúlpam capiatúr suam:
Cóntinete uós domi, prohibéte a uobis uím meam.
HE. (*aside*) Míra edepol sunt, ní hic in uentrem súmpsit confidéntiam.
Vaé misero illi quóius cibo iste fáctust imperiósior.
ER. Túm pistores scrófipasci quí alunt furfuribús sues,
Quárum odore praéterire némo pistrinúm potest,
Eórum si ego quoiúsquam scrofam in público conspéxero,
Éx ipsis dominís meis pugnis éxculcabo fúrfures.
HE. (*aside*) Sátur homost, habét profecto in uéntre confidéntiam. 812
ER. Túm piscatorés qui praebent pópulo piscis foétidos,
Qui áduehuntur quádrupedanti crúcianti canthério,
Quórum odos subbásilicanos ómnis abigit ín forum,
Eís ego ora uérberabo súrpiculis piscáriis;

---

801 is extemplo *BVE*. 807 furfure *M*. 812 *preceded by* 811 *in M*. 815 abegit *BJ*.

---

804 pro̅h̅i̅bete, § 104, probably, otherwise dactyl in fourth foot, see § 66. No diaeresis. **805 nĭ hĭc**, hiatus, § 86, or else *hĭc* (pron.) as in 98, 547. **806 quo̅i̅u̅s**, § 105, or *quoiŭ'*, § 93. **807 quĭ alunt**, hiatus, § 86. **809 e̅o̅rum**, § 101. **810 me̅i̅s**, § 100. **814 canthērio**. **816 e̅i̅s**, § 100.

V́t sciant, aliéno naso quam éxhibeant moléstiam.
HE. (*aside*) Básilicas edíctiones átque imperiosás habet.
ER. Túm lanii autem, quí concinnant líberis orbás ouis,
Quí locant caedúndos agnos ét duplam agninám danunt,
Quí petroni nómen indunt uérueci sectário,
E*ō*rum ego si in uiá petronem pública conspéxero,
Ét petronem et dóminum reddam mórtalis misérrumos.
HE. (*aside*) Eúgepae! edíctiones aédilicias híc quidem habet,
Mírumque adeost ni húnc fecere síbi Aetoli agoránomum.
ER. Nón ego nunc parasítus sum, sed régum rex regálior;
Tántus uentri cónmeatus méo adest in portú cibus.
Séd ego cesso hunc Hégionem oneráre laetitiá senem?
Quí homine *hominum* adaéque nemo uíuit fortunátior.
HE. (*aside*) Quae íllaec est laetítia, quam illic laétus largitúr mihi?

---

818 lanu B^1, lanii B^2, lanũ *VE*, lanum *J*.

---

821 ēorum, § 101. **823** Hiatus after *Eugepae*, § 85 (6); dactyl in seventh foot, § 66, no other example in the play. **824 sibi Aetoli**, hiatus, § 86 (9); most edd. transpose, *Aetoli sibi*. **827** Dactyl in fourth foot and no diaeresis, § 66. **828 Quī homine**, hiatus, § 86. **hominum** Camer., *met. gr.* Sch. reads *Quin hoc homine*.

ER. (*knocking at inner door*) Heús ubi estis? écquis *hic est*? *écquis* hoc aperit óstium? 830
HE. (*aside*) Híc homo ad cenam récipit se ad me. ER. Áperite hasce ambás foris,
Príus quam pultando ássulatim fóribus exitium ádfero.
HE. (*aside*) Perlúbet hunc hominem cónloqui. (*aloud*) Ergásile! ER. (*from passage*) Ergasilum quí uocat?
HE. Respíce. ER. Fortuna quód tibi nec facit néc faciet, hoc mé iubes; 834
Sed qui ést? HE. Ad portum néscio quem náctus es, ubi cénes; 837
Eó fastidis. réspice ad me. Hégio sum. ER. (*coming out*) Ó mihi 835
Quántumst hominum *homo* óptume optumórum, in tempore áduenis.
Cédo manum. HE. Manúm? ER. Manum, inquam, cédo tuam actutúm. HE. (*giving it*) Tene. 838

---

832 uel assultatim *BJ*, uel absultatĩ †assultatim *E*, †absultatim †assultatĩ *V*. 837 Nescio quem ad portum *M*. Nescio...fastidis *after* 836 *in M*. 836 quantumst *at end of* 835 *in BJ*. optumorum optume *M*.

---

830 hĭc (adv.) as always. **hic est? ecquis** Bx. *met. gr.*, see Comm. **hŏc**, cf. 660, 762. **831** Hiatus at diaeresis and change of speakers, § 84 (1), 85 (5). **832 Prius**=*priŭ'*, § 93. **833—835** With the opening of the dialogue the tr. sept. are interrupted for a few lines. **833** Iam. oct., § 51, with hiatus at diaeresis, § 84 (1). **834** Iam. oct. **facĭt néc**, § 142. Sch. Bx. omit *hoc*. **837** Iam. sept., § 48. **Ad portum nescio quem** transposed *met. gr.* **ēs**, § 128. **835** The tr. sept. are resumed. **ēō**, § 101. Hiatus at diaeresis, § 84 (1), and at change of speakers, § 85 (5). **836** I have inserted *homo* (cf. Ter. Ph. 853) *met. gr.*, and transposed *optumorum optume.*

ER. (*shaking it*) Gaúde. HE. Quid ego gaúdeam? ER. Quia ego ímpero; (*shaking it harder*) age gaudé modo.
HE. Pól *maestissumí* maerores mi ánteuortunt gaúdiis.
ER. Iám ego ex corpore éxigam omnis máculas maerorúm tibi.
(*Shaking very hard*) Gaúde áudacter. HE. Gaúdeo, etsi níl scio quod gaúdeam.
ER. Béne facis; iubé— HE. Quid iubeam? ER. Ígnem ingentem fíeri.
HE. Ígnem ingentem? ER. Ita díco, magnus út sit. HE. Quid? me, uólturi,
Tuán causa aedis íncensurum cénses? ER. Noli iráscier.
Iúben an non iubés astitui aúlas, patinas élui,
Láridum ac pernás foueri fóculis feruéntibus,
Álium piscis praéstinatum abíre? HE. Hic uigilans sómniat.
ER. Álium porcinam átque agninam et púllos gallináceos?
HE. Scís bene esse, sí sit unde. ER. Péctinem atque ophthálmiam,
Hóraeum scombrum ét trugonum et cétum et mollem cáseum?

---

840 Noli irascier *at end of v. in M.* 844 me uolt uri? *BJ*, uoluri *VE.* 847 atque epulas *M.* 850 Pernam atque opthalmia *M.*

---

839 Dactyl in fourth, § 66. **840 maestissumi** to fill up the line; see Comm. **841 Iăm ego**, hiatus, § 86. **842 sciŏ**, cf. § 110. **843 fĭĕri**, § 130. Hiatus at diaeresis. **845 Tuān**, § 111, 92. **846 Iubĕn**, § 138. Hiatus at diaeresis. **847 fōculis**, see Comm. **848** No diaeresis. **851 trūgōnum**, see Comm.

HE. Nóminandi istórum tibi erit mágis quam edundi cópia
Híc apud me, Ergásile. ER. Mean me caúsa hoc censes dícere?
HE. Néc nihil hodie néc multo plus tu híc edes, ne frústra sis;
Proín tu tui cottídiani uícti uentrem ad me ádferas.
ER. Quín ita faciam, ut *tū́*te cupias fácere sumptum, etsi égo uotem.
HE. Égone? ER. Tu ne. HE. Túm tu mi igitur érus es. ER. Immo béneuolens.
Vín te faciam fórtunatum? HE. Málim quam miserúm quidem.
ER. Cédo manum. HE. (*giving it*) Em manúm. ER. Di te omnes ádiuuant. HE. Nil séntio.
ER. Nón enim es in sénticeto; eó non sentis. séd iube
Vása tibi pura ádparari ád rem diuinám cito
Átque agnum adferrí propere unum pínguem. HE. Quor? ER. Vt sácrufices.
HE. Quoí deorum? ER. Mihi hércle; nam ego nunc tíbi sum summus Iúppiter,
Ídem ego sum Salús, Fortuna, Lúx, Laetitia, Gaúdium;

---

855 coctitiani *B*, quottidiani *E*, cotidiani *VJ*. 862 proprium pinguem *M*. 864 fortunax *VEJ*.

---

852 magis = *magĭ'*, § 93. **853 Me͞an'**, § 99, 92. **854 frustră**, § 152. **855 Pr͞oin**, § 104. **tu͞i**, § 111. **860 ēs**, § 128. **e͞o** probably, § 101, with hiatus at diaeresis, § 84 (1). **861** Hiatus at diaeresis, § 84 (1). **863 de͞orum**, § 101, or *Mihi* elided.

Proín tu diuom hunc sáturitate fácias tranquillúm tibi.
HE. Ésurire míhi uidere. ER. Mi équidem esurio, nón tibi.
HE. Iúppiter te díque perdant. ER. Te hércle—mi aequomst grátias
Ágere ob nuntiúm ; tantum ego nunc pórto a portu tíbi boni.
Núnc tu mihi placés. HE. Abi, stultus ; séro post tempús uenis.
ER. Ígitur olim si áduenissem, mágis tu tum istuc díceres.
Núnc hanc laetitiam áccipe a me, quám fero ; nam fílium
Tuóm modo in portú Philopolemum uíuom saluom et sóspitem
Vídi in publicá celoce, ibidémque illum adulescéntulum
Áleum una et tuóm Stalagmum séruom, qui aufugít domo,
Quí tibi subrupuít quadrimum púerum filiolúm tuom.
HE. Ábi in malam rem, lúdis me. ER. Ita me amábit sancta Sáturitas,
Hégio, itaque suó me semper cóndecoret cognómine,

---

865 deum *BJ.*

---

865 diuom Sch., *met. gr.*; the word occurs in Aul. 50, Poen. 1177. **866** Bx. Sch. read *equidem*; otherwise *ĕsúrio*, § 142. **870 Abĭ**, § 142. **871 magis**=*magĭ'*, § 93. **873 Tūōm**, § 111. **874 celōce**, so dactyl in fourth foot, § 66; no diaeresis. **875 tūōm**, § 111. **877 ĭn**, § 138: no diaeresis. **878 sūō**, § 111.

V́t ego uidi. HE. Meúm*ne* gnatum? ER. Tuóm gnatum et geniúm meum.
HE. Ét captiuom illum Álidensem? ER. Μὰ τὸν Ἀπόλλω. HE. Et séruolum
Meúm Stalagmum, meúm qui gnatum súbrupuit? ER. Ναὶ τὰν Κόραν.
HE. Iám diu— ER. Ναὶ τὰν Πραινέστην. HE.—uénit? ER. Ναὶ τὰν Σιγνίαν.
HE. Cérton? ER. Ναὶ τὰν Φρουσινῶνα. HE. Víde sis— ER. Ναὶ τὰν Ἀλάτριον.
HE. Quíd tu per barbáricas urbes iúras? ER Quia enim item ásperae
Súnt, ut tuom uictum aútumabas ésse. HE. Vae aetatí tuae!
ER. Quíppe quando míhi nil credis, quód ego dico sédulo.
Séd Stalagmus quoíus erat tunc nátionis, quom hínc abit?
HE. Sículus. ER. At nunc Sículus non est; Bóius est—boiám terit;
Líberorum quaérundorum caúsa ei, credo, uxór datast.
HE. Díc, bonan fidé tu mi istaec uérba dixistí? ER. Bona.
HE. Di ínmortales, íterum gnatus uídeor, si uera aútumas.

---

888 Sicuius. Ē. et nunc si cuius *B*, Sicuius et nunc sicuius *VE* (si cuius *E*), Cuius et nunc. PAR. Sicuius *J*.

---

879 Meūm, § 102; at end of line the same word is dissyl. Fl. Bentl. read *Meumne*, which improves the rhythm. **Tūōm**, § 111. **880 Mă**. **881 meūm**, § 102, twice. **883 Vidĕ**, § 137. **885 tūōm**, § 111. **889 ēī**, § 100.

ER. Aín tu? dubium habébis etiam, sáncte quom
ego iurém tibi?
Póstremo, Hegió, si parua iúri iurandóst fides,
Víse ad portum. HE. Fácere certumst; tu íntus
cura quód opus est.
Súme, posce, próme quiduis; té facio cellárium.
ER. Nam hércle nisi mantíscinatus próbe ero, fusti
péctito.
HE. Aéternum tibí dapinabo uíctum, si uera aútu-
mas.
ER. V́nde id? HE. A me meóque gnato. ER.
Spónde*n* tu istud? HE. Spóndeo.
ER. Át ego tuom tibi áduenisse fílium respóndeo.
HE. Cúra quam optumé potest. ER. Bene ámbula
et redámbula. [*Exit* HEG., *L.*
Íllic hinc abiit; míhi rem summam crédidit—cibá-
riam.
Di ínmortales, iam út ego collos praétruncabo té-
goribus!
Quánta pernis péstis ueniet, quánta labes lárido,
Quánta sumini ábsumedo, quánta callo cálamitas,
Quánta laniis lássitudo, quánta porcináriis!
Nám si alia memorém, quae ad uentris uíctum con-
ducúnt, morast.

---

901 PARASITVS, *as heading*, B^2VE. 902 tergoribus *M.* 904 absumendo *M.* 905 *A begins to be decipherable.*

---

892 a͞in, § 106. **898 me͞oque**, § 101. **899 tu͞om**, § 111. **901 ĭllĭc**, § 151. **902 tegoribus** Turnebus, *met. gr.*, for MSS. *terg.*, see § 66.

Núnc ibo, ut pro praéfectura meá ius dicam lárido,
Ét, quae pendent índemnatae, pérneis auxilium út feram. [*Exit into house.*

---

907 UTPROP...FE...RAMEAIUS *A*, ut praefecturam et ius *M*. 908 PERNIS *A* (*Studemund*), perne eis *B*, pernies *VE*, pernis *J*.

---

907 meā, § 99. 908 pernēis, § 100.

ACTVS V.

PVER.

[*Enter a Boy from the house; he soliloquises.*]

Diéspiter te díque, Ergasile, pérdant et uentrém tuom
Parasítosque omnis ét qui posthac cénam parasitís dabit.
Cladís calamitatísque intemperiés [modo in] nostram aduenít domum.
Quasi lúpus esuriens métui ne *uel* ín me faceret ímpetum;
Nimisque hércle ego illum mále formidabam; íta frendebat déntibus.
Aduéniens totum déturbauit cúm carne carnárium,
Arrípuit gladium, praétruncauit tríbus tegoribus glándia,
Aulás calicesque omnís confregit, nísi quae modialés erant;

---

911 CLADESCALAMITATESQ. *A*, cladis calamitas q' *M* (quę *V*). MODOIN *A*, modam *V*, modom *E*. 912 TIMUI *A*. *After this v. parts of a line, om. in M, have been deciphered in A,* UBIUOLT......IMPETUM. 913 *A seems to have had* FORMIDAVI. 914 deturbauit totum *M*. 915 tergoribus *M*. 916 confringit *BVE*.

Act V. Sc. 1. Iambic octonarii, § 51: all the lines have caesura in 5th foot, only three (910, 919, 921) have diaeresis at end of 4th foot. **912** Proceleusmatic in 1st foot; **uel** Sch., *met. gr.* **913 Nimĭsque,** § 142. **914 carnē,** § 119. **915 tribus** = *tribŭ,* § 93.

Cocum pércontabatúr, possentne sériae feruéscere;
Cellás refregit ómnis intus réclusitque armárium.
(*Calling into house*) Adséruate istunc súltis, serui;
ego íbo, ut conueniám senem.
Dicam út sibi penum áliud ornet, síquidem sese utí
uolet:
Nam, hic quídem ut adornat, aút *ei* iam níhil est
aut iam níhil erit. [*Runs off, R.*

HEGIO. PHILOPOLEMVS. PHILOCRATES.
STALAGMVS.

[*Enter* HEG., PHILOP., PHILOC. *and* STAL. *from the*
L., HEGIO *speaking to* PHILOP.]

HE. Iouí disque agó gratiás merito mágnas,
Quom té re*d*ducém tuo patrí reddidérunt
Quomque éx miseriís plurumís me exemérunt,
Quas, dúm te caréndum hic fuít, sustentábam,
Quomque húnc (*pointing to* STAL.) conspicór in po-
téstate nóstra

---

917 serire *VEJ*. 920 ALI...ADORN...*A*. 922 DEISQ. *A*, diisque *M*. 925 QUAEADKUCC......MKUCFUI *A*, Quae adhuc te carens dum hic fui *M*. 926 conspicio *M* (*A illeg.*).

---

917 Cocŭm pérc., § 142. **918 rēclusit**: the *e* is long not as being followed by *cl*, which in Pl. would not lengthen a short syllable, but owing to the original form of the particle, *red*, whence *reccludo*, *redduco*, etc. **920 sibī** iambus as often. **921 ei**, *met. gr.*; see Comm.

Sc. 2 opens with bacchiac tetrameters, § 60; then follow two trochaic octonarii, 928, 929 (see § 69), introducing the troch. septenarii, which are continued to the end of the play. **922** Second Paeon in third foot; no diaeresis. **923 re*d*ducem** Schneider, *met. gr.*, see on 918. **tūō**, § 111. **924** Ionic a maj. in 1st foot; no diaeresis. **926 conspicōr** (§ 123) Geppert, *met. gr.*

Quomque haéc (*pointing to* Philoc.) *re* repértast fidés firma nóbis.
PHILOP. Sátis iam dolui ex ánimo et cura, sátis me [et] lacrumis máceraui,
Sátis iam audiui tuás aerumnas, ád portum mihi quás memorasti:
Hóc agamus. PHILOC. (*to* Heg.) Quíd nunc, quoniam técum seruauí fidem
Tíbique hunc reducem in líbertatem féci? HE. Fecisti út tibi,
Phílocrates, numquám referre grátiam possím satis,
Proínde ut tu proméritu's de me et fílio meo.
PHILOP. Immó potes,
Páter, et petere id á te ego potero et di eám potestatém dabunt,
Ýt beneficium béne merenti nóstro merito múneres;
Sícut tu huic (*pointing to* Philoc.) potés, pater mi, fácere merito máxume.
HE. (*to* Philoc.) Quíd opust uerbis? língua nullast quá negem quidquíd roges.
PHILOC. Póstulo abs te ut mi íllum reddas séruom, quem hic relíqueram
Pígnus pro me, quí mihi melior quám sibi sempér fuit,

---

928 cura me satis et *BJ*, CURASATISMELACRUMIS *A*. maceraui hoc *M* (*A illeg.*). 931 *A ends*. 933 meo *om. VEJ*. 934 et poteris et ego potero *M*. 935 meriti *VEJ*.

---

927 re Spengel, *met. gr.* Seyffert however considers the line an iam.-bac., § 73. **928 satis**=*satĭ'*, twice, § 93. Notice the five anapaests in this line, softening transition from bacchiacs to trochaics. **929 Satis**=*satĭ'*, § 93. **tūās**, § 111. **930 Hōc** as in 967. **933 Prōinde**, § 104. **meo** monosyll. elided. **934 ēam**, § 99.

Pró benefactis éius uti ei prétium possim réddere.
HE. Quód bene fecistí, referetur grátia id quod póstulas.
Ét id et aliud quód me orabis ímpetrabis; átque te
Nólim suscensére quod ego irátus ei fecí male.
PHILOC. Quíd fecisti? HE. In lápicidinas cónpeditum cóndidi,
Vbi resciui míhi data esse uérba. PHILOC. Vae miseró mihi:
Própter meum capút labores hómini euenisse óptumo.
HE. Át ob eam rem míhi libellam pró eo argenti né duis;
Grátiis a me, út sit liber, dúcito. PHILOC. Edepol, Hégio,
Fácis benigne. séd quaeso hominem ut iúbeas arcessí. HE. Licet.
(*Calling into house*) Vbi estis uos? íte actutum, Týndarum huc arcéssite.—
(*To the young men*) Vós ite intro: intéribi ego ex hac státua uerbereá (*pointing to* STAL.) uolo
Érogitare, meó minore quíd sit factum fílio.
Vós lauate intéribi. PHILOP. Sequere hac, Phílocrates, me intró. PHILOC. Sequor.
[*Exeunt* PHILOP. *and* PHILOC. *into house.*

940 ei *om. VJ.* 941 *follows* 938 *in BE.* 948 aducito *BVE*, ad ducito *J.* 951 inter ibo *M.* ueruere auolo B^2 (*om.* B'), ueruerce auolo *V*, ueruece auolo *EJ.*

943 No diaeresis. **946 mĕūm**, § 102. **947 prŏ ĕo ārg.**, for the hiatus see § 86. **948 Gratiis** Böthe, *met. gr.* **949 Facis**=*facĭ'*, § 93. **950 Vbĭ estis**, hiatus, § 87: to avoid which Bx. Sch. read *Heus ubi estis?*

HEGIO. STALAGMVS.

HE. Áge tu illuc procéde, bone uir, lépidum mancupiúm meum.
ST. Quíd me oportet fácere, ubi tu tális uir falsum aútumas?
Fúi ego bellus, lépidus; bonus uir númquam neque frugí bonae
Néque ero umquam; né spem ponas mé bonae frugí fore.
HE.Própemodum ubi locí fortunae tuaé sint facile intéllegis:
[Sí eris uerax, tua éx re facies éx mala meliúsculam.]
Récte et uera lóquere; sed neque uére neque *tu* récte adhuc
Fécisti umquam. ST. Quód ego fatear crédin pudeat quom aútumes?
HE. Át ego faciam ut púdeat; nam in rubórem te totúm dabo.
ST. Éia, credo ego ínperito plágas minitarís mihi;
Tándem ista*ec* aufér, dic quid fers, út feras hinc quód petis.

957 neque spem *VEJ*. 960 Recta *B*. 962 rumorem *B*, roborem *VEJ*.

Sc. 3. Tr. sept. **955 ubī** as in Bac. 431, Poen. 702, Ps. 490, Rud. 1236, 1347, Truc. 360. **956 bonus** = *bonŭ'*, § 93. **957 erŏ unquam,** hiatus, § 87, to avoid which Bx. reads *numquam* comparing Ps. 136, Men. 1027. **958 tūāē**, § 111. **959 Sī eris,** hiatus, § 86. **960** Dactyl in 4th foot, § 66. **tu,** *met. gr.* **962** No diaeresis. **964 istaec** Schmidt, *met. gr.* In Trin. 413, 665 A has *istaec*, BCD *ista*; cf. Am. 1101.

HE. Sátis facundu's; séd iam fieri dícta conpendí uolo.
Hóc agamus. iam ánimum aduorte ac míhi quae dicam edíssere.
Sí eris uerax, *éx* tuis rebus féceris meliúsculas.
ST. Núgae istaec sunt; nón me censes scíre quid dignús siem?
HE. Át ea supterfúgere potis es—paúca, si non ómnia.
ST. Paúca ecfugiam, scío: nam multa euénient et meritó meo,
Quía ecfugi et tibí subrupui fílium et eum uéndidi.
HE. Quoí homini? ST. Theodóromedi in Álide Polyplúsio
Séx minis. HE. Pro di ínmortales! ís quidem huius ést pater
Phílocratis. ST. Quin mélius noui quám tu et uidi saépius.
HE. Sérua, Iuppitér sụpreme, et me ét meum gnatúm mihi.
(*Calling into house*) Phílocrates, per tuóm te genium óbsecro, exi; té uolo.

---

965 dictis compendium *M.* 966 aduorte haec mihi *M.* 971 *follows* 973 *in M.* 972 Quia et fugi *M.* 973 theodoro medico *M.* 975 quam te et *M.* 977 ingenium *M.*

---

965 Satis=*satĭ'*, § 93. MS. reading involves *compendīūm*, see Comm. **967 Hōc.** **968 Sī eris**, hiatus, § 86. **tūīs**, § 111; see Comm. **971 scĭō**, § 110: no diaeresis. **972 Quia ĕcfūgi**, § 138. **973 Quŏĭ homini**, hiatus, § 86. **977 tūōm**, § 111; hiatus at diaeresis, § 84 (1).

PHILOCRATES. HEGIO. STALAGMVS.

[*Enter* PHILOCR. *from the house.*]

PH. Hégio, adsum; sí quid me uis, ímpera. HE. Hic gnatúm meum
Tuó patri ait se uéndidisse séx minis in Álide.
PH. (*to* STAL.) Quám diu id factúmst? ST. Hic annus íncipit uicénsumus.
PH. (*to* HEG.) Fálsa memorat. ST. Aút ego aut tu; nám tibi quadrímulum
Tuós pater pecúliarem páruolo pueró dedit.
PH. (*to* STAL.) Quíd erat ei nomén? si uera dícis, memoradúm mihi.
ST. Paégnium uocitátust; post uos índidistis Týndaro.
PH. Quór ego te non nóui? ST. Quia mos ést obliuisci hóminibus
Néque nouisse, quóius nihil*i* sít faciunda grátia.
PH. Díc mihi, isne istíc fuit quem uéndidisti meó patri,
Quí mihi pecúliaris dátus est? ST. (*nodding*) Huius fílius.
HE. Víuitne is homo? ST. Argéntum accepi, níl curaui céterum.
HE. (*to* PHIL.) Quíd tu ais? PH. Quin ístic ipsust Týndarus tuos fílius,

---

982 paruulum *M.*

Sc. 4. Tr. sept. **979 Tu͞o**, § 111. **a͞it**, § 106. **981 tĭbī.** **982 Tu͞os**, § 111, or *tŭŏ'*, § 93. **983 e͞i**, § 100. **987 me͞o**, § 101. **988 mĭhī.** **990 ais** dissyl., § 106. **tu͞os**, § 111 or *tŭŏ'*, § 93.

Ýt quidem hic arguménta loquitur; nam ís mecum a pueró puer
Béne pudiceque éducatust úsque ad adulescéntiam.
HE. Ét miser sum et fórtunatus, sí *uos* uera dícitis.
Eó miser sum quía male illi féci, si gnatúst meus.
Éheu, quom ego plús minusque féci quam *me* aequóm fuit.
Quód male feci, crúcior; modo si inféctum fieri póssiet!
(*Looking off*) Séd eccum incedit húc ornatus haúd ex suis uirtútibus.

TYNDARVS. HEGIO. PHILOCRATES. STALAGMVS.

[*Enter* TYND. *heavily chained, and carrying a pick; he does not see the others.*]

TY. Vídi ego multa saépe picta quae Ácherunti fíerent
Crúciamenta; uérum enim uero núlla adaequest Ácheruns
Átque ubi ego fui, in lápicidinis; íllic ibi demúmst locus,
Ýbi labore lássitudost éxigunda ex córpore.

---

997 haud suis *B*, audax suis *VEJ*. 1001 lassitudo est omĩs *M* (omnis *J*).

---

993 uos Camer., *met. gr.* **994 ēō**, § 101. **995 quom ego,** hiatus, § 86. **me** Bx., *met. gr.* **996 fĭĕri**, § 130. No diaeresis. **997 Séd ĕccum**, § 138. **sūīs**, § 111.

Sc. 5. Tr. sept. **998 Ācherunti**, § 133. **fĭĕrent**, § 130. **999 enĭm uéro**, § 142. **Ācheruns**, § 133.

Nam úbi illo adueni, quási patriciis púeris aut monérulae
Aút anites aut cóturnices dántur, quicum lúsitent,
Ítidem mi haec aduénienti upupa, quí me delectém, datast.
(*Sees the others*) Séd erus eccum ante óstiumst; erus álter eccum ex Álide
Réd*i*it. HE. *O* salue, éxoptate gnáte mi. TY. (*astonished*) Hem, quid 'gnáte mi'?
Áttat scio quor té patrem adsimulés esse et me fílium;
Quía mi, item ut paréntes, lucis dás tuendi cópiam.
PH. Sálue, Tyndare. TY. Ét tu, quoius caúsa hanc aerumnam éxigo.
PH. Át nunc liber ín diuitias fáxo uenies; nám tibi
Páter hic est: hic séruos, qui te huic hínc quadrimum súrpuit,
Véndidit patrí meo te séx minis; is té mihi
Páruolum pecúliarem páruolo pueró dedit.
Íllic indicium fécit; nam hunc ex Álide huc reddúximus.
Quín huius filium íntus eccum, frátrem germanúm tuom.

1004 delectet *M.* 1008 *A begins.* 1009 -GUO *A*, ex iguo *B.* 1014 reducimus *M.* 1015 QUID *apparently in A, which omits* 1016—1022. TY. Quid huius filium? PH. Intus *M.*

1002 ĭllo, § 151. **1003 cōturnices,** Lucr. IV. 641. **1005** Dactyl in 4th, § 66. **1006 O** Speng. to avoid hiatus; cf. Men. 1132, Trin. 1163, etc. **1007 scĭŏ,** § 110; dactyl in 4th foot, to avoid which edd. transpose, *esse ads.*; no diaeresis. **1011 surpuit,** § 107. **1014 ĭllĭc,** § 151. **1015 hūĭūs,** § 105.

TY. (*confused*) Quíd tu ais? addúxtin illum húius captiuom fílium?
PH. Quín, inquam, intus híc est. TY. Fecisti édepol et recte ét bene.
PH. Núnc tibi pater hic (*pointing to* HEG.) ést. hic (*pointing to* STAL.) fur est tuós qui paruom hinc te ábstulit.
TY. Át ego hunc grandis grándem natu ob fúrtum ad carnuficém dabo.
PH. Méritus est *ergá te.* TY. Ergo edepol méritam mercedém dabo.
(*To* HEG.) Séd dic, oro, páter meus tun és? HE. Ego sum, gnáte mi.
TY. [Núnc demum in memóriam redeo, quóm mecum recógito.]
Núnc edepol demum ín memoriam régredior audísse me
Quási per nebulam—Hégionem meúm patrem uocárier.
HE. Ís ego sum. PH. Conpédibus quaeso ut tíbi sit leuior fílius
Átque hic grauior séruos. HE. Certumst príncipio id praeuórtier.

1016 filium captiuum *M.* 1023 *ends with* RREDISSEME *in A* (*Studemund*), audissem me *BJ.* 1025 ISEGOSUM *A*, Ego sum *M.* 1026 ATQ. HUIC *A.* principium *M.*

1016 ăĭs, § 106; probably **illum** ‖ **hūĭūs**, § 105, with hiatus at diaeresis, § 84 (1), to avoid which Bx. reads *illunc.* **captiuom filium** transp. *met. gr.* **1018 tŭōs**, § 111, or *tŭŏ'*, § 93. **1020 erga te** Sch., *met. gr.* **1021 pátĕr**, § 138. **Egō**, § 120, but Böthe reads *oro te*, with *pater mĕūs* and *egŏ*. On **ēs** see § 128. **1023 regrediōr**, § 123. **1024 mĕūm**, § 102, hiatus after *nebulam*, § 85 (4).

(*To* Tynd.) Eámus intro, ut árcessatur fáber, ut istas cónpedis
Tíbi adimam, huic dem. ST. Quoí peculi níhil est, recte féceris. [*Exeunt into house.*

CATERVA.

[*Enter all the actors; they address the audience.*]

Spéctatores, ád pudicos móres facta haec fábulast,
Néque in hac subigitátiones súnt neque ulla amátio
Néc pueri suppósitio nec argénti circumdúctio,
Néque ubi amans aduléscens scortum líberet clam suóm patrem.
Huíus modi paucás poetae réperiunt comoédias,
Vbi boni melióres fiant. núnc uos, si uobís placet,
Ét si placuimús neque odio fúimus, signum hoc míttite;
Quí pudicitiae ésse uoltis praémium, plausúm date.
[*Exeunt omnes.*

1030 subi cogitationes *VE*, subite cogitationes *J*.

1027 ēāmus, § 99.
Sc. 6. **1031 nec ărgénti,** § 142. No diaeresis. **1032 sūōm,** § 111. **1033 Hūīūs,** § 105, or *hūiŭ'*, § 93.

NOTES.

ACROSTIC ARGUMENT.

One of these is prefixed to each of the plays except the Bacchides, the beginning of which has been lost. They are considered from internal evidence to be the work of a time long subsequent to Plautus; moreover the idea of an acrostic argument is evidently one which would occur only to a literary student, and the plays of Plautus were not studied as literature until at least a century after his death. The form CAPTEIVEI is here adopted chiefly, no doubt, to gain two extra lines for the explanation of the plot, but partly also on account of its archaic air. In inscriptions dating towards the end of the republic EI for I is found but rarely, and much less frequently in non-final than in final syllables.

ii. **Alium**=*alterum*, 8.
v. **in ibus**, see R. 377.
vi. **uersa**=*mutata*, 37.
vii. **amittatur**=*dimittatur*, see on 36.

PROLOGUE.

This is not the work of Plautus; it is assigned by Ritschl to the middle of the 1st century B.C., when the plays of Pl. were revived on the Roman stage; cf. the prologue to the Casina:

> Nos, postquam populi rumore intelleximus
> studiose expetere uos Plautinas fabulas,
> antiquam eius edidimus comoediam.

In the original play there was probably no prologue, the necessary explanations being given by the parasite Ergasilus in a passage at l. 94 which was afterwards cut out; even as it now stands some explanations are given there for the second time. The way in which this prologue was compiled from the rest of the play may be seen by comparing the following lines: 4 with 96, 8 with 876 and 1011, 20 with 982 and 1013, 24 with 93, 27 with 98 and 100, 28 with 101, 31 with 169 and 170, 33 with 167 and 168, 34 with 111, 43 with 686.

There is no prologue extant to the Curc. Ep. Most. Per. or Sti.; in the Trin. Rud. Cist. Aul. and Am. the prologue is spoken by a god, in the Merc. and Mil. by one of the characters in the play; here and in the rest of the plays it was spoken by a member of the company (*grex*), probably one of the younger actors (cf. prol. ad Ter. Heaut.) who was dressed for the part (prol. ad Ter. Hec.) and carried an olive branch as being a suppliant for the favour of the audience.

1. **Hos quos**: antecedent attracted into case of relative (R. 1067), as happens frequently (at any rate in early Latin) when its own clause is separated from it by the relative clause; cf. 110, 807, Verg. Aen. I. 573 *urbem, quam statuo, uestra est*, Trin. 985 *illum, quem ementitus es, ego sum ipsus Charmides*, Truc. 745 *illis, quibus inuidetur, i rem habent*, Trin. 137 *ille, qui mandauit, eum exturbasti ex aedibus.* Generally, as here, when the main sentence comes, the antecedent is repeated in its proper case.

2. **Illi**, whether taken as pron. or adv., is generally regarded as corrupt, following so closely upon *hos* or *hic*; see however, as to pronouns, on 548. Fl. suggests *uincti quia*, Speng. *inuiti qui*, Bx. *in uinclis qui.* Possibly *ei inquam qui* may be right, *inquam* being used in the repetition of a phrase with a small variation, as in Aul. 758, Ps. 516.

adstant 'stand up,' see on 637.

i stant: παρὰ προσδοκίαν, intended to raise a laugh by disappointing the audience of the explanation they expected.

3. **testes estis** = *testamini* and governs substantival clause *me...loqui*, which again governs *hoc.*

uerum is a secondary predicate, i.e. is predicated with or through the primary predicate *loqui.* Roby, 1017 *c*, suggests the name *sub-predicate*, to distinguish this from the secondary predicates which are used to complete the predication of verbs of indeterminate meaning.

5. **is**: the pronoun is put for emphasis before, and outside of, the relative sentence of which it is the subject: see R. 1045 and cf. 19, Poen. 924 *sed ego nunc est, quom me commoror.*

suo sibi: *sibi* repeats and emphasizes the notion of *suus*, 'his own': cf. the French 'mien à moi'; the phrase is an irregular colloquialism, without grammatical construction: it occurs about ten times in Pl. (in Truc. 698 we have *ubi male accipiar mea mihi pecunia*), also in Ter. (Ad. 958 *suo sibi gladio hunc iugulo*) and in Columella.

6. **operam datis**: see on 344. On the disorderly and impatient character of a Roman audience, see Mommsen H. R. II. p. 422.

7. **nati fuerunt**=*nati sunt*, as often in Pl.; see R. 1453 and cf. Poen. 1347 *sciui et miratus fui*, Merc. 488 *aurum Hector qui expensus fuit*, Mil. 118 *capiunt praedones nauem illam ubi uectus fui*, Ps. 689 *quod subito conmentus fui*, Curc. 566 *quod fui iuratus, feci*, etc.

8. **surrupuit**=*surripuit*, the spelling of all MSS. elsewhere in this play: taking all the plays, the spelling of A, as well as of BCD, is more often *-rip-* than *-rup-*; in the participle all have *-rupt-* more often than *-rept-*. For the change from *ă* to *ŭ* in composition, cf. *salio* with *insulio*, *capio* with *aucupari mancupium recupero*, *calco* with *inculco*, *c(a)lam* with *occulo*, *taberna* with *contubernium*, etc.

9. **Alide**, the native pronunciation; we use the Attic form *Elis*.

10. **iam hoc tenetis**: the same question is addressed to the audience in Poen. prol. 116 and in Mercury's explanation, Am. 485; for *teneo* 'grasp' 'understand,' cf. 697.

11. **illic ultumus** 'that man at the back' who is supposed to have answered 'no.'

accedito 'come closer'; this, the MSS. reading, is altered by Ussing and others to *abscedito*, as being inconsistent with next v.; but *accedito* will stand if we suppose the man at the back to answer that there is no room in front, whereupon the actor retorts 'if there isn't room to sit down, there is room to walk out.'

12. **ubi sedeas**: *ubi* refers to *locus* and=*in quo*=*talis ut in eo*, hence the consec. subj., R. 1682. Before 155 B.C. the auditorium (*cauea*) of a Roman theatre was merely a sloping bank of earth: in that year the censor Cassius began to build a stone theatre with tiers of seats or steps (*subsellia*, *gradus*) for the audience, but the senate on the motion of Scipio Nasica ordered its demolition and decreed '*ne quis in urbe propiusue passus mille subsellia posuisse sedensue ludos spectare uellet*,' Val. Max. II. 4. 2; so that, as the epitome of Livy says, bk 48, *aliquandiu populus stans ludos spectaret*. Meanwhile provincial towns like Tusculum and Faesulae, which were not so strict in their conservatism, had their stone theatres, and after some years the *caueae* in Roman theatres were filled with seats like these, but made of wood. Hence we find *subsellia* mentioned in the prologues (not by Pl.) to the Poenulus and Amphitruo. But as we also find references to a sitting audience in the body of some of the plays (e.g. Aul. 719, Ep. *ad fin.*, Truc. *ad fin.*) we may conclude that the spectators in the time of Pl. either sat on the ground or brought seats or cushions with them (as in Greece, Theophr. Char. 2).

ambules = *abeas*, As. 488 *age ambula ergo*, Ps. 263 *ambula tu*, Trin. 1108 *cito ambula, actutum redi*, Ter. Heaut. 379 SY. *abeas si sapias.* CL. *eo*... SY. *ambula*, etc.; *bene ambula* is a polite farewell, e.g. in 452 and 900.

13. **mendicarier**: for this old form of the infin. pass. see on 438; the meaning is 'to break his voice and so come to beggary by losing his employment.'

14. **me rupturus sum**: cf. Cas. 809 *dirumpi cantando hymenaeo*, Cic. Fam. VII. 1. 4 *dirupi me paene in iudicio Galli Caninii*, Hor. Ep. I. 19. 5 *rupit Iarbitan Timagenis aemula lingua*, and Pl. Merc. 138 *tua causa rupi ramices; iam dudum sputo sanguinem.*

15. **ope** 'wealth,' in which sense the singular is very unusual; it is found however in a fragment of Ennius, *uidi ego te, adstante ope barbarica, tectis caelatis laqueatis, auro ebore instructam regifice* (Androm. fr. 9 in Cic. Tusc. III. 19, 44) and in a passage of Vergil imitated therefrom, Aen. VIII. 685 *hinc ope barbarica uariisque Antonius armis.*

censerier: one of the duties of the censors was to take the *census* or register of all Roman citizens who were *sui iuris*, enquiring the number of each man's children and estimating the value of his property. According to the estimate thus formed, the citizens were distributed into the five Servian classes, while below these classes came the *capite censi*, those who having no property were registered 'by the head.' To this lowest class the actor implies that *illic ultumus* belongs, for he turns from him to address the rest of the audience as 'you who are rated (not by the head but) by your property,' referring chiefly, no doubt, to the Senators who from 194 B.C. had the orchestra reserved for them (Liv. XXXIV. 44. 5).

16. **Accipite relicuom**: this phrase has two meanings, (1) 'hear the sequel,' cf. Cic. Fam. VIII. 17. 2 '*Cur hoc?*' *inquis; immo reliqua expectate*, (2) 'receive the balance due to you,' cf. Cic. Fam. II. 13. 3 *mihi erat in animo, quoniam...publicanis... superioris lustri reliqua conseruaram, proficisci in Ciliciam.* Here it is used, of course, in the first sense, but the second meaning occurs to him and suggests the metaphor which follows; cf. Cist. 190 *nunc quod relicuom restat uolo persoluere ut expungatur nomen, ne quid debeam.* Grammarians call this play upon words *paronomasia.*

alieno uti (sc. *aere*) = 'to be in debt'; cf. Curc. 371 *subduxi ratiunculam, quantum aeris mihi sit quantumque alieni siet*, Cic. Fam. V. 6 *me scito tantum habere aeris alieni ut cupiam coniurare*, Att. VII. 3 *omnes qui aere alieno premantur.*

nil moror, with clause or infin. as object, has two meanings: (i) 'I don't care if' (i.e. I have no objection to), cf. Livy III. 54 *nihil ego quidem moror, quominus decemuiratu abeam*, Ov. Her. XII. 186 *nec moror ante tuos procubuisse pedes*, Antony in Cic. Phil. XIII. 17. 35 *nil moror eos saluos esse et ire quo iubetis.* (ii) 'I don't care to' (i.e. I have an objection to), cf. Most. 830 *nihil moror ductarier*, Cas. 748 *nihil moror barbarico bliteo (cenare)*, Cist. 517 *nil moror...mi...fieri pluris liberos*, Trin. 337 *nil moror eum tibi esse amicum cum eiusmodi uirtutibus.* Here it has the latter meaning.

17. **dixeram** may mean 'as I *had said* before I was interrupted,' but the pluperf., especially of this verb, is often used by Pl. where we should expect the imperf. or perf. (aorist); cf. 194, 305, 938, Merc. 760 *uxor rurist tua quam dudum deixeras te odisse atque anguis*, Am. 383 *te esse aiebas Sosiam.* SO. *Peccaueram*, Ps. 617 *seruos eius qui est mercatus mulierem, qui...quindecim dederat minas, quinque debet*, Aul. 635 *nihil equidem tibi abstuli.* EV. *At illud, quod tibi abstuleras, cedo.*

18. **dominum**: antecedent transferred to the relative clause; cf. 180, 278, etc.

20. **Peculiarem** = 'belonging to, or included in, a *peculium*.' Cf. As. 540 *etiam opilio, qui pascit alienas ouis, aliquam habet peculiarem, qui spem soletur suam*, Aul. 465 *gallus gallinacius, qui erat anui peculiaris.* In Per. 202 the slave of a slave is called *peculiaris eius.* The ancient power of a Roman father over his children was unlimited; he could legally scourge and imprison his son, sell him into slavery or put him to death, whether the son was of full age or not. Such being the *patria potestas*, it followed that the son could no more hold property independently of his father than the slave independently of his master. A citizen's children and his slaves were, as regards him, alike in the eye of the law; both were said to be *in potestate*, and the word *familia* included both. Their property was his, but both might by his permission keep a private purse, called in either case *peculium.* The word is a diminutive of *pecunia*, which is derived from *pecus* and dates from a time when flocks and herds formed the chief possessions of, and the measure of value for, the community.

quasi with numerals = 'about': Cic. I. Verr. 8 *quasi decem fiscos*; Bx. quotes Most. 617 *debet quasi quadraginta minas.*

22. **pilas**: the *pila* was a small hand-ball with which the Romans played various games resembling fives or shuttle-cock: cf. the Greek proverb, quoted by Brix, θεῶν παίγνια ἄνθρωποι.

habent 'treat' 'use,' as in 314.

24. **Postquam belligerant**, see on 487; for change of conjugation in *belligerant* (*bellum gerere*) cf. *aedificare, nauigare* (*nauem agere*), *aucupare* (*auem capere*), *auspicari* (*auem specere*), *morigerari* (*morem gerere*), etc.

25. **Vt fit** 'as commonly happens.'

28. **Si** 'to see if' 'to try if' 'in the hope that,' as in 100, Verg. Aen. I. 181 *prospectum late pelago petit, Anthea si quem iactatum uento uideat*, IX. 512 *saxa quoque infesto uoluebant pondere, si qua possent tectam aciem perrumpere*, Caes. B. G. VI. 29 *L. Minatium cum omni equitatu praemittit, si quid celeritate itineris proficere possit*, etc.

posset...mutet, unclassical sequence of tenses, not however uncommon in Plautus; cf. Poen. 601 *quasi tu...oraueris...ut commostraremus tibi locum...ubi ames*, Ps. 795 *Orcus recipere ad se hunc noluit ut esset hic qui mortuis cenam coquat*, and cf. Mil. 131 *dedi mercatori, qui ad illum deferat, ut is huc veniret.*

quo mutet suom, cf. 171; MSS. have *cum quo*, which not only spoils the metre but does not suit the sense, *cum* being used of the person with whom one exchanges something, not of that which is given or received in exchange. *Mutare* is used either with acc. of that which is given up and abl. of that which is received in exchange or *vice versa*: thus it sometimes means 'to give in exchange' sometimes 'to receive in exchange.' Cf. the uses of ἀλλάττειν, e.g. Soph. Ant. 944 οὐράνιον φῶς ἀλ. ('to quit') and Eur. Hec. 483 Ἅιδα θαλάμους ἀλ. ('to enter'). For the former meaning of *mutare*, cf. Ov. Fast. VI. 165 *exilio mutant urbem* (*Romam*), Verg. G. II. 522 *exilioque domos et dulcia limina mutant;* for the latter meaning, that of the text, cf. Hor. Od. II. 16. 18 *quid terras alio calentes sole mutamus?*

30. **indaudiuit**: *endo* or *indu* is an old form of *in*, seen in *ind-igeo, ind-ipiscor, indi-gena, ind-oles, indu-stria*, etc. Lucretius uses *indugredior, induperator, indupedio. Indaudire* means 'to half-hear' 'to hear an uncertain rumour,' as in Mil. 212 *nam os columnatum poetae esse indaudiui barbaro* (viz. *Naevio*); cf. its frequent use in composition with inchoative forms, R. 1983.

de 'of' 'belonging to,' R. 1908. Cf. Cic. Mil. 24, 65 *gladio percussus ab uno de illis*, Fam. XIII. 16 *qui de tuis unus esset.*

31. **Summo** superlative from *sup-*: *summus* = *sup-mus* = *supimus*, cf. *infimus, extimus, intimus, citimus, ultimus*, etc.

32. **Nil** adverbial 'in no respect,' cf. 16.

parsit = *pepercit*: Pl. always, and Ter. sometimes, use the former form: there is a play upon the word, which is rendered by Sonnenschein 'he was not saving of his money, so that he could be saving of his son.'

33. **Reconciliare**: *concilio* from *concilium* (probably from *concire* as *exilium* from *exire*, *proelium* from *proire*, 60) originally meant to 'bring together' two or more parties or things, and then was used of one, 'to procure' or 'bring over': *sibi legionas* Cic. Fam. XII. 13; especially by payment, cf. Ep. 472 *conciliauisti probe* 'you have bought cheaply,' Ps. 133 *exite, ignaui, male habiti et male conciliati*, 'kept at a loss and bought at a loss,' of slaves. And as *conciliare* = *emere*, so *reconciliare* = *redimere*, here and in 168, 576, etc.

34. **ambos**: emphasized, for at first sight there seems no reason why Hegio should have bought a captive like Tynd., who was a slave and therefore would not be taken in exchange for his son; but finding that these two captives were master and slave, and hoping that this fact would facilitate the exchange, he bought them both.

quaestoribus, Roman allusion; it was part of the *prouincia* (see on 156) of the quaestors to sell booty taken in war; cf. Bac. 1075 *nunc hanc praedam omnem iam ad quaestorem deferam.*

35. **Hisce** = *hi-ce*, old form of nom. pl. A final *s* in the nom. pl. of *-o* stems of all kinds is frequently found in early inscriptions. But in the early language an *s*, following a vowel, was frequently not pronounced (see Introd. § 93), and so came sometimes to be omitted in writing (cf. *ille, ipse, pote* for *illus, ipsus, potis*). Thus *heis magistreis uireis*, etc., found in early inscriptions, were replaced later on by *hi magistri uiri*, etc. *Hisce* is found in Ps. 539, Rud. 294, etc., *illisce* in Most. 499. In Mil. 374 the best MSS. have *hisce oculis* (nom. pl.).

hunc = 'this which you see'; the audience, to whom the captives have been separately introduced, have already noticed that the master is clad as a slave and the slave as a master.

36. **amittat** = *dimittat*; only early writers use it in this sense; Pl. does so frequently, e.g. 332, 589, 655, Mil. 1413 *si te saluom hinc amittemus.* It is used with the classical meaning in 23, 143.

38. The Prologue is very careful in his explanations; Philocrates is the Elean *eques*, dressed in the clothes of his slave Tyndarus, and Tynd. is Hegio's son, stolen in infancy and sold as a slave to the father of Philocrates.

39. **imaginem** and (*m*)*imitari* are supposed to be connected in etym. with μιμεῖσθαι ($\surd$*ma* 'to measure') 'to measure or form oneself upon some one else,' 'to imitate.'

40. **expediet**: *expedire* is lit. 'to free the feet from a snare,' cf. Cic. Verr. II. 2. 42, 102 *uidete in quot se laqueos induerit, quorum ex nullo se unquam expediet.* Here it means 'to set

going' 'put in operation,' cf. Tac. Hist. III. 73 *neque alienis consiliis regi neque sua expedire.*

42. **fratrem**: i.e. Hegio's other son, who had lately been taken prisoner by the Eleans.

44. **Inprudens**: i.e. *improuidens* 'not foreseeing it.' For the sentiment, cf. Ter. Hec. 879 *equidem plus hodie boni feci inprudens, quam sciens ante hunc diem umquam.*

saepe iam in multis locis: pleonasm, cf. 328, 998.

46. **sua sibi**: see on 5.

48. Probably interpolated: it only repeats 47 and confuses the construction.

conmenti: sc. *sunt.*

de 'in accordance with': cf. S. C. de Bac. *de senatuos sententiad*, Most. 758 *de exemplo meo ipse aedificato*, Cic. Verr. v. 21 *de consilii sententia.*

49. **ad**=*apud*: cf. 699, Poen. 726 *commeminisse ad praetorem*, Ter. Heaut. 979 *esse ad sororem*, Cic. Att. x. 16. 1 *ad me fuit*, pro Lig. 10, 30 *ad parentem sic agi solet*, Livy VII. 7 *ad hostes bellum apparatur.*

51. **Homunculi** 'poor mortals,' cf. Cic. Fam. IV. 5 *coepi egomet mecum sic cogitare* '*Hem! nos homunculi indignamur...*'

quanti 'how little,' this sense being conveyed by the context, not the word itself: so Rud. 155 *homunculi quanti estis!* Cic. ad Q. F. I. 2. 8 *sed haec tibi praecipiens quantum profecerim, non ignoro.*

recogito: *re*='over and over again,' as in *remordere*, Verg. Aen. I. 261 *quando haec te cura remordet*, and *recinere*, Hor. Od. III. 27. 1 *impios parrae recinentis omen ducat*; so *reputare*, Trin. 674 *etiam atque etiam ut reputes*, and *remandere* 'to chew the cud,' *reuoluere*, etc.

quom recogito: see on 1022.

52. **Haec res agetur**: in this line both *res* and *fabula* are used in a double sense: *res*, besides 'subject-matter,' means 'reality' (Cic. Tusc. v. 11, 32 *rem opinor spectare oportet, non uerba*) and *fabula*, the ordinary word for a 'play,' also means a 'fiction' (Hor. Od. I. 9. 16 *iam te premet nox fabulaeque Manes*). He begins by saying 'this is the matter (*res*) which we are going to act,' then thinking of the other meaning of *res* and punning upon the double meaning of *fabula*, he adds 'but to you it will not be a reality but a story or fiction.'

53. **quod** is acc. after *monitos* (*esse*): *moneo*, besides acc. of person, takes an acc. of thing, if expressed by a neuter adjec-

tive or pronoun, R. 1094. The similar double acc. after *rogo* etc., is not thus limited, K. 208, R. 1122. In the passive the acc. of the thing is retained: compare Cic. Fam. III. 3 *Fabius ea me monuit*, Q. F. II. 1 *tribunus me primum sententiam rogauit*, with De Am. 24 *quae ab natura monemur* and Att. I. 13 *scito primum me non esse rogatum sententiam*.

uoluerim: for the subj. see K. 452 *c*, R. 1686.

54. **operam dare**: see on 344.

55. **Non pertractate**: this word, which only occurs here, is usually translated 'in the ordinary hackneyed way': there are two objections to this, (1) the rest of the line then becomes mere repetition, (2) *pertractare* means 'to treat a subject' not 'in a hackneyed way,' but 'carefully' 'thoroughly,' and sometimes 'diffusely.' Accordingly the older edd. took *pertractate* in a good sense and altered *non* into *nam*; reasonably, in my opinion, although all recent edd. follow the MSS. Cf. 185, where all edd. have introduced this very change.

56. **spurcidici**: this compound seems not to occur elsewhere: Lucr. IV. 180 has *suauidicis uersibus*, and Ter. Ph. 213 *saeuidicis dictis*. Cf. 671.

inmemorabiles 'that *should* not be spoken.' Brix quotes Rud. 654 *edepol infortunio hominem praedicas donabilem*, Aul. 633 *uerberabilissume*. The term usually has simply a passive signification 'that can be' spoken, etc.: but sometimes an active one, cf. 402, K. Append. I.

57. **periurus leno**: e.g. Labrax in the Rudens: cf. Rud. 1385 *ne tu, leno, postules te hic fide lenonia uti*.

meretrix mala: e.g. the Bacchides in the play of that name and Phronesium in the Truculentus.

58. **miles gloriosus**: a frequent character in the New Comedy and so a favourite one with Pl. The Athenian public was no doubt more familiar than the Roman with the bragging soldier of fortune who had served in the wars between the successors of Alexander.

60. **proelia**: the old form of the word may have been *proilium* (cf. in early inscriptions, *foidere foiderati coipint Coilius* for *foedere*, etc.), perhaps from *pro* and *ire* (cf. *concire concilium*).

61. **paene iniquomst**: 'would be almost dishonest.' *Iniquos* is the usual word for a false weight: cf. Persius I. 130 *fregerit heminas Arreti aedilis iniquas*, Juv. XIV. 126 *seruorum uentres modio castigat iniquo*. 'In the dramatic world comedy greatly preponderated over tragedy: the spectators knit their

brows when, instead of the expected comedy, a tragedy began.' Mommsen, H. R. II. 423. Cf. Am. prol. 51 (spoken by Mercury),

> Post, argumentum huius eloquar tragoediae.
> quid contraxistis frontem? quia tragoediam
> dixi futuram hanc? deus sum, commutauero;
> eandem hanc, si uoltis, faciam ego ex tragoedia
> comoedia ut sit omnibus isdem uersibus.
> utrum sit an non uoltis? sed ego stultior,
> quasi nesciam uos uelle, qui diuos siem.

The meaning of the text is 'it would be almost a swindle for us to come here in the dress of comedy and then suddenly try to palm off a tragedy upon you.'

est: we say 'it would be' in a supposed case, the Romans said 'it is': see R. 1535, and cf. inf. 396, 868, Cic. Phil. II. 11, 17 *longum est persequi ceteros* and (quoted in Mayor's note) Sest. 5 *longum est ea dicere; sed hoc breue dicam*, Tusc. Disp. I. 17 *si te rogauero aliquid, non respondebis?* A. *Superbum id quidem est* (i.e. 'would be'); so *magnum est*, *satis est*, etc. This usage is most marked where the *est*-clause forms the apodosis of a conditional sentence in the subjunctive, as in 906, Mil. 764 *otium rei si sit, possum...*, Poen. 921 *nunc si eadem hic iterum iterem, inscitiast*, Trin. 1186 *si pro peccatis centum ducat uxoris, parumst.*

67. **iudices**: *iudex*=*ius-dex*: for the omission of *s* cf. *i-dem* (masc.) *di-duco tre-decim*, etc.: for the term. *-dex*, from *dicere*, cf. *uin-dex*, *in-dex*.

68. **duellum**: old form of *bellum*, derived from *duo*. So *bis* for *duis*, *Duellona* for *Bellona* in the S. C. de Bac. (B.C. 186), *Duellius*=*Bellius* (Cic. Or. 45, 153), *duonoro* for *bonorum* in the epitaph of Scipio, son of Barbatus, R. 76. The *u* became a consonant (*v*, pronounced *w*), and the *d* dropped off as in *(d)uiginti*, *Iovis* (*Diovis*), *Ianus* (*Dianus*). For the interchange of *v* and *b*, cf. *ambo* ἄμφω, *nubes* νέφος, *scribo* γράφω, *uenio* βαίνω, *uolo* βούλομαι, etc., R. 75, 91. For the sentiment cf. Cas. 87 *ualete, bene rem gerite, et uincite uirtute uera, quod fecistis antidhac*, and Am. 16 *aequi et iusti hic eritis omnes arbitri.*

ACT I. SCENE I.

Ergasilus: the name is evidently taken from Pl.'s Greek original. As Ὀνήσιλος corresponds to ὀνήσιμος, so Ἐργάσιλος to ἐργάσιμος, which=*scortum*: cf. Hdt. I. 93, II. 135.

69. **Scorto** 'the Mistress': for the case see K. 224, R. 1068, 1069: it might also be put in apposition to *nomen*, as in English. In the Menaechmi the parasite opens the play with the words

Iuuentus nomen fecit Peniculo mihi, i.e. 'the sponge,' because he made a clean sweep of the tables.

70. **inuocatus** 'uninvited.'

71. **derisores** 'jeering or jesting parasites,' who earned their meals by their witticisms and by making fun of others; cf. Hor. Ep. I. 18. 11 *imi derisor lecti*. In Sti. 171, Gelasimus the parasite says *nunc si ridiculum hominem quaerat quispiam, uenalis ego sum cum ornamentis omnibus*. Erg. himself was a *ridiculus homo* (cf. 482), but 'of all the parasites in Pl. he approaches nearest to the character of the faithful client of the house' (Sellar).

absurde hoc dictum (*esse*) 'the jesters, I know, say that this is a very inappropriate nickname,' referring to his unattractive appearance. The primary meaning of *absurdus* is 'out of tune.' Cf. a line in Cic. Progn., *absurdoque sono fontis et stagna cietis*, De Or. III. 11, 41 *uox quasi extra modum absona et absurda*: it is derived from *ab* and *sur-*, cf. *su-sur-rus*, σῦριγξ, Sanscr. *svâras* 'a sound.' Notice alliteration and the repetition of the same word under different forms (*dictum dicere*).

72. **aio** = *a(g)io*, as is shewn by *ad-agium*: so *maior* = *magior*.

73. **Sibi** with *inuocat* 'to his aid.'

talos: games with dice were played by the Romans at table after the *cena* and during the *mensae secundae*. Cf. Most. 301 *accumbe igitur. Cedo aquam manibus, puere; appone hic mensulam; uide tali ubi sint*, Mil. 165 *adcuratote ut sine talis domi agitent conuiuium*. The dice were of two kinds, *tali* (ἀστράγαλοι) and *tesserae* (κύβοι); the latter were exactly like modern dice, but the *tali* were oblong and rounded at the two ends so that they must rest on one of the other four sides, which were marked 1, 3, 4, 6. With *tesserae* six was the highest throw, ace the lowest, and three *tesserae* were generally but not always used (cf. ἢ τρὶς ἓξ ἢ τρὶς κύβοι, 'all or nothing'). But with *tali* four were always used, the highest throw being when they all came up different, the lowest when they all came up the same. The highest throw in both games was called the '*Venus*,' and the player when throwing called upon the name of the person he or she loved: cf. Curc. 355 *prouocat me in aleam, ut ego ludam: pono pallium: ille suum anulum opposiuit, inuocat Planesium*, As. 779 *talos ne quoiquam admoueat homini nisi tibi. Quom iaciat, 'te' ne dicat, nomen nominet*, 904 *iace talos, ut porro nos iaciamus*. DE. *Maxume. Te, Philaenium, mihi* (throwing)... *Hoc Veneriumst*.

74. **inuocatum**: a pun, the mistress being *inuocata* ('invoked'), the parasite *inuocatus* ('uninvited'): the same pun occurs Rud. 811.

77. **Quasi mures**: cf. Per. 59 *quasi mures semper edere alienum cibum.* So Diogenes called the mice his parasites, Diog. Laert. vi. 40.

78. **Vbi res prolatae sunt** 'during the vacations,' in the law-courts and senate. These were of two kinds, (i) the *dies festi*, days set apart for *ludi*, *feriae*, *epulae* and *sacrificia*, (ii) long set vacations, of which there were probably, at this time, two in the year, one in spring and one in autumn. Erg. is here referring to the autumn vacation, when everyone went out of town. Cf. Cic. Mur. 13, 28 (*iuris*) *prudentia, quae neque extra Romam umquam neque Romae rebus prolatis quidquam ualet*, Att. xiv. 5 *legari noluerim ante res prolatas*, Q. F. iii. 8. 4 *in his supplicationum otiosis diebus...Res prolatae.*

80. **caletur**, in class. Latin *calet*, impers., 'the weather is warm.' The contrary change is more frequent in early Latin, active forms being used of many verbs which were afterwards deponent; see on 593.

81. **Suo sibi**: see on 5.

latent......uiuont: asyndeton, see on 406, 505, R. 2204, K. App. iii.

ros si non cadit: cf. Varro R. R. iii. 17 *locus* (for rearing snails) *est melior quem et non coquit sol et tangit ros...Paruos iis cibus opus est.*

83. **occulto**: *oc-cul-o* is from $\surd$*cal* 'to cover,' whence also *cilium* 'eyelid,' *caligo*, *celare*, *clupeus*, *καλύπτω*, etc.

84. **ruri**: locative, R. 332, K. 30, 49.

rurant: not found elsewhere and probably coined by Pl. for the sake of the assonance with *ruri*; a deponent, *ruror*, is quoted once from Varro.

homines quos ligurriant 'men for them to sponge upon'; consec. subj., R. 1690, K. 452.

85. **uenatici**: sc. *canes*, cf. Mil. 268 *odorans quasi canis uenaticus*, Cic. Verr. iv. 13 *mirandum in modum—canes uenaticos diceres—ita odorabantur omnia et peruestigabant, ut...*

86. **res redierunt**: the technical expression for the opening of term, opposed to *res prolatae sunt*, cf. Cic. Or. Quum Sen. Gr. Egit, 11 *res quom redissent*, Sest. 62 *atque ut iidem ad res redeuntes ut uenirent rogarentur.*

Molossici: a race of hounds from Epirus used chiefly for hunting wolves and other big game. *Molossici*, therefore, is not contrasted with *uenatici* but is added by way of strengthening it, 'during vacation we are eager enough, but at the beginning of term we are as keen as Molossian hounds, on the scent of a meal.' Uss. says they were fat and stayed in the house, being used as watch- and sheep-dogs; but, although they were certainly used as house-dogs (see Hor. Sat. II. 6. 114 and Lucr. v. 1062 sqq.) their original and general use was for hunting; cf. Hor. Epod. VI. 5 *nam qualis aut Molossus aut fuluus Lacon, amica uis pastoribus* (i.e. as destroying wolves), Verg. G. III. 405 *acremque Molossum*, Mart. XII. 1. 1 *retia dum cessant latratoresque Molossi et non inuento silua quiescit apro*, and in an epigram attributed to Martial, *concita ueloces fugeret quum damma Molossos*, Stat. Ach. II. 73 *uelut ille cubilia praedae indubitata tenens multo legit arua Molosso uenator*, Lucan IV. 440 *uenator tenet ora leuis clamosa Molossi.* These hounds are also mentioned in the poems of Gratius and Nemesianus on the chase; the former says, speaking of the British hound, *ad magnum quum uenit opus promendaque uirtus et uocat extremo praeceps discrimine Mauors, non tunc egregios tantum admirere Molossos* (i.e. *quantum Britannicos*).

87. **Odiosici, incommodestici**: comic terminations added to imitate *uenatici*.

88. **colaphos**: κολάφους. The Latin form of the word was *alapa* (for the omission of the initial *c*, cf. *lamentum*, 96).

colaphos perpeti: cf. 472 *plagipatidas* and Ter. Eun. 244 *at ego infelix neque ridiculus esse neque plagas pati possum.* In Per. 61 the parasite says of his ancestors, also parasites, *his cognomentum erat duris Capitonibus.*

89. **Potis** (sc. *est*) = *potest.*

frangique aulas in caput: an ordinary experience for a parasite. Cf. Per. 61 (quoted above), Curc. 396 *an aula quassa cum cinere effossus siet* (*oculus*), Am. frag. in Non. *optumo iure infringatur aula cineris in caput.* The clause is best constructed with *perpeti* (cf. 132) but may also be taken with *potis*, in which case it would be an example of the construction in Verg. G. IV. 337 *nymphae caesariem effusae nitidam*, Aen. II. 273 *perque pedes traiectus lora tumentes*, etc., on which see R. 1126, K. 210.

aula (spelt *olla* by later writers, cf. *Claudius* and *Clodius*, *plaustrum* and *plostrum*, etc.) was a large jar or pot with a lid, made of baked earth and used for many purposes, esp. cooking; cf. 846, 916.

90. **Porta Trigemina**: notice the Roman allusion; four lines further on, he says *Nam haec est Aetolia.* The *Porta Trigemina* was in the short piece of the wall between the Aventine Mount and the river; through it the road led to Ostia. It was probably so called from having three arches, but it was connected in legend with the Trigemini Horatii.

ad saccum ire='to work in the Docks.' *Saccus* means generally a 'bag' or 'sack'; it is used of 'money-bags,' e.g. Hor. Sat. I. 1. 70, II. 3. 149 and Mart. x. 74. 6, and of 'corn-sacks,' Cic. 2 Verr. I. 38, 95 and Phaedr. II. 7. 3 *tumentes multo saccos hordeo.* From the former meaning *ad saccum ire* has been explained 'to go begging,' but more probably *saccus* is here used in the latter sense; for just outside the Porta Trigemina was the Emporium or Wharf, where corn and other imports were landed and where there would be plenty of demand for unskilled labour, as at our own docks.

92. **[nam] postquam**: *nam* is omitted by Uss. as having crept in from 94: if retained, there must be a full stop after *periculumst* and 93—97 must be taken as a long parenthesis, which is not a Plautine construction.

rex, a parasite's patron: cf. 825, As. 919 *regem perdidi*, Sti. 454 *tam confido quam potis me meum obtenturum regem ridiculis logis*, Ter. Ph. 338 *nemo satis pro merito gratiam regi refert*, Hor. Ep. I. 17. 43 *coram rege suo de paupertate tacentes.*

potitus est: for this sense, of 'meeting with' an evil, cf. Ep. 562 *hostium est potita*, Am. 178 *eum nunc potiuit pater seruitutis*, Lucr. IV. 766 *mortis letique potitum.*

94. Uss. suggests that the play in its original state had no prologue (see note on 1), and that the necessary explanations were given here by Ergasilus.

96. **lamentariae** does not appear to occur elsewhere; *(c)lamentum* (for the omission of the initial *c*, cf. *alapa colaphus* (88), *laena* χλαῖνα, *rudus crudus*, R. 110) is from √*cal* 'to call,' whence *clamo*, *clarus*, *Kalendae*, *nomen-cla-tor*, καλεῖν, etc.

99. **Inhonestum**: cf. 129 *qu. carcerarium*: the trade of the *mango* was despised at Rome. For the asyndeton, see on 406.

100. **si** 'in the hope that,' see on 28.

101. **qui mutet filium**: cf. 28. *Qui* is an old form of the abl. (from *quis*, while *quo* is from *qui*, R. 379, 383), the abl. being one of price, R. 1198. In the older writers it is of all genders (cf. 1004) and sometimes plural (cf. 1003).

102. **nimis quam**: *nimis* conveys an idea of 'excess,' either of the proper limit ('too'), or of the usual limit ('very'): here it means the latter, and *nimis quam*='how very': cf. Truc. 469 *nimis quam paucae*, Most. 500 *n. q. formido* (verb), 1123 *n. q. es orator catus*, 'how very few' 'how very much' 'how very shrewd' (see Rams. Most. Exc.); so *admodum quam*, *mire quam*, *sane quam*, etc. Roby, however (1649), takes these to be instances of attraction; the whole expression being adverbial

each member is made adverbial; he compares ἱδρῶτος θαυμαστοῦ ὅσου, θαυμαστῶς ὡς χαίρω, etc.

103. **recipit...recipiam**: a pun,

While he's on *hostile shore*, 'tis plain
Without a *host I'll, sure*, remain.

nihil est = an emphatic *non est*: cf. 16, 32.

104. *in* **iuuentuti**, Müller's emendation; Brix and Sch. read *necullast s. iuuentutis*, Uss. *nullast spes iam iuu.*, others *nullast iuu. s.* or *nulla iuu. est s.* But *in* would easily fall out before *iuu.* and the gen. *-tis* may have arisen from the initial *s* of *spes* being added to the old abl. form *-ti*. In Truc. 495 the MSS. have *sine uirtuti*, and *salutei uirtutei*, as well as *partei*, *fontei*, etc., are found as ablatives in inscriptions probably later than Pl. For the phrase cf. Per. 309 *ecquid estne speculae in te?* Ter. Ad. 455 *in te spes omnis sitast*, Cic. Fam. XII. 1. 1 *cuius omnis spes in uobis est.*

105. **Ille demum** 'he and he alone': cf. 1000, 1023 and Sall. Cat. 20 *idem uelle atque idem nolle, ea demum firma amicitia est.*

antiquis moribus, abl. of description, K. 234, R. 1232. For *antiquos* as a term of praise, cf. Trin. 295 *moribus uiuito antiquis*, Ter. Ad. 442 *antiqua uirtute ac fide*, Cic. Rosc. Am. 9, 26 *homines antiqui, qui ex sua natura ceteros fingerent*, 10, 27 *uestigia antiqui officii*, Att. IX. 15 *uide quam sim antiquorum hominum.*

107. **moratus moribus**: notice the repetition.

108. **aperitur ostium**: the entrance to most Roman houses was by a passage (*prothyrum*) which led from the street or forecourt (*vestibulum*) into the *atrium*. At each end of the *prothyrum* were doors, whereof the outer was properly called *ianua*, the inner *ostium* (cf. Per. 755 *ante ostium et ianuam*), but this distinction is not always observed. The word for the door itself, whether of the *ianua* or *ostium*, is *fores* (see on 831). The creaking of these doors in opening was the conventional signal for the appearance of an actor from the interior of a house, the phrases being *crepuerunt fores*, *crepuit* or *concrepuit ostium*; but not *crepuit ianua*, for the *ianua* was always open by day: cf. Most. 435 *sed quid hoc? occlusa ianuast interdius?* Sti. 308 *quid hoc? occlusam ianuam uideo!*

109. **saturitate ebrius** 'drunk with gorging': cf. Cas. 747 *cena ebria*: "he intentionally uses the wrong word to raise a laugh, as in Mil. 26 *brachium* for 'thigh,' 94 *ualgis sauiis* 'crooked-legged mouths,' 818 *sorbet* for *stertit*, etc." Tyrrell on Mil. 26. Cf. also 810 and Sti. 581 *ut me hodie iugularem fame.* The parasite uses *saturitas* again, 771, 865, 877.

ACT I. Scene II.

110. **sis.** Cf. Cic. Or. 45 *libenter etiam copulando uerba iungebant, ut 'sodes' pro 'si audes,' 'sis' pro 'si uis.'*

istos, quos...his, antecedent attracted into case of relative; see on 1. There, as here, the grammar is corrected and the meaning made plainer by throwing in a second antecedent in the proper case.

111. **Heri**: √*hes*, cf. *hes-ternus*, χθές, yester-day.

quaestoribus, see on 34.

112. **His** after *istos*: see on 548.

singularias only occurs here: on the analogy of *binarius* 'containing two,' *senarius* (*versus*) 'containing 6 feet,' *quinarius, denarius* (*nummus*) 'containing 5 or 10 *asses*,' *singularius* means 'containing one' and *sing. catenae* are 'separate chains' as opposed to those by which the captives were at present chained together (*iuncti*, 113).

114. **si...si**: asyndeton (see on 406, 903), for *si...siue* or *siue...siue*: cf. Rud. 1256 *deos quaeso, ut quidquid in illo uidulost, si aurum, si argentumst, omne id ut fiat cinis.*

115. **uti adseruentur**: generally explained as depending on *uide* or *cura* understood, cf. the use in Greek of ὅπως, e.g. Ar. Av. 131, Nub. 824, 1177: but more probably it means 'provided that,' cf. Cic. Verr. 5, 47 *ager efficit cum octauo, bene ut agatur, uerum, ut omnes Di adiuuent, cum decimo.*

116. **Liber captiuos** 'a free man who has been taken prisoner,' not 'a captive who is allowed some liberty' as Uss. says.

117. **fugiundi**: this old form is found in Pl., Ter. and Sallust: also (after *i* and in *ferundus, gerundus*) frequently in the MSS. of Caes., Cic. and Livy.

118. **postilla** = *postea*; cf. Curc. 529 *numquam postilla uidi.*

119. Notice alliteration in this line and the next.

120. **uidere ita** = 'seem so,' as Brix points out: so with *esse* we frequently find *ita, sic*, etc., used as predicates. Cf. 228, 236 and note on 699. Brix quotes Am. 574 *Hic homo ebrius est.* SO. *Vtinam ita essem*, Bac. 1180 *ita sum.* Cf. also Ter. Ph. 527 *sic sum*, 529 *ego hunc aliter esse credidi.* Hegio is reproaching the Lorarius for having saved no *peculium*, with which to buy his freedom.

121. There is a play upon the word *dare*, 'perhaps as I have nothing else to give you, you would like me to give you the slip': for *dare in pedes* cf. Bac. 374 *me contuli in pedes,*

Ter. Ph. 190 *hinc me conicerem in pedes*, Cic. Fam. XIV. 12 *in uiam quod te des hoc tempore, nihil est.*

122. **Si dederis**: supply *te in pedes.*

quod dem: viz. severe punishment.

123, 124. These lines have been considered spurious: the MS. reading *praedixisti* does not scan.

faxis: cf. 149 *dixis*, *induxis*, 622 *faxit*, 801 *faxo*, 172 *faxint*, 576 *reconciliasso*, 168 *reconciliassere*. Roby, 622, explains these forms as futures, indicative subjunctive or infinitive, formed by adding *-so* or *-sso*, *-sim* or *-ssim*, *-sere* or *-ssere*, to the stem: cf. the Greek future. See, however, Peile, Gr. and Lat. Etymol. p. 318.

caueam means both a 'bird-cage' and a 'prison.'

126. **ad fratrem**: see on 497.

127. **nocte hac**='last night': cf. Am. 730 *quor igitur praedicas te heri me uidisse, qui hac noctu in portum aduecti sumus?* Mil. 381 *mi haud falsum euenit somnium, quod noctu hac somniaui*, Cic. Fam. VII. 1 *his ego tamen diebus dirupi me paene.*

quippiam turbauerint: cf. Cic. Q. F. III. 1. 7 *ne quid ille turbet, uide*, Rhet. ad Herenn. IV. 50, 63 *ne quid isti barbari perturbent.* Brix quotes Most. 1017 *numquid Tranio turbauit*, Bac. 1091 *quae meus filius turbauit*, etc.

129. **Aegrest mi**=*dolet me*: cf. 701, Curc. 169 *male uales, ere, quod mi aegrest*, Men. 626 *dic, mea uxor, quid tibi aegrest?* For the adv. used as predicate, see on 699.

facere: the usual word for following a trade or calling: Cic. post Red. in Sen. 5 *f. piraticam*, II. Verr. 5. 28 *f. mercaturas*, Q. F. III. 1. 2 *f. topiariam*, Fam. VI. 18 *f. haruspicinam, praeconium.*

130. **miseriam miserum** : notice the repetition.

131. **conciliari**: see on 33.

133. **maerore maceror**: alliteration and assonance: *maerore* is abl. of efficient cause, K. 241, R. 1228.

134. Notice assonance of similar endings.

et: the general rule (R. 2202) is that with three or more co-ordinate words either no conjunction is used or each is connected with the preceding or *que* is annexed to the last: but Pl. frequently uses *et* before the last of a series of coordinate words: e.g. Ps. 44 *animo corde et pectore*, Cur. 37 *nupta uidua uirgine iuuentute et liberis*, 283 *subito, propere* *et celere*, Trin. 272 *rem fidem honorem gloriam et gratiam*, Am. 841, etc.

135. **Ossa atque pellis**: cf. Aul. 564 *ossa ac pellis totus est, ita cura macet.*

misera macritudine, abl. of efficient cause, K. 241, R. 1228; *macritudo* is apparently not found elsewhere. Brix reads *miser aegritudine*, Uss. *miser macr.*, Scaliger *miser, a macr.* (which might be paralleled, e.g. from Liv. II. 14 *inopi tum urbe ab longinqua obsidione*), Sch. *miser, I macr.*, referring to the shape of the letter I (which, however, is a joke that would be more intelligible to the eye than to the ear); Onions, in Classical Review, Dec. 1887, suggests *miser, a, macr.*, taking *a* as an ejaculation.

138. **bene ament**: cf. 315, 913 (note).

139. **defleam**: *de*='thoroughly,' 'completely,' as in *debellare* 'to subdue thoroughly,' *defatigare* 'to tire out,' etc. The subj. in *fleam defleam* would come under R. 1618. Cf. 839 and Per. 135 *tum tu me sine illam uendere.* SA. *Tune illam uendas?* Ter. And. 894 *Tamen Simo audi.* SI. *Ego audiam?* Very similar is the repetition in the subj. of another's question, R. 1770, e.g. 556 and Most. 545 *quid nunc faciundum censes?* TR. *Ego quid censeam?* Trin. 1079 *hicine nos habitare censes?* CH. *Vbinam ego alibi censeam?* Ep. 693 *quid ago?* AP. *Quid agas?* Ter. Ad. 83 *quid fecit?* DE. *Quid ille fecerit?*

142. **denique**: used with ablatives, locatives, and adverbs of time='then and not till then.' Cf. Cic. Fam. IX. 14. 5 *tantum accessit ut mihi nunc denique amare uidear, antea dilexisse.* Also used (like *demum*, 105) with demonstrative pronouns, e.g. Cic. Fam. x. 10 *is enim denique honos mihi uideri solet, qui...*

144. **potitust**: see on 92.

145. **quanti**: locative, R. 1186; sometimes called genitive of price.

149. **dixis, induxis**: see on 124.

istuc animum induxis: for this construction cf. Cic. Att. VII. 3 *id, quod animum induxerat paullisper, non tenuit.* One of the accusatives is the direct object of the verb, the other is governed by the *in* in composition, but it is difficult to decide which is which: i.e. we may take the phrase as equivalent to (1) *ducere istuc in animum*, or to (2) *ducere animum in istuc.* The former seems the better explanation as we also find **in** *an. inducere* used in the same sense, e.g. Rud. 22 *hoc in animum inducunt suom*, Ter. Heaut. 1028 *ne istuc in animum inducas tuom*, Hec. 292, 603; also in Sall. Cat. 54 *Caesar in an.*

induxerat laborare, Q. Cic. de Pet. 11 *deinde id, quod natura non habes, induc in animum*, Cic. Sull. 30, 83 *in an. inducam defendere*, and in some MSS. of Cluent. 15, 45 *neque enim legare eiusmodi matri poterat in an. inducere*; and frequently in Lat. prose from Livy downwards. Cf. also 548 *ne tu, quod istic fabuletur, aures inmittas tuas*. (2) The second explanation, *ducere animum in istuc*, is supported by Ter. Hec. 689 *nunc animum rursum ad meretricem induxti tuom*, Cic. de Am. 59 *amici iacentem animum excitare inducereque in spem*; also by the analogy of *animum aduortere* (which = *animum uortere ad*, see on 329). With either explanation one of the accusatives is governed by the *in* in composition; see R. 1118.

150. Notice repetition of *unicus*.

151. **quom**, 'because,' with indic.; see on 923. Notice the order of the words *malum q. amici tuom d. malum*, called Chiasmus, i.e. the making of a Greek χ, or cross. Cf. 199, 399, 566, 567, 773, 796, 846, 960.

152. **Huic dolet** = *hic dolet:* an impersonal use of verbs of feeling, more common in Pl. than in later writers.

153. **Quia** is used almost invariably by Pl. after verbs of feeling and similar expressions, where later writers would use *quod;* cf. 203, 259. Brix on Trin. 290 *lacrumas mi eliciunt quia*, quotes the following among other instances:—*lacrumo* Mil. 1328, *gaudeo* Am. 958, *suscenseo* Trin. 1164, *consolor* Trin. 394. These *quia-* or *quod*-clauses are really in apposition to a neut. pronoun or equivalent expression in the principal clause (K. 416) sometimes expressed, as here, but usually understood. Cf. the following: 203 *nos pudet quia...* Ep. 107 *idne pudet te quia...* Most. 48 *inuidere mihi hoc quia...* Aul. 418 *istuc male factum arbitror quia non latus fodi*, Cist. 103 *irata est quia...* Cato (ap. Gell. VII. 3) *idne irascimini si...* Cas. 378 *iniquomst quia...* Mil. 1210 *istuc acerbumst quia...* etc. *Quia* was originally neut. plur. of the relative, as *quod* is neut. sing.

remissus: *remittere exercitum* is to send the levies back home, cf. Ep. 206 *a legione omnes remissi sunt domum*; and *imperare* (155) is to call them out. The same phrases were used of the summoning and dismissal of the comitia centuriata, which was originally a military organization.

edundi: see on 117.

154. **qui posset**: for the subj. see R. 1680, K. 452 *b*.

156. **prouinciam**: etymology doubtful: it may be connected with *uinco*, it cannot be a contraction of *prouidentia* which, according to all analogy—e.g. *praes praed-is* (*prae-*

uid-), *aetas* (*aeuitas*), *cunctus* (*co-uinctus*), *upilio* (*oui-pilo*)—ought to make, and does make, *prudentia.* It denotes, when used with reference to a Roman magistrate, the *sphere of action* within which he was called upon to discharge the duties of his office.

157. Schoell brackets this line; two objections to it are evident: the MSS. read *Quod* which makes nonsense, while if *Quoi* be read the construction is clumsy, at the least; again a dactyl is followed by an anapaest (Int. § 46, v.), and the accent on *Phílopolemús* is unnatural (cf. 95, 873). *Quod obt.* was probably a gloss on *prouinciam*, expanded into a verse by some unskilful hand. Most editors however retain the line, some explaining *omnes quoi obt.* as equivalent to *omnes ut cuique obt.*, others referring *quoi* to *Philop.* which follows. Brix and Uss. attempt to avoid this difficulty by transposing *fugitant...prouinciam* and *postquam...tuos*, while Fl. escapes the metrical difficulty by reading *post Ph. quam.*

obtigerat: the Roman magistrates, unless they came to some mutual arrangement, cast lots for their provinces: cf. Cic. Vat. 5 *in eo magistratu quom tibi aquaria prouincia sorte obtegisset.*

158. The lines 159—164 would come more naturally from Erg., to whom the MSS. assign them, than from Hegio (and Spengel therefore (Philol. 37. 424) arranges thus:—ER. 154, 155. HE. 156, 157. ER. 158—164. HE. 165—171); moreover the repetition in *fugitare hanc prouinciam* seems awkward. Possibly these words were a gloss upon *mirandumst* and displaced some similar words with which Erg. began his speech; as for instance HE. *Non pol mirandumst.* ER. *Namque ad hanc prouinciam...;* but it is more probable that the whole passage 152—167 is an interpolation.

159. **multigeneribus**: nom. *multigener*, like *bigener*, *degener*. Pl. uses the word again in Sti. 383. Lucr. uses the form *multigenus, -a, -um.*

opus est: the original meaning was 'there is work to be done with,' hence the abl.; but as this came to mean that the thing in question 'is needed,' *opus* was also constructed with the nom., as in 164. Afterwards the word seems to have acquired the meaning 'need,' as it is used by Livy and later writers with a gen. (R. 1225, 1226, 1255, 1256 and pref. to vol. II. p. 71).

160. **primum dum**, 'first of all now,' 'to begin now,' not uncommon in Pl., cf. Rud. 32, Trin. 98, Mil. 297. *Dum*, according to Ramsay, Most. App. II., is here an adverb 'now,' 'at this present time;' in this sense it is found subjoined to

other words ('enclitic' *dum*) and is generally written in one word with them. This use is most frequent with imperatives, e.g. 570 *age dum*, Most. 661 *pulta dum fores*, 666 *euoca dum aliquem*, 1124 *sine me dum istuc iudicare*, Men. 378 *sine me dum hanc compellare* (Cic. and later writers use only *age dum*, *agite dum*); but *dum* is also found subjoined to other words besides imperatives, as in *primum dum*, *nec dum*, *qui dum*, *non dum*, etc. Cic. Att. VII. 12, has *itaque a te nihil dum certi exquiro*.

Pistorensibus: in this passage we have a series of puns, the proper names being formed from words connected with dining and at the same time resembling the actual names of different tribes, etc. Thus *Pistorenses* is formed from *pistor*, and resembles *Pistorienses*, the people of Pistorium (now *Pistoia*) in Etruria. *Pistor* is from *pinsere* 'to pound,' since mortars were used before the invention of mills; according to Pliny N. H. XVIII. 11, 28 there were no persons at Rome who were bakers (as distinguished from millers) by trade, nor any slaves specially kept for this purpose in private houses, till B.C. 173 (Sm. Dict. Antiq. 'Pistor'). As this line obviously refers to such persons, it must be an interpolation and Schoell brackets it, partly on this account, partly because of its form, coming between the *opus est* of 160 and of 162.

162. **Paniceis** (=*Panicis*) formed from *panis*; perhaps with a pun on *Poenici*, as Sch. suggests.

Placentinis from *placenta* 'a cake'; also='a man of Placentia,' a Roman colony in Cisalpine Gaul, founded 219 B.C.

163. **Turdetanis**: the name of a civilized tribe in Spain; the edible referred to is the '*turdus*,' which was considered a great delicacy. Martial, XIII. 5, ranks it first of all birds, and in Hor. Ep. I. 15. 40, the glutton Maevius says *obeso nil melius turdo*.

Ficedulensibus: the *ficedula* was also thought a great delicacy; cf. Juv. XIV. 9, Mart. XIII. 5. According to Gellius XV. 8 it was the only bird of which epicures ate the whole. It is not clear what town or tribe is referred to; perhaps Ficulea, an ancient town of the Sabines.

164. **maritumi milites**: i.e. fish. For the case see on 159 and cf. Cic. Fam. II. 6 *dux nobis et auctor opus est*, etc.

166. **priuatus**: not a 'private' as opposed to an officer, but a 'private person' as distinguished from a public official: cf. Cic. Phil. XI. 10 *clarissimo uiro priuato imperium extra ordinem non dedi*, Invent. I. 25 *quaeritur seruos sit an liber, pecuniosus an tenuis, priuatus an cum potestate*.

168. **In his diebus**, 'shortly': cf. Ps. 317 *in hoc triduo*. The phrase is sometimes used of the immediate past, cf. Cic. Fam. VII. 1 (quoted on 127).

reconciliassere: a fut. infinitive, see on 124. Some of these futures were taken as presents and conjugated as new verbs, viz. *arcesso*, *lacesso*, *capesso*, *facesso*, perhaps *incesso* and *petesso* (from *arcio=ad-cio*, *lacio*, *capio*, *facio*, *incedo* and *peto*), R. 625. So *incipisso* (532) from *incipio*.

169. **eccum**=*ecce eum;* so *eccos*, *eccas*, *ecca*, *eccillum*, *eccistam*, etc. The accusatives depend on *ecce* as if it were *uide*. For *eccum* with, or as, a nom. see on 997. *Eccum* often, as here, refers to an absent person, see on 1015.

171. **Hoc** is abl.: see on 28.

pote (sc. *esse*)=*posse;* the MSS. have *fore*, which could not be followed by acc. and inf., and is perhaps due to *foras* at end of next line. Müller proposed, and Uss. and Sch. adopt *pote;* cf. Aul. 309 *censen talentum magnum exorari pote?*

172. **faxint**: see on 124.

foras: acc. of motion to, R. 1110, lit. 'to out of doors.' It is acc., as *foris* is locative, of an obsolete noun *fora;* see R. 1169.

173. **hodie**: Schoell. Most editors insert *es*, but (*h*)*odie* might easily fall out before *adce-* and seems to be required by the sense either here or in next line.

quod sciam: the subj. is consecutive, R. 1694; for *quod*, see on 670.

174. **natalis dies**: birthdays were marked by festivities; cf. Pers. 767 *hoc age; accumbe, quia hunc diem suauem meum natalem agitemus amoenum*, Ps. 164 *nam mi hodie natalis dies est; decet eum omnes uos concelebrare.*

175. **Propterea**, etc.: the natural corollary of the preceding lines would have been an invitation to, not from, Hegio. So in Sti. 486 the parasite invites himself, *uin ad te ad cenam ueniam?* The reading in the text is due to Schoell; most editors read *te uocari ad me ad c.*, distributing the dialogue as in the MSS., but *uocari uolo* would be a roundabout expression for *uoco*, and the arrangement in the text of 172—177 (suggested by Spengel, Philol. 37. 426) seems more suitable to the characters of Erg. and Hegio.

176. **Facete dictum**, as in Poen. 637, Ter. Eun. 288; it means 'well put,' 'neatly expressed,' cf. Cic. Off. I. 29 *facete dicta, quae uocant ἀποφθέγματα.* For *facete* see on 276.

pauxillo contentus esse: the MSS. have *pauxillum c. e.* which can hardly mean 'be contented with a little,' although Uss. thinks it possible, comparing the use of the acc. with *dignus*. It can only mean 'be a little contented,' which makes nonsense of Erg.'s answer *ne perp. modo*. So we must either emend *pauxillo* and *perpauxillo*, which is difficult on account of the repetition of the acc., or we must take *contentus esse* in the sense of 'contentedly eat,' *contentus* being used absolutely and adverbially; either of these uses might be paralleled by itself, the former e.g. by Poen. 460 (quoted on 643), the latter by Hor. Sat. I. 1. 3, I. 4. 108, but the combination of them is very awkward.

177. **Ne perpauxillo modo**=*modo ne perp.* (cf. Ter. Ad. 835 *ne nimium modo*), and *modo ne*=*dummodo ne* 'provided that...not,' cf. Cic. Att. v. 4. 3 *quae de Sicinio audisti ea mihi probantur; modo ne illa exceptio aliquem incurrat bene de nobis meritum.*

179—183 would come in better, as Sch. points out, after 190 if 183 were expunged. In 179 most editors have HE. *Age sis roga.* ER. *Emptum, nisi...*, but the arrangement in the text is that of the MSS. and is retained by Uss. and Sch. As the proposal comes from Erg. it is he, and not Heg., who would be impatient to settle the matter.

179. **sis**: see on 110.

roga emptum='strike the bargain,' lit. propose or stipulate that the thing (Erg.'s company) be bought. *Rogare* is used of the person who asks the formal question in a *stipulatio* (see on 898), and the phrase *rogare emptum* occurs in the Digest, XVIII. 1. 41 *cum ab eo qui fundum alii obligatum habebat, quidam sic emptum rogasset.* Somewhat analogous is the phrase *rogare consules*, used of the presiding magistrate proposing to the comitia the names of candidates for the consulship. Ergasilus regards Hegio's dinner as the price for which he sells his own company (the usual view, cf. Sti. 171 where the parasite says *nunc si ridiculum hominem quaerat quispiam, uenalis ego sum cum ornamentis omnibus;* also Sti. 195 and 220 sqq.) and wishes Hegio to strike the bargain by formal question (as in Ep. 471 *Estne empta mihi istis legibus?* PE. *Habeas licet*); but he remembers that he may yet get a better invitation, and adds, as an afterthought, *nisi...magis* 'on condition that I do not get a better offer'; this was not an unusual condition in an agreement for sale, especially in the case of land: cf. Dig. XVIII. 2. 1 *ille fundus centum esto tibi emptum, nisi si quis intra Kal. Jan. proximas meliorem condicionem fecerit.*

nisi qui: *qui* is used as an indefinite pronoun, substantive or adjective, only after *si nisi ne num*, R. 380.

180. **mi atque amicis**: Gelasimus in the Sti. says (580) *cum amicis deliberaui iam et cognatis meis; ita mi auctores fuere ut egomet me hodie iugularem fame*: cf. Men. 700 *ibo et consulam hanc rem amicos, quid faciundum censeant*, Poen. 794 *ibo, amicos consulam quo me modo suspendere aequom censeant.*

condicio, the antecedent, is put into the relative clause, in agreement with the relative, cf. 18, 278. K. 330, 331.

ferre condicionem (from *condico*; not *conditio*, a rare and late word derived from *condo*) is to 'offer terms,' 'to make an offer.' Cf. Rud. 1030 *ecquid condicionis audes ferre?* Men. 591 *condiciones tetuli tortas*; so in Hor. Od. I. 1. 12 *Attalicis condicionibus*='most extravagant offers.' It is used of an invitation to dinner in Mart. XI. 52. 1 *cenabis belle, Iuli Cerealis, apud me; condicio est melior si tibi nulla, ueni.*

181. **meis legibus**: *lex*=the saying or words which accompanied any formal act; cf. Cic. de Or. I. 39, 178 *in mancipii lege* 'in the formula appropriate to *mancipatio*,' and I. 58, 256, *Manilianas uenalium uendundorum leges.* So it comes to mean 'terms,' 'conditions,' cf. Most. 351 *ego dabo ei talentum!...sed ea lege, ut...* As. 746 *istum ostende quem conscripsti syngraphum...leges perlege*, Aul. 255 *mihi despondes filiam?* EV. *Illis legibus, cum illa dote, quam tibi dixi*, Livy XXI. 12 *has pacis leges.* In the words *meis legibus* Erg. refers to the condition (*lex*) as to a better offer (*condicio*) contained in the clause *nisi...magis.* Sch. and Uss. make this clause depend upon *addicam*, putting a stop after *emptum;* this makes Erg. say 'if I don't get a better offer, I will accept yours on my own conditions'; what he does say, in effect, is 'I will accept your offer on my own conditions, viz. provided I don't get a better.'

addicam: *addicere* is used of the auctioneer, 'to knock down'; cf. Cic. Rab. Post. 17 *ecquis est ex tanto populo qui bona C. Rabirii Postumi nummo sestertio sibi addici uelit?*

182. **Profundum**: a pun on *fundum*, alluding of course to the parasite's insatiable appetite, which in Curc. 121 is called *barathrum.*

183. **Em**: see on 373.

uel iam: i.e. 'I am ready to come *now*, if you like.'

184. **leporem**: the metaphor is from trapping hares; a man sets a trap or snare, but instead of a hare he finds a

weasel in it. So Erg. hunting for a good dinner, has only succeeded in getting an invitation to a bad one. A hare was a dainty: cf. Cas. 138 *mi lepus*, as a term of endearment, Hor. Sat. II. 4. 44 *fecundae leporis sapiens sectabitur armos*, and ib. II. 8. 89 *et leporum auulsos, ut multo suauius, armos.*

185. **conmetat**: frequentative of *conmeare*, Ter. Heaut. 444, etc. The meaning seems to be 'my food, the *ictis*, is very tough, for it lives a hard life in stony places.' It is difficult to see the point of this; probably H. is made to use an unusual expression in order to give the parasite an opening for his joke in 187.

186. **istoc uinces me**: Brix quotes Sti. 756 *numquam edepol med istoc uinces.*

ne postules: see on 739. The subjunctive is probably jussive, cf. on 434.

187. **calceatis** refers to *scruposam uiam*, 185.

tamen is properly used in a sentence which limits or modifies a concessive sentence, but the two sentences are sometimes compressed into one and *tamen* retained to mark the implied opposition. Thus this line = *quanquam cum c. d. ueniam necesse sit, ueniam tamen.* So 603 *procul tamen audio* (= *etsi procul es, tamen audio*) and 297, 393, 404, Cas. 787 *cras habuero uxor ego tamen conuiuium* ('though not to-day, still...'), Most. 174 *equidem pol uel falso tamen laudari multo malo* ('though I be praised falsely, yet...'), Cic. Att. I. 16. 2, *quum illum plumbeo gladio iugulatum iri tamen diceret* ('though the sword were of lead, still...'), Rab. Post. 41 *quae quidem (dignitas) in miserrimis rebus huic tamen tribuenda maxima est* ('though his circumstances are very bad, still...'), Phil. II. 117 *sed ex plurimis malis hoc tamen boni exstitit*, Clu. 7. 22 *petiuit ut sibi restituerent...eum filium quem tamen unum ex multis fortuna reliquum esse uoluisset.* Compare the use of *tamen* with participles, on which cf. Cic. pro Sest. 140 and Halm's note.

188. **Asper uictus** means unsavoury food, but the parasite pretends to take it very literally.

189. **Sus terrestris**: alluding to the way pigs root up the ground. Some parts of swine were considered great delicacies; see 849, 904.

190. **Multis holeribus** (abl. of description, R. 1232) explains *terrestris cena*; a 'dinner from the earth' is one which consists mainly of vegetables, more fit for invalids than guests, as Erg. suggests.

191. **Numquid uis?** a formula of leave-taking, see on 448.

temperi is locative case of *tempus*, R. 524.

192. **subducam ratiunculam**: cf. Curc. 371 *subduxi ratiunculam*, Cic. Att. v. 21. 11 '*subducamus summam*'...*assidunt: subducunt: ad nummum conuenit.* The diminutives *ratiunculam quantillum* are intended to represent a comic fear lest his resources should not be equal to the expense of entertaining such a valiant trencherman as Erg. The usual explanation, which refers them to the large price paid for the captives (see 258), does not account for Hegio's change of plan (cf. 194 with 126).

193. **trapezitam**: Gr. τραπεζίτης, lit. 'one who sits at a table,' i.e. a money-changer or banker. Cf. St Mark xi. 15.

siet: archaic and uncontracted form of the present subjunctive: see R. 722 and cf. Sanscr. *syâm*, Gr. εἴην (=ἐ(σ)ιην as *siem*=*esiem*).

194. **ire**: a colloquial use of the present where we should expect the future, common in Pl. Cf. Most. 620 *dic te daturum, ut abeat*... TH. *Egon' dicam dare?* Ps. 1118 *leno ubi esset domi me aibat arcessere.* Brix on Trin. 5 gives a long list.

dixeram: for the tense see on 17, and cf. Cic. Verr. IV. 48 *tamen quod antea de istius abstinentia dixeram, sigillis auolsis reliquum argentum reddidit.*

iuero: R. § 1465, says the completed future is used frequently in the comic poets, and occasionally in later writers, with but little if any difference of meaning from the simple future, especially (*a*) of a predicted result, e.g. 314, (*b*) of an action during something else, e.g. 293, (*c*) of an action performed at once, the completion being as it were anticipated, e.g. 495, and (*d*) of an action postponed, the future element being predominant, e.g. 341 and the passage in the text.

ACT II. SCENE I.

195. **aerumnam**: etymology doubtful; according to Fest. it=αἰρομένη, excited mind, the suffix being the Greek participial termination -ομενος. Cf. *al-umnus* a nursling, *au(c)-tumnus* the increasing year, *pilumnus* armed with *pila* (in Carmen Saliare), *columna* (*culmen, cel-sus*), *uertumnus* (*uertere*), R. 825. According to Doederlein (Lat. Synon. IV. 420) it is a contraction of *aegrimonia*, and *alumnus* of *alimonium*, but it is difficult to account for the omission of the *g*, as well as for the fact that no such contraction occurs in the case of the many other words in *-imonia* (see R. 935). There is

a Sanscr. root *yas* 'to strive' and *yat* 'to vex.' For the meaning of *aerumna* cf. Cic. Fin. II. 35. 118 *Herculis perpeti aerumnas; sic enim maiores nostri labores non fugiendos...nominauerunt.*

exsequi, 'undergo,' lit. 'follow through to the end' (for this force of *ex* in composition cf. Trin. 406 (*argentum*) *exessum, expotum, exunctum, elutum in balineis*, and the verbs *emerere* 'to serve out one's time,' *enumerare, explere*, etc., R. 1949). The meaning 'undergo,' 'suffer,' seems rare, but cf. Trin. 686 *egestatem ex.*, Ps. 995 *mortem ex.*, Truc. 459 *probrum ex.*, Cic. Att. IX. 12 *cur non omnes fatum illius exsecuti sumus?* Phil. II. 22 *exsequi cladem illam fugamque;* and cf. on 1009.

196. **id pati**, where we should expect *eam*, but *id* refers generally to the preceding sentence or idea. Instances where the phrase is a vague one, like *id facere*, are not uncommon; cf. *id facietis* in this line, inf. 898, Most. 112 *si quid nummo sarciri potest, usque mantant neque id faciunt donicum parietes ruunt*, Cato R. R. 5 *scabiem pecori et iumentis caueto: id ex fame...fieri solet;* but we also find, in 223, *si id prouenit*, Ter. And. 527 *orabo gnato uxorem; id si inpetro...*, Lucr. II. 269 *ut uideas initum motus a corde creari ex animique uoluntate id procedere primum.* And there are numerous instances where *id* refers to a sum of money; e.g. As. 88 *uiginti iam usust filio argenti minis; face id ut paratum iam sit.*

animo aequo: cf. Rud. 402 *animus aequos optumumst aerumnae condimentum.*

labos (connected with *labo* and ἀλφ-άνω) is of course used of mental, as well as of bodily, trouble; cf. Cic. Tusc. II. 15 *labor est functio quaedam uel animi uel corporis, grauioris operis et muneris*; for the termination *-os* cf. *honos, arbos*, and see R. 183, 193.

197. **credo**: parenthetical, as in 961, 963; cf. 326.

liberi is contrasted with *serui* and includes (1) *ingenui*, those who are free born, (2) *libertini*, those who were once *serui* but have been freed.

198. **morigerari**, formed from *morem gerere* (for change of conjugation see on 24), 'to adapt oneself to,' 'to give in to,' usually with dat. pers. as in 404, but also with dat. rei, as here and Am. 131 *pater nunc intus suo animo morem gerit*, Cic. Orat. 48 *uoluptati aurium morigerari debet oratio.* The active form *morigero* occurs in Am. 981. Notice the repetition *morigerari mos.*

199. **Eam queit**: the MSS. read *Eamque et*, which cannot be translated or scanned. Schoell emends *eam queit* (=*quit*,

cf. Acrostic Arg. and 162, 908) explaining 'mos morigerandi tam ero quam servo levare potest servitutem.' This is the best of the various emendations which have been proposed.

erili imperio, ingeniis uostris: notice asyndeton (note on 406) and chiasmus (note on 151).

200. **Indigna**; unfit for free men like you to put up with.

201. **opus est**: see on 158.

multam iram editis: Keine's emendation of the corrupt reading of the MSS. The meaning is 'there isn't need for much howling; you are showing plenty of indignation by means of your eyes.' With the phrase *iram edere oculis* cf. Ter. Ad. 312 *ut ego iram hanc in eos euomam omnem*, Liv. XXI. 28 *trepidationis aliquantum edebant.*

202. **utare**: the second pers. sing. of the subjunctive is often used indefinitely, in general statements not addressed to anyone in particular; 'you' = 'one' (R. 1544, K. 363, Madvig 370); cf. 420 *uideas* = 'one sees,' Ter. Ad. 254 *abs quiuis homine, quomst opus, beneficium accipere gaudeas* (= 'one is glad'), And. 460 *fidelem haud ferme mulieri inuenias uirum.* Sall. Cat. 58 *quem neque gloria neque pericula excitant, nequiquam hortere* (= 'one exhorts'). When this usage occurs in a conditional or other subordinate clause, in which the verb would otherwise have been in the indicative, the verb in the hypothetical or other leading proposition will be in the indicative, as in the text (R. 1546, Madv. 370 obs.). Cf. Cic. de Sen. 11 *haec* (*mens atque animus*), *nisi tanquam lumini oleum instilles, exstinguuntur senectute*, Lucr. II. 36 *nec calidae citius decedunt corpore febres textilibus si in picturis ostroque rubenti iacteris quam si plebeia ueste cubandum est.*

203. **quia** = *quod:* see on 153.

cum catenis, 'wearing chains'; for this sense of *cum* (R. 1881) cf. 187 *cum calceatis dentibus*, Mil. 16 *illum dicis cum armis aureis*, Ps. 158 *te cum securi caudicali praeficio prouinciae* ('you with the axe'), Cic. Verr. IV. 24 *praetor cum tunica pulla sedere solebat*, Mil. 4. 11 *lex...esse cum telo...uetat*, Poen. 852 *haud amice facis, qui cum onere offers moram*, where *cum onere* = 'to a man with a burden,' *onusto.*

pigeat: for the distinction between *pudet* and *piget* cf. Donat. ad Ter. Ad. 392, *pudet quod turpe est: piget quod dolet*, Non. V. 10 *pudet uerecundiae est, piget poenitentiae.* They are often used together in contrast, as here: cf. Ps. 282 *nimio id quod pudet facilius fertur quam illud quod piget; non dedisse istunc pudet, me quia non accepi piget.*

205. **solutos sinat**: for this construction, see on 345.

emerit: subjunctive because dependent on subjunctive, R. 1778.

207. **officium**: contracted from *opificium*, as *officina* 'a workshop' from *opificina* (which occurs Mil. 880). Others derive from *officere* which, however, is only used in a bad sense while *officium* is only used in a good one.

Nostrum officium quod est: this may be taken as a relative definition (R. 1763, sq.) the order of the words being *scimus* (*id*) *quod est nostrum officium*; but more probably it is a dependent question, *nostrum officium* being accusative (lit. 'we know our duty, what it is'; for this idiom see on 376). *Quod est* is a colloquialism; in classical Latin it would be *quid sit.* For the substantival use of *quod* see on 833. The use of the indicative in dependent questions is not uncommon in Pl. Setting aside those passages in which the indic. can be explained by taking the clause as an independent question or exclamation (e.g. 557, where we might punctuate *Viden tu hunc? quam inimico uoltu intuitur!* and 964 *dic quid fers*, which might be translated 'tell me, what do you bring?' cf. R. 1761), there yet remain many instances in which the indicative is used although the clause is certainly dependent; e.g. 236, Men. 207 *scin quid uolo ego te accurare?* Sti. 410 *uidete, quaeso, quid potest pecunia*, Most. 145 *cor dolet quom scio ut nunc sum atque ut fui.* And in some passages the indicative is even used side by side with the subjunctive; cf. Am. 17 *quoius iussu uenio et quam ob rem uenerim, dicam*, Cist. 58 *eloquere utrumque nobis, et quid tibi est et quid uelis nostram operam*, Mil. 514 *ut nesciam utrum me expostulare tecum siet an...me expuregare haec tibi uidetur aequius*, Most. 194 *rem uides, quae sim et quae fui ante*, 951 *scio quo me ire oportet et, quo uenerim, noui locum*, Per. 512 *nescis quid te instet boni neque quam tibi Fortuna faculam lucrifera adlucere uolt.*

si sinat: the apodosis is *scimus*, not *est*, and *scimus si sinat* is an instance of an illogical condition, the proper apodosis being omitted and some allied fact substituted, R. 1574: 'we know our duty (and would do it) if he would let us go unchained'; so in Verg. Ecl. IX. 45 *memini numeros, si uerba tenerem* 'I remember the measure (and could sing the song) if I only had the words.'

fingitis=*paratis*, a rare meaning; cf. 47 *conpararunt et confinxerunt dolum.* Uss. quotes Lucil. XXVIII. 57 *sed fuga fingitur; ut timido pede percitu' uadit!*

agitis: cf. Am. 50 *quam rem oratum huc ueni, primum proloquar.* In both passages the subordinate clause may be taken as either a dependent question (see above) or a relative definition (*sentio rem, quam agitis*). The distinction between these is clearly marked in Ter. And. 536 *ausculta paucis et, quid ego te uelim et tu quod quaeris, scies*, where *quid uelim* is a dep. question and *quod quaeris* a rel. definition ('the answer to your question'; *quid quaeras* would mean 'your question,' R. 1763).

208. **Apage**=ἄπαγε, 'go to!' our slang 'get out!'

209. **Immo**: 'nay,' see on 287.

210. **exorare**: *ex* here='through to the end' (cf. *exsequi*, 195) and so 'successfully'; cf. *expalpare* 'to get by coaxing,' *expugnare* 'to gain by fighting.' *Exorare*, like *orare*, takes (1) acc. pers., 'to persuade' 'prevail upon,' (2) acc. rei, 'to ask successfully' 'to obtain,' and sometimes (3) both accusatives, as here and Bac. 1199 *hanc ueniam illis sine te exorem*, Ter. And. 901 *sine te hoc exorem*.

211. **hisce**: this evidently does not refer to the Lorarius and his subordinates, who are included in *uobis*. Brix suggests that the house-slaves of Hegio were standing by, examining the strangers curiously.

arbitris: 'as by-standers,' with both *hisce* and *uobis*. *Arbiter* is from *ad-bito* (cf. 380 *rebitas*, 604 *adbites*) 'one who comes up'; so a 'by-stander' 'witness,' as here and Trin. 146 *circumspice dum te, nequis adsit arbiter*; so, a person to whom a dispute is referred, an 'arbiter,' as in Ter. Heaut. 500 *ambigunt de finibus; me cepere arbitrum*. On *ar* for *ad*, cf. *aruena arueho aruentores aruocatus arfines aruolare arfari aruorsarius*, for *aduena* etc. In the SC de Bac. (186 B.C.) *arfuerunt arfuisse* occur, R. 160.

212. **locum loquendi**: notice the assonance; for the construction cf. Cic. Att. I. 18 *nactus locum resecandae libidinis*, IX. 7 *gaudeo, si est nunc ullus gaudendi locus*, and the genitives after *signum spatium tempus*, R. 1313.

214. **incipisse**: see on 168.

215. B gives this v. to Phil. distributing 216—219 as in the text: but before the Lorarii Tynd. must speak as the master (*concede huc*).

mihi: so-called dat. of the agent, which, however, really expresses the 'person affected,' i.e. an indirect object; *haec mihi uidenda sunt* 'these are, as regards me, things to be seen,' *haec mihi uisa sunt* 'these are, as regards me, seen things,' R. 1146, K. 222.

216. **Obnoxii**: from *ob noxam*, as *obuius* from *ob uiam*, *opportunus* from *ob portum*, *opprobrare* from *ob probrum*, *obse-*

crare from *ob sacra*, R. 990; used primarily of one who is under liability to another on account of a fault, cf. Sti. 497 *perii hercle...nihil obnoxie* 'not through my own fault,' Tru. 835 *ego tibi me obnoxium fateor, culpae conpotem;* hence applied to other obligations, such as for favours received, as here, ='beholden' 'obliged'; cf. As. 284 *ut nobis sint obnoxii, nostro deuincti beneficio*, Verg. G. I. 396 *fratris radiis obnoxia Luna.*

217. **quae** = *eorum quae*; this ellipse of an antecedent pronoun is less harsh where the antecedent would have been in the same case as the relative, e.g. 743 *breue spatiumst perferundi* (*ea*) *quae minitas mihi*, Verg. Ecl. II. 71 *aliquid saltem potius* (*eorum*) *quorum indiget usus*, or where the antecedent is the subject or direct object of the principal verb, e.g. Ps. 1217 *qua facie fuit* (*ille*) *quoi dedisti sumbolum?* inf. 985 *mos est obliuisci* (*eius*) *neque nouisse* (*eum*), *quoius*... But in cases like the text it is rarer; cf., however, 265, 941, Am. 318 *os* (*eius*)... *quem percusseris*, Aul. 605 *ut* (*eorum*), *quae fierent*, *fieret particeps*, Men. 192 *ut superior sis mihi quam quisquam* (*eorum*) *qui impetrant*, Lucr. I. 883 *aliquid* (*eorum*) *nostro quae corpore aluntur*, Am. 652 *omnia adsunt bona* (*ei*) *quem penest uirtus*, Curc. 590 *cupio dare mercedem* (*ei*) *qui...conmonstret*, Mil. 1077 *meri bellatores gignuntur* (*ex iis*), *quas*...

218. The MSS. reading, *copia est ea facitis*, is unmetrical and would be the only instance in Pl. of *compos* with the abl.; but the true reading is quite uncertain. Some editors read *copiae facitis*, altering elsewhere so as not to interrupt the cretic tetrameters; others *copia est atque ea facitis*, which makes the rest of the line a mere repetition of *copia est* and retains the abl. with *compos*. The reading I have suggested in the text might have been corrupted thus:—*copiaeistaeaffatĩfacitis*, *copiaesteafacifacitis*, then *copia est ea facitis*. A genitive *aliae* occurs in Cic. Liv. and Lucr.; see on 398. For *iste* = *istarum rerum*, see on 934. Schoell reads *copia est: consili facitis n. c.*

facitis: for *quom* with indicative, see on 923.

219. **si uidetur**: 'if you please,' a polite command.

220. **arbitrari**: 'to be a by-stander' and so 'to hear' or 'see,' cf. Aul. 607 *hinc ego et huc et illuc potero, quid agant, arbitrarier*. The word does not occur again in this sense (derived from the original meaning of *arbiter*, 211) until Appuleius. Notice the repetition *arbitri arbitrari*.

223. **id** referring to *dolos*: see on 196.

225. **Tamen**: i.e. though you are in the master's place, yet you must shew a servant's zeal and diligence.

uiso opust: see on 159 and R. 1256.

sine arbitris: carelessly used for 'without discovery,' for there would be no use in their making pretences when no one was by.

226. **docte** 'cleverly'; cf. 40, 787. Notice the double alliteration.

227. **Tanta...agundumst**: generally taken as an instance of Parataxis for Syntaxis, i.e. as meaning 'so important is our undertaking *that*' etc.: see on 504. But *tanta* may equally well refer to what precedes, as in 826, 869, and a parallel passage, Ep. 83.

haud somniculose 'in a wide-awake way'; cf. Ter. Ad. 392 *nimium inter uos...pernimium inter est; tu, quantus quantu's, nil nisi sapientia es, ille somnium.*

229. **Nam**: the ellipse is ('you have every reason to hope so,) for'; see on 464.

tuo caro capite 'thy dear self,' *meum carum caput* 'my dear self'; the head was considered the seat of life and so was used for the whole person: in 946 *propter meum caput = propter me*; cf. Most. 293 *triginta minas pro capite tuo dedi*, Sti. 751 *fugit hoc libertas caput*, Ps. 723 *siquidem hoc uiuet caput*, Mil. 725 *o lepidum caput*, and in Ter. *festiuom caput, ridiculum caput*, etc. For *uae capiti tuo*, see on 885.

230. **offerre uilitati** must mean 'to expose to contumely'; *uilitas*, 'lowness of price,' is used to mean 'a holding cheap,' but rarely, and only in late writers. It is probably so used here for the sake of the antithesis to *carus* 'dear.' The usual explanation is 'to offer for sale at a low price,' but *offerre* does not mean 'to offer for sale' and *uilitas* is abstract, not concrete.

232. **maxuma pars homines habent** is hardly Latin; Schoell omits the words *maxuma pars*, considering them to have crept into the text as a gloss upon *fere*; if they were retained, *fere* would be superfluous and *homines* must be altered to *hominum.* It may be remarked that *homines, maxuma pars, habent* would stand; for where different assertions are made in the same sentence about the different parts of the whole subject (a plural or collective noun), the whole is often put in the nom. with the parts in apposition to it: e.g. Liv. XXIV. 7 *interfectores pars in Forum pars Syracusas pergunt*, 21 *multitudo, pars procurrit in uias, pars in uestibulis stat* (where we should say 'part of the multitude'); and where the assertions about the different parts are not only different but contrary, i.e. where it is clear that

what one part does the other contrasted part does not do, it is natural to omit the latter, as in Liv. XXVI. 33 *quod senatus iuratus, maxima pars, censeat...id uolumus.*

235. **Ex**: used of the earlier state or condition from which transition occurs, cf. 305, 538, Cist. 384 *si possum tranquillum facere ex irato mihi*, Ps. 965 *sed eccum qui ex incerto faciet mihi quod quaero certius*, Liv. XXI. 39 *otium ex labore, copia ex inopia, cultus ex illuuie.*

236. **Nunc...autumo**: the sense is 'I have promised to act towards you as you wish me (228), now I am saying how I want you to act towards me.' Tynd. seems to think he has been expressing himself rather strongly, and this line and the next are apologetic in tone.

uolo: indicative in dependent question, see on 207.

237. **Quod...patri**: the sense is 'excuse my reminding you of this duty; so forgetful is human nature that I should do so to my own father.'

suadeam: hypothetical subj., sometimes called potential, R. 1536.

238. **si te audeam**, sc. *patrem nominare*; most editors transpose *te si*, but Brix defends the MSS. order, see on 303. *Si audeam=si uelim*, 'I might deservedly call you by that name if I wished'; cf. *sodes* (*si audes*) 'if you please,' and 662, Rud. 1030 *ecquid condicionis audes ferre?* 'are you willing to make any offer?' Trin. 244 *da mihi hoc, mel meum, si me amas, si audes*, Truc. 425 *non audes aliquid dare munusculi*, Poen. 757 *mitte ad me, si audes, hodie Adelphasium*, etc.: cf. on 287.

patrem nominem: cf. Cato ap. Gell. v. 13 *patrem primum, deinde patronum proximum nomen habere.* In 443 Tyndarus (the supposed master) calls Phil. (the supposed slave) *patronus* and *pater*. So in Rud. 1266 the master says to the slave *mi anime, mi Trachalio, mi liberte, mi patrone, immo potius mi pater*: cf. also Ter. Ad. 455 *in te spes omnis nobis sitast: te solum habemus, tu es patronus, tu pater.*

239. **secundum proxumus**: pleonasm.

240. **Audio**: an expression of assent, 'quite so.' Cf. Mil. 218 PE. (arousing PA. out of a brown study) *Vigila inquam, expergiscere inquam, lucet hoc inquam.* PA. *Audio*, 'it has dawned' 'Quite so, (it has dawned upon me what to do'), Ter. Ph. 160 *at non cotidiana cura haec angeret animum.* PH. *Audio*, 236 *'inuitus feci, lex coegit'; audio, fateor*, Eun. 371 PA. *Pro illo te ducam.* CH. *Audio.* PA. *Te esse illum dicam.* CH. *Intellego*, Cic. Rosc. Am. 18, 52 *numquid est aliud?*

'Immo uero,' inquit, 'est; nam istum exhaeredare in animo habebat.' Audio; nunc dicis aliquid quod ad rem pertineat. In Curc. 610 *quid agis, bone uir?* C. *Audio,* it may be used, as here, in accepting a compliment. Sometimes the assent is ironical, as in Ps. 291 *pietas prohibet.* BALLIO. *Audio,* Ter. And. 552 SI. *Irae sunt inter Glycerium et gnatum.* CH. *Audio.* SI. *Ita magnae ut sperem posse auelli.* CH. *Fabulae.*

Et propterea: referring to *tu es pater*, 'my fate depends on you, therefore be careful.'

ted: see on 405.

memineris: what follows, i.e. the change of characters.

243. **Vtqui**: this enclitic *qui* has nothing to do with the relative but is an affirmative particle which in classical Latin survived only in *atqui*; it is found with *ut* in 553, As. 505 *an ita tu es animata utqui expers matris imperio sies?* Bac. 283 *adeon' me fuisse fungum utqui illi crederem?* Curc. 218 *Aesculapi ita sentio sententiam utqui me nihili faciat,* Trin. 637 *an id est sapere utqui beneficium a beneuolente repudies?* Ter. And. 148, Lucr. I. 755 (see Munro's note); it is also found with *hercle* (e.g. Men. 1092), with *edepol* (e.g. Am. 776), with *pol* (e.g. Am. 705), with *ecastor* (e.g. As. 930), and with *quippe* (e.g. Aul. 348).

fuisse, 'to cease to be'; see on 516.

uelint: consec. subj. R. 1700, K. 415; *ut...uelint* is in apposition to *animum.*

244. **pro**, 'in virtue of,' R. 2072. Cic. Att. x. 8 B *pro iure nostrae amicitiae te peto.*

245. **erga** in Pl. and Ter. sometimes, as here, follows its substantive, if that stands by itself: thus Trin. 1128 *amicum erga*, but inf. 407 *erga suom gnatum.*

247. **honore honestes.** I take these words to refer to T.'s feelings, not to his outward bearing: 'do not feel less respect for me (and so serve me less faithfully) than when you were my slave.' Others take them of his outward bearing and understand *ego te* after *quam*, 'do not treat me with more respect than (I did you) when you were my slave,' which would be a very harsh elision. With the phrase *honore honestes* (for the abl. see R. 1236), cf. 393, 422, Cur. 182 *luce lucebit.* Slightly different are 356 *tanto honore honestas,* 420 *quantis laudibus collaudauit,* 595 *maculari maculis luridis,* Men. 93 *eo uinclo uincies,* 203 *hoc animo animatos esse,* Rud. 187 *hoc ornatu ornatam,* Ter. Heaut. 286 *uestitam ueste lugubri,* etc. Such repetitions, generally for the sake of emphasis, are common in Pl.; see on 248, 250, 840 and Index, s.v. 'Repetition.'

seruibas: for this form of the imperfect, see R. 607.

248. **ut...ut**: repeated after the insertion of the subordinate clauses in order to mark the construction. Cf. Rud. 1256 (quoted on 114), Aul. 791 *nunc te obtestor Euclio ut, si quid ego erga te imprudens peccaui aut gnatam tuam, ut mihi ignoscas*, Bac. 777 *per omnes deos adiuro ut, ni meum gnatum tam amem atque ei facta cupiam quae is uelit, ut tua iam uirgis latera lacerentur probe*, Cas. 511 *ut id, quod alius condiuit cocus, ego nunc uicissim ut alio pacto condiam*, Ps. 580 *ut, ubiquomque hostibus congrediar..., facile ut uincam*, Trin. 141 *ut, quod meae concreditumst taciturnitati..., ut mihi necesse sit iam id tibi concredere*, Ter. Ph. 153 *adeon' rem redisse ut, qui mihi consultum optume uelit esse, Phaedria, patrem ut extimescam.*

meminisse memineris: so in Aul. 181 *properare propero*, Poen. 433 *pergin' pergere?* See above, on *honore honestes*.

250. **Memoriter meminisse**: so Am. 417 *memorat memoriter*, Cas. 267 *cupide cupis*, Cur. 688 *propere propera*, Mil. 1035 *uolgo uolgem*, Men. 151 *caueo cautius*, Most. 968 *misere miseret*, Pers. 426 *ualide ualet*, Poen. 606 *sapienter sapit*, Ps. 358 *cursim curram*, 1297 *madide madeam*, Truc. 354 *nitide nitet*, etc. See on 247.

ACT II. SCENE II.

252. **Vbi sunt**: the captives had gone to one side of the stage (219), which was of considerable width. The back-scene in the Pseudolus represents three or four houses (Ps. 952).

253. Philocrates throughout this scene assumes the familiar manner of the slave in comedy (cf. 121, sqq.) This familiarity was tolerated at Athens and represented, probably with exaggeration, in the New Comedy whence Pl. took his plays; but it was of course quite opposed to Roman ideas.

in quaestione essemus 'be out of the way' 'be to seek': cf. Pers. 52 *caue fuas mihi in quaestione*, Ps. 663 *uide sis ne in quaestione sis, quando arcessam, mihi*, Mil. 1279 *uide ne sies in expectatione*, Cael. ap. Cic. Fam. VIII. 14 *quod iudicium nunc in expectatione est, etiam in bona spe.* Cf. also *in promptu habere, in usu esse*, etc., R. 1390.

254. **circummoeniti**: 'words with *ū* in the root syllable were in the older language written with *oi* or *oe*,' R. 264. Cf. *poena punire, moenio munio, Poeni Punicus*, and in inscriptions *oenus, moerum, coera, loedos*, etc.

255. The fun in this, the best scene in the play, if not the best scene in any play of Pl., is derived from two sources. The first and most obvious source is the deception practised upon

Hegio by the captives and the intentional ambiguity of many of their remarks to him (e.g. 273, 302, 346, 382, 405, 417, 427), and the complacence with which he speaks of his own cleverness in the matter (e.g. 255, 452—455). The second source resembles the so-called 'irony' of Sophocles; for as Sophocles' audience knew the outlines of the legendary stories from which he took his plots, and so were able to detect in many of the lines a hidden meaning of which the characters were unconscious, so here the spectators, having been informed by the Prologue that Tyndarus is Hegio's son (a fact of which the characters are unaware), notice in some of his remarks a significance of which he himself is unconscious, and while he is, as he thinks, deceiving Hegio, the spectators are enjoying his ignorance of the real state of things and his unintentional truthfulness (e.g. in 305, 310, 316). In the present line Hegio's sententious wisdom is all the funnier from the fact that before him stand the master and slave each in the other's clothes (37), and the process of deceiving him has already begun.

quom etiam = *etiam quom* in next line. For the repetition of *cauet* cf. Ps. 940 *memorem inmemorem facit qui monet quod memor meminit.*

256. **cautor captus est**: notice the assonance. As the same phrase occurs Ep. 359 *ipse cautor captust*, Bücheler considers this line spurious; it only repeats 255, and the use of the perf. in speaking of a repeated action (*captus est* = ἐξηπατήθη, gnomic aorist) is rare, if not unparalleled, before the age of Augustus, R. 1479. For *captus* = *deceptus* see on 653.

257. **causa ut**: cf. Liv. v. 55 *ea est causa ut ueteres cloacae nunc priuata passim subeant tecta*, and *occasio ut*, inf. 424; the subj. is consecutive, R. 1696.

258. **Quos mercatus sim**, 'inasmuch as I have bought you' R. 1714, K. 454. It would be subj. even if it did not depend on a preceding subj.

259. **quia** = *quod;* see on 153.

uitio uortere: *uitio* is predicative dative, R. 1162, vol. 2 p. xxv—lvi, K. 225; the phrase is found with a dat. pers. and acc. rei, and instead of, or in apposition to, the latter we may have a dependent sentence introduced by *quod* (*quia*), *si* or *ut*. Cf. Mil. 1350 *tibi istuc uitio uortat*, Rud. 700 *nobis uitio uortas si...*, Liv. VIII. 32 *neminem id Q. Fabio uitio uersurum si... mouisset*, Lucr. v. 1357 *uitio uertere ut...uellent*, Cic. Fam. VII. 6 *ne sibi uitio illae uerterent quod abesset a patria.* For the old form *uortere*, see on 703.

260. **si...si**: the second *si*-clause is subordinate to the first, i.e. would remain conditional if the first were made into

a principal sentence, as in Merc. 814 *faxim, si itidem plectantur uiri, si quis duxerit...*, but generally where there are two or more *si*-clauses they are co-ordinate with one another; e.g. Trin. 95 *siquid sceis me fecisse inscite aut improbe, si id non me accusas, tute obiurgandu's*, Am. 941, Ps. 265, Merc. 807; cf. Aul. 229 *ubi tecum coniunctus siem, ubi onus nequeam ferre pariter, iaceam ego.*

fuat: old form of present subj., R. 722, formed from the root *fu-* (whence *fu-i, fo-re*) as *sim* (*siem*) is from the root *es* (whence *es-se, er-am, er-o*); cf. *duim*, 331.

263. **sunt quae uolo**: *est qui, sunt qui* and similar phrases are used both with indic. and subj. (consecutive, R. 1686, K. 452 *c*), cf. 53, 327. It is not always easy to make out any difference of meaning, but the subj. is said to be used where the antecedent is indefinite, the indic. where it is definite; cf. Hor. Sat. II. 2. 182 *sunt qui non habeant, est qui non curat habere*, 'there is a certain man (viz. myself) who,' etc. Notice the alliteration in this line, 263.

264. **Quarum rerum** after *quae*; cf. note on 539 and Pers. 392 *si hoc accurassis lepide, quoi rei operam damus*. For the genitive (of the object of action implied in substantives and adjectives) see R. 1314, K. 262.

falsilocum does not seem to occur elsewhere; such compounds occur frequently in the older writers and Lucretius, but most of them, however regularly formed, failed to obtain a permanent place in the language.

265. **Quod sciam** is generally used to limit a sweeping assertion (R. 1694), as in 173, Cic. Fin. II. 3 *Epicurus se unus, quod sciam, sapientem profiteri est ausus*, but here (judging from what follows) a definite neuter antecedent must be supplied, *eius quidem quod sciam*; see on 217 and cf. Men. 1106 *nil reticebo quod sciam.*

nescibo: old form of the future, in classical times only found in *ibo quibo nequibo*, R. 603. Cf. 619, 785.

nescium: passive, 'unknown,' as in Rud. 275 *in locis nesciis nescia spe sumus*, and in Tac., e.g. Ann. I. 59 *nescia tributa*; here probably used in this uncommon sense for the sake of repeating *nescibo*. Kennedy, Lat. Gr. p. 281, gives a list of adjectives so used.

266. **tostrina** = *tonstrina*; the MSS. B and D here preserve the old spelling; so *Pisaureses, cesor* (for *Pisaurenses, censor*) occur in Republican inscriptions, *tosillae* (*tons.*) in Cic., *mostrum* (*mons.*, cf. *Mostellaria*) in Verg., and *mostrare* (*mons.*) several times in Pl. (R. 168). *Tondere* = to 'fleece' or 'cheat';

cf. Bac. 242 *tondebo auro usque ad uiuam cutem*, 1095 *is me scelus auro usque attondit dolis doctis indoctum.*

cultros: probably used generally, 'his implements,' whether scissors (*forfices*) for clipping *per pectinem*, or razors (*nouacula*) for shaving *strictim*; cf. Cic. Off. II. 7 *cultros metuens tonsorios.*

adtinet: not used as a vb. active in Cic. Its subject is not *senex* but *Philocrates*, a very awkward change which Brix defends; the instances he quotes, Pers. 616, Merc. 406, Trin. 597, are scarcely similar, and most editors emend; thus Böthe *nunc iam hic*, Geppert *hic nunciam*, Uss. *hic iam* and Schoell *nunc senex eist* (=*ei est*) which seems the easiest emendation.

267. **Ne id quidem inuolucri**: *id* δεικτικῶς, 'not so much' 'not a scrap,' cf. Most. 385 *non hoc longe* 'not an inch,' Ter. Ad. 163 *huius non faciam* 'not a snap.' For the partitive gen. see on 376.

inicere: in composition the initial *i* of *iacio* is dropped (R. 144) and the *a* becomes *i*, as in *capio incipio*, etc. (R. 204).

268. **utrum strictimne an**: in classical Latin we should not have both *utrum* and *ne*, but it is not uncommon in Pl. and Ter., *utrum* having its literal meaning 'which of two,' and *ne*, *an* marking the alternatives; cf. Bac. 75 *utrum ego istuc iocon adsimulem an serio*, Most. 668 (quoted on 333), Ps. 709 *dic utrum Spemne an Salutem te salutem*, Rud. 104 *utrum tu masne an femina 's*, Ter. Eun. 721 *utrum praedicemne an taceam.*

strictim adtonsurum: before 300 B.C. the Romans wore their beards untrimmed, hence *barbatus* often='an ancient Roman,' cf. Cic. Coel. 14, 33 *aliquis mihi ab inferis excitandus est ex barbatis illis, non hac barbula sed illa horrida quam in statuis antiquis et imaginibus uidemus*, Sest. 8, 19 *unum aliquem ex barbatis illis exemplum imperii ueteris, imaginem antiquitatis*, Liv. V. 41 *barba, ut tum* (B.C. 387) *omnibus promissa erat*, Iuv. XVI. 31 *dignum barba dignumque capillis maiorum*, where see Mayor's note. But in 300 B.C. a barber was brought to Rome from Sicily (Varr. R. R. II. 11) and it soon became, and thenceforth continued, the custom to have the beard either clipped over a comb (*tondere per pectinem*) or clean shaved (*radere, tondere strictim, ad cutem*, ἐν χρῷ κείρειν). Pliny, VII. 59, says that Scipio Africanus (B.C. 234—183) was the first Roman who was shaved every day.

adtonsurum dicam esse: a periphrasis for *attonsurus sit*, cf. 533, 541, Am. 825 *nescio quid istuc negoti dicam*, Aul. 804 *seruom esse ubi dicam meum Strobilum, non reperio*, Cur. 12 *quo te dicam ire*, Merc. 516 *quid nomen tibi deicam esse*, Trin. 2 *finem fore quem dicam nescio.*

269. **frugi est** 'is worth anything,' without any idea of moral rectitude, cf. Bac. 654 *nullus frugi esse homo potest nisi qui et bene facere et male tenet. Improbus sit cum improbis...* Sometimes, however, it implies moral rectitude, as in Poen. 963 *si frugi esse uis, eas liberali iam adseres causa manu*; cf. Cic. Tusc. Disp. III. 8, IV. 16. *Frux* means primarily fruits, secondarily 'profits' 'success,' and the dat. was used predicatively, 'a source of profit' (often, as in 956, with *bonae*); hence came its use as an indeclinable adjective (294).

usque admutilabit=*strictim attondebit*; cf. Pers. 825 *me usque admutilasti ad cutem,* Mil. 768 *qui admutiletur miles usque*, and Bac. 242, 1095, quoted on 266. *Admutilare* is only found in Pl.

probe: a slang expression, of an action done satisfactorily or thoroughly without reference to the nature of the act itself; cf. 635, Am. 282 *adpotum probe* 'well drunk,' Most. 1089 *probe me emunxti* 'have properly befooled me.' *Usque probe* seems an instance of Plautina abundantia.

270. **Quid tu?** 'what of you?' always followed by a question about the person spoken to, with which question, however, *tu* should not be joined: cf. 717, Ps. 610 *quid tu? seruosne es an liber?* Rud. 1304 *quid tu? num medicus quaeso es?* Pers. 215 *quid tu? confitere ut te autumo?* Tru. 797 *quid tu? cur eum accepisti?* So also 279, 281, Mil. 1021 *quid ego? hic astabo?* 961 *quid ea? ingenuan an liberast?* etc.

mauelis=*malis*: Pl. also uses *mauolo, mauolet, mauellem*; for the omission of *g* in *ma(g)uolo*, cf. *(g)ui(g)uo, bre(g)uis* (βραχυς), etc. R. 129.

271. **longissume** sc. *absit.*

272. **quamquam**, corrective, 'and yet,' R. 2215.

273. **familiaris filius** 'son of the house'; cf. *pater-, mater-familias.* Of course Phil. actually was *fam. filius.*

274. **Eugepae**=εὖγε παῖ: cf. Trin. 705 *euge, euge, Lysiteles,* πάλιν 'bravo, encore!'

Thalem Milesium: the chief of the seven sages, about 636—546; he is a type of wisdom in Greek literature, (e.g. Ar. Nub. 180) and so in the adaptations of Pl. e.g. Bac. 122 *quem ego sapere nimio censui plus quam Thalem,* Rud. 1003 *stultus es.* GR. *salue, Thales.*

talento 'even if I could get him for a talent'; a talent is no doubt fixed upon for the sake of the pun on *Thalem,* but it would certainly be a small price for such a slave. Hegio values Phil., thinking him to be Tynd., at 20 minae or one third of a talent (353), and Tynd. when 4 years old was sold for 6 minae (974). Slave-girls were worth from 20 minae (Ps. 52) up to 60 or even 100 *minae* (Pers. 662), and in Xen. Mem. II. 5. 2 a talent is paid for an overseer for mines. Cf. Mommsen H. R. Bk. iii. ch. 13.

275. **ad** 'in comparison with,' 'Thales was a fool *to* him,' cf. Mil. 968 *ad tuam formam illa una dignast*, Ter. Eun. 361 *at nihil ad nostram hanc.*

nimius nugator 'a very trifler,' see on *nimis* 102, and on *nugas* 531.

276. **facete** 'cleverly' 'neatly'; cf. 176 and As. 581 *ut adsimulabat Sauream me esse, quam facete!* In Pl. *facetus* has only two meanings, (1) dexterous, apt, clever, (2) dainty, delicate.

orationem contulit 'has adapted his speech,' see on 253; *conferre* in this sense is not found elsewhere in Pl. but cf. the phrase *iter conferre*, and Cic. Verr. v. 30, 77 *tu supplicia, quae debentur hostibus uictis, ad tuum non ad populi Romani tempus conferes.*

277. **Quo de genere**: *quo genere* would be more usual (295), but cf. Ov. Met. IX. 613 *de tigride natus*, XI. 312 *alipedis de stirpe dei nascitur Autolycus.* In qualifying a noun *de* (*summo*) *genere* is usual, cf. Rud. 1197 *de genere summo adulescens.* Brix suggests *quo, dic, genere.*

Polyplusio, in Gr. πολυπλουσίου 'the Goldmores'; apparently the real family name of Philocrates (973). There were so many Greeks at Rome, especially among the slaves, that the Greek words and puns in Pl. would be easily understood by his audience.

278. **illi**=*illic*, in Elis, as in 334, 341; *illi isti* (Pl. for *istic*) *hic illic istic* are locative cases of the pronouns *ille iste hic illic istic*, R. 524.

unum pollens: *unus* is used to emphasise (1) verbs, as in Cic. Or. 29 *Demosthenes unus eminet inter omnes oratores*, (2) superlative adjectives, as in Cic. Fam. IV. 13 *unus omnium doctissimus.* I know no other example of its use with a positive adj., but *solus* is often so used by Terence. Uss. suggests that the two adjectives were taken together and the superlative termination added only to the last but intended to apply to both.

279. **Quid ipsus**: see on 270, and for the old form *ipsus* see R. 371.

ab summis uiris: sc. *honoratur*, implied in *summo honorest.*

281. **Quid diuitiae?** 'what of his riches?' see on 270.

sebum: a play upon *opimae*, 'rich enough for the old man to melt tallow out of them'; the riches of Phil. are emphasised (cf. 277, 285, 299, 318) in order to make Hegio more anxious for the ransom and so more ready to send the pretended Tynd. home as messenger. Hegio has not yet explained that he meditates an exchange.

282. **quom abimus**: the historic present, which is regularly found with *dum* (R. 1458), is also used (in Pl. and Ter. frequently) with *quom* and *postquam*; cf. 887, Men. 1136 *hunc censebat te esse, credo, quom uocat te*, Am. 668 *illam hic reliqui quom abeo*, Ter. Eun. 342 *quom huc respicio ad uirginem illa sese...huc aduorterat*, 522 *quid habuisset quom perit*, Cic. Rosc. Am. 41 *quom occiditur Sex. Roscius ibidem fuerunt.* For examples with *postquam*, see on 487.

283. **Orcum**: identified by the Romans with the Gr. god Hades or Pluto.

284. **Salua res est** 'it's all right'; see on 539.

philosophatur 'is quibbling' 'is hair-splitting,' cf. Ps. 974 *saluos sum, iam philosophatur*, Rud. 986 *philosophe*, 'quibbler.'

285. **Quid erat ei nomen?** Sch. reads *quod* without remark, but according to Brix (on Trin. 889) and Uss. (on Am. 360) the substantive *quid*, and not the adjective *quod*, is used by Pl. in this phrase; cf. 983, Mer. 516 (quoted on 268).

Thensaurochrysonicochrysides, lit. 'son of gold-that-surpasses-treasuries-of-gold.' In Pers. 699 Sagaristio gives his name as

> Vaniloquidorus Virginisuendonides
> Nugipolyloquides Argentiexterebronides
> Tedigniloquides Nummorumexpalponides
> Quodsemelarripides Numquampostereddides.

The repetition of *-chryso-* is suspicious; Geppert suggests *-crypsides*, Böthe *-crocsides*, Spengel *Thensaurocroeso-*, Sch. *Thensaurochersi-*.

287. **Immo** always marks dissent, but 'this dissent comprises every modification from a direct and vehement contradiction to a slight correction of, or improvement upon, what has been said, such correction or improvement tending in many cases not to overthrow but to strengthen and confirm the assertion to which it refers,' Ramsay, Most. Exc. iv. Thus here and in 857 we have a simple correction, in 209 this correction is less direct, in 608 it is more emphatic. In 289 there is a correction of an understatement, in 354 this correction is more emphatic. Then we have a simple refusal in 341, a courteous contradiction in 933, and a vehement denial in 567.

audaciam 'unscrupulousness,' esp. in the pursuit of gain. Cf. Cic. Off. I. 19 *animum paratus in periculum si sua cupiditate, non utilitate communi, impellitur audaciae potius nomen habeat quam fortitudinis.* The connection of ideas is natural, for *audacia* and *auaritia* are from the same root; *audeo* (*auideo*, cf. *cau(i)tor nau(i)ta au(i)ceps*) is from *auidus* which, like *auarus*, is from *aueo*. Cf. the use of *audeo*=*uolo*, 238.

288. It is evident from 633 sqq. that this line, if genuine, must be an 'aside.'

germano nomine 'his real name.' Cf. Poen. 137 *gerrae germanae* 'real nonsense,' Cas. 615 *in germanum modum* 'in true fashion,' Rud. 737 *ex germana Graecia* 'of pure Greek blood.'

289. **Quid tu ais?** 'what's that you say?' as in 1016; sometimes it is used in turning for an opinion to another person, *tu* being emphasised, as in 627, 990. On the other hand *quid ais tu* has almost always the same meaning as *quid ais*, 'look here'; see on 613.

Immo used in substituting a strong expression for a weak one; cf. Ter. Eun. 812 *credin?* GN. *Immo certe*, Ph. 145 *non multum habet quod det fortasse?* GE. *Immo nil*, Ad. 482 *quaere rem.* GE. *Immo hercle extorque.*

pertinax a comic use of the word; *tenax* being used in the sense of 'niggardly' he strengthens it into *pertinax* which has quite a different meaning. For this sense of *per* in composition, see R. 986.

290. **ut magis noscas**: final subj. expressing the 'purpose, not of the principal action itself, but of the mention of the action,' R. 1660. So 803, 854, Cic. Att. I. 1 *ut frontem ferias, sunt qui etiam Caesonium putent competitorem fore.*

genio suo: each man had his own Genius, a deity who presided over his birth and watched over him during life and to whom he offered sacrifices, esp. on his birthday (Tibull. II. 2); according as his fortunes were good or bad his Genius was white or black (Hor. Ep. I. 7. 94). Hence a parasite's patron was called his Genius as watching over his fortunes: see on 879. Women also had their Genii, but they were called Iunones. Notice that this Roman idea is attributed by Pl. to an Elean.

ubi quando=*ubi aliquando* 'when at any time'; so we have *si quando* and *num quando*, and generally *qui quis ubi unde* are used indefinitely after *si* and *ne*, and the first two after *nisi* and *num.*

291. **Samiis**: a secondary predicate, R. 1017 *c*. From Samos the Romans got their household crockery, common earthenware intended for use not ornament; cf. Sti. 693 *quibus diuitiae domi sunt, scaphiis, cantharis, Batiochis bibunt: nos nostro Samiolo poterio si nunc bibimus, tamen efficimus pro opibus nostra moenia.*

293. **hac** sc. *uia*: cf. 953, Ter. Heaut. 329 *argentum eadem hac inueniam uia.* So with *ea illa alia recta* etc.

eadem sc. *opera*, expressed in 450; cf. on *una opera*, 563.

exquaesiuero: for the fut. perf. see on 194. The form *-quaero* is found in composition in six or seven passages of Pl., instead of the regular *-quiro*, R. 262.

294. **hominem frugi** 'a sensible man,' see on 269. Notice the alliteration here.

296. **tua ex re**: see on 347.

feceris: probably indicative, R. 1533 *bb*; cf. on 695.

297. **tamen**: elliptical, as in 187, '(even if you do not confess) still.' Notice the repetition *scis scire.*

298. **quamquam** 'and yet,' as in 272.

302. **cum istoc** = *cum istius opibus*, an example of brachylogy of which the stock instance is Il. XVII. 41 κόμαι Χαρίτεσσιν ὁμοῖαι. Cf. also Tibull. III. 4. 70 *nec similes chordis reddere uoce sonos.*

303. **Memini quom**: cf. Cic. Fam. VII. 28 *memini quom mihi desipere uidebare*; the *quom*-clause is the object of the verb. Brix quotes Poen. 723 *uidistis leno quom aurum accepit*, Truc. 112 *nam ipsi uident quom eorum adgredimur bona*, Bac. 469 *quin ego quom peribat uidi.* Cf. also on 516 *nunc illud est quom.*

audebat sc. *me laedere*; cf. 238, 343, 399, As. 96 *qua tu seruom Sauream potes, circumduce*, 248 *si mutuas non potero, certum est sumam fenore*, Ps. 120 *si neminem alium potero, tuom tangam patrem.*

304. **uiden** = *uidesne.*

Fortuna humana: the older writers do not seem to have felt the ambiguity of these different cases; cf. Lucr. I. 57 *eadem rursum natura perempta resoluat* (where *perempta* is neut. plur.) and Munro's note. For the sentiment cf. Herod. I. 207 κύκλος τῶν ἀνθρωπηΐων ἐστὶ πρηγμάτων· περιφερόμενος δὲ, οὐκ ἐᾷ τοὺς αὐτοὺς εὐτυχέειν, Soph. Trach. 127 ἀλλ' ἐπὶ πῆμα καὶ χαρὰ πᾶσι κυκλοῦσιν, οἷον ἄρκτου στροφάδες κέλευθοι, Hor. Od. I. 34. 12 *ualet ima summis mutare et insignem attenuat deus obscura* *promens; hinc apicem rapax Fortuna cum stridore acuto sustulit, hic posuisse gaudet.*

305. **fueram, insueram**: for the tense see on 17. Tynd. is unintentionally telling the truth.

e summo: see on 235.

307. **Et quidem** 'aye, and,' cf. 562.

proinde ut=*talem qualis*, adv. instead of adj., see on 699, and cf. Am. 960 *proinde eri ut sint, ipse item sit.*

familia=the whole body of slaves (*famuli*) in a house (*fam. urbana*) or on an estate (*fam. rustica*).

309. **hoc te monitum**: see on 53.

uoluerim: Brix for MSS. *uolueram*, on the analogy of 53, but there *est quod* precedes (see on 263); *uolueram* might be supported by such passages as Cic. Sest. 30, 64 *cesseram si alienam a me plebem fuisse uoltis.* Cf. however 344, 599.

310. **gnatus tuos**: i.e. Philopolemus. Tyndarus thinks he is lying, the audience know that he is unconsciously telling the truth.

314. **habueris, curauerit, profuerit**: for simple futures, in speaking of a predicted result; see on 194. Here *erit* follows (315), cf. As. 280 *erum in obsidione linquet, inimicum animos auxerit*, Ter. Hec. 599 *et me hac suspicione exsoluam et illis morem gessero.* *Habeo*='treat' 'use,' as in 22.

315. **bene profuerit**: cf. 138, 913. Notice alliteration here.

317. **faterin**=*faterisne.*

320. **faxint**: note on 124. The subj. is jussive, R. 1596.

321. **tam etsi**: this or *tam et si* is the usual spelling of BCVE, *tametsi* of D. The word is always a spondee (or anapaest) in Pl., never a bacchius.

patri decere: a rare construction, cf. Pers. 214 *decet lenonis familiae*, Am. 820 *nostro generi non decet*, Ter. Ad. 928 *ita nobis decet*, Heaut. 965 *ubi quoi decuit primo.* Sch., for metrical reasons, reads *decŏre* (neut. adj.) quoting Priscian VI. p. 235 and Rud. 193 *indecŏre.*

323. **Potius** after *decere magis*, pleonasm; cf. 239, 687, Trin. 274 *eo...magis lubet cum probis potius quam cum improbis uiuere*, As. 689 *magis decorumst libertum potius quam patronum onus in uia portare*, Sti. 80 *malint potius quam*, Cist. 45 *at satius fuerat eam uiro dare nuptum potius.*

illi=*illic*, see on 278.

324 is interpolated from Aul. 166: *nostrum*, which is suitable there, ought to be *meorum* here.

325. **omnino...omne...homini**: notice the assonance, intended apparently for emphasis.

327. **Est ubi** 'sometimes,' see on 263.

328. **multa multis saepe**: pleonasm, as in 44, Cas. 349 *uidi ego dis fretos saepe multos decipi*, Mil. 885 *multos saepe uidi...*, Poen. 129 *saepe ego res multas tibi mandaui.* Notice the double alliteration in this line.

329. **hoc animum aduorte**: of these two accusatives *animum* is the object of the verb and *hoc* is governed by the preposition in *aduorte*, K. 205, R. 1118; cf. Lucr. III. 54 *aduortunt animos ad religionem*: Brix however takes *hoc*=*huc* (see on 480), like Verg. Aen. VIII. 440 *huc uertite mentem.*

330. **Filius meus**: Philopolemus. **Alide**: see on 573.

331. **nummum**: *nummus* in Pl. is the name both of a gold and of a silver coin; the gold *nummus* was the Philippus, of which Philip of Macedon coined large quantities about 350 B.C. Being the first gold coin of any importance it soon became current everywhere, and specimens have been found all over Europe, from the British Isles to the Crimea. Like the Persian daric and the Lydian and Attic stater, it weighed two drachmae. In Pl. it is usually called *nummus aureus* or *Philippeus*, but in a few passages, where a certain sum in Philips has been often mentioned in the context, *nummus* alone is used. In all other cases *nummus* by itself in Pl. means the silver *nummus* (*nummus argenti*, As. 487, Aul. 108, Ps. 97, 299), by which was meant the Attic silver didrachm=$\frac{1}{50}$ of a mina or about eighteen pence (cf. Truc. 561 *de mina una diminui modo quinque nummos, mihi detraxi partem Herculaneam*, i.e. a tenth part). *Nummus* is the Latin form of νοῦμμος, used in Sicily and Magna Graecia for νόμισμα (that which is established by law or custom (νόμος), the authorized medium of exchange). Νοῦμμος meant not only 'money' in general, but was applied particularly to the chief silver coin; hence the Romans after the time of Pl. used *nummus* not only for a sum of money but also for their most important silver coin, *nummus sestertius*, worth about 2*d.*; but this sense is unknown to Pl. Thus, when *nummus* is used for a definite coin or amount, it means in Pl. a didrachm, in later writers a sesterce. And it was also used both by Pl. and by later writers for any trifling sum, as we use 'a shilling' and 'a farthing.' This is the meaning in the text and in Pers. 660 *nummus abesse hinc non potest* 'I won't take a shilling less,' Most. 112 *si quid nummo*

sarciri potest, Cic. Att. v. 21, quoted on 192, etc. See Ramsay, Most. Exc. XIV.

duis: from *duo* (=*do*); so *creduis* (605), *perduint*, etc. 'Plautus also has forms from this verb with the more regular *a*, e.g. *duas*, *creduas*,' R. 589. Cf. *edim* (461) and *edam*, *sim* and *fuam* (260).

332. **amittam**: see on 36.

333. **oras**=*dicis*, its original meaning (cf. *orator*) as in Cas. 499 *ex copia piscaria consulere quid emam meliust.* ST. *aequom oras*, Most. 668 *uidendumst primum utrum eae uelintne an non uelint.* TH. *Bonum aequomque oras*, Ps. 388 *nolo bis iterari; sat sic longae fiunt fabulae.* CA. *Optumum atque aequissumum oras*, Rud. 1151 *nugas mulier magnas egeris.* GR. *Ius bonum oras* (cf. Ep. 25 *ius dicis*). Notice alliteration and repetition in this line.

334. **publicam seruitutem**: prisoners captured in war were public property; some were sold to private persons (cf. 27), some were employed in public buildings etc., and the condition of the latter at Rome was much better than that of the former (cf. Liv. XXVI. 47, Ulp. frag. tit. 20). The δημόσιοι at Athens were employed as subordinate clerks in the civil service and as policemen. For the cognate acc. see on 391.

illi=*illic*, cf. 278.

335. **Priuatam medici**: sc. *seruitutem; medici* is objective gen. corresponding to a dative after the verb *seruire*, R. 1318.

huius: most editors give this speech to Tyndarus, either taking *huius*='myself,' or explaining *pol...cluens* as an aside; but it comes very well from Phil. who has assumed the pert manner of the slave in comedy (see on 253).

cluens is from *clueo* 'to hear' (see on 689) and means 'one who hears and obeys' 'a dependent': as to the *clientela*, see on 444; the relation was hereditary on both sides, but any citizen or stranger who wanted a protector (and all strangers would) might attach himself to a *patronus* by voluntary commendation, cf. Cic. Or. I. 39 *qui Romam in exilium uenisset, cui Romae exulare ius esset, si se ad aliquem quasi patronum applicauisset*.... Plautus is evidently thinking not of Aetolia but of Rome; for in Greece the social position of the *medicus* was high, but at Rome in early times the only doctors were Greek freedmen or slaves from Sicily and Magna Graecia (there was a famous medical school at Croton, Hdt. III. 131); such freedmen would be *clientes* of their former masters, and any Greek physician settling in Rome would also voluntarily seek the protection of some powerful citizen.

336. **in procliui**: *procliue* is a 'downward slope' and, as it is easier to walk down hill than up, *in procliui esse*='to be easy'; we use 'uphill' in the sense of 'hard' but not *vice versa.* There is a play upon the literal and metaphorical meanings of the word; 'this business is as easy as it is for rain-water to run downhill in a storm.'

337. **is homo**: Sch. emends *citissume* considering *is homo* imported from 341; he thinks that Pl. would have used the acc. (cf. 609) and that *is homo* is a strange expression for one's son (but cf. 989).

338. **ab re** 'against my interests,' cf. As. 224 *haud est ab re aucupis*, Trin. 238 *ab re consulit.* So *in rem* (386), *ex re* (296, 959).

tum scies: cf. Bac. 1023 *specta, tum scies.*

339. **redierit**: future perf., cf. Ter. Ph. 419 *haud desinam donec perfecero hoc.*

postulo 'expect'; see on 739.

341. **illi**=*illic*, in Elis, 278. **Immo**: see on 287.

misero: future perf. for future simple, of an action postponed; see on 194.

343. **iusseris**: sc. *perferri*, see on 303.

344. **nihil est**, 'it is of no use,' cf. Cas. 286 *nihil est me cupere factum nisi tu factis adiuuas*, Poen. 914 *nihil est nisi, dum calet, hoc agitur*, Tru. 769 *nihil est irasci quae te non flocci facit.*

operam: *opera* in this play is used in two senses, closely related, (i) 'labour' 'exertion,' as in this passage, in 425 and in 437 *dare operam* 'to take pains'; so *eadem opera* (450), *una opera* (563), *mea op.* (409), *tua op.* (410); hence opposed to *dicta* as 'deeds' to 'words' in 429; (ii) a 'service,' in *dare operam* 'to render a service' 362, 705, *dare op. malam* 'to do an ill turn' 701. Hence the use of *dare op.* in the sense of 'pay attention to' 'listen to' in 6, 54, 618 (cf. the two meanings of 'attend to').

luseris: cf. Cas. 424 *si nunc me suspendam meam operam luserim*, Ps. 369 *in pertussum ingerimus dicta dolium; operam ludimus.* The usual phrase is *perdere operam.*

345. **rem omnem**: Sch. for *omne* of MSS., cf. 377. *Omne* will not scan and could hardly be used indefinitely by itself like *omnia.*

transactam reddet, as distinguished from *transiget*, lays stress upon the state which is the result of the action, as distinguished from the action itself. The construction is common in Pl. and Ter.; it is found (i) with verbs of incomplete meaning, e.g. 709 *arbitror*, Mil. 886 *regionem consili repertam haberent*, Cic. Div. II. 28 *illud exploratum habeto*, 'consider as,' Ps. 926 *hanc explicatam rem dabo*, Cas. 439 *factum et curatum dabo*, Cist. 328 *perfectum ego hoc dabo negotium*, Ter. Eun. 212 *effectum dabo*, Verg. Aen. III. 69 *placataque uenti dant maria*, Am. 1145 *missum facio Tiresiam*, Cic. Or. I. 10 *missos facio mathematicos*, As. 122 *perfectum reddat quod promiserit*, Ps. 530 *ecfectum hoc hodie reddam*, Cur. 385 *hoc ecfectum tibi tradam*, (ii) with verbs of desire, e.g. 53, 309, 425 *uolo*, Liv. XXV. 3 *ordinem publicanorum offensum nolebant*, Cur. 304 *te conuentum cupit*, (iii) with other verbs, as 707, Cic. Phil. II. 12 *gaudeam factum*, Ter. And. 684 *inuentum tibi curabo et mecum adductum Pamphilum*, Cap. 207 *sino*, Men. 995 *sublimen raptum oportuit*, Ter. Ad. 214 *morem gestum oportuit*. Generally in these constructions the participle is a secondary predicate (R. 1402), but in some cases we must suppose *esse* omitted.

347. **ex sententia** 'to his liking'; for *ex* 'according to', cf. 296, 447, 997, Cic. Fam. XII. 4 *ex opinione hominum*, and such adverbial expressions as *ex bona fide*, *ex lege*, *ex more*, etc. The phrase is used either adverbially or adjectivally, cf. the pun in Cic. Or. II. 64 *ridicule illud L. Nasica censori Catoni, quom ille 'Ex tui animi sententia* ('on your word') *tu uxorem habes?'*, *'Non Hercule,' inquit, 'ex animi mei sententia.'*

348. **hodie**, 'ever,' a colloquialism; used to strengthen negatives, especially *numquam*.

tuom concredas: Sch., for *suom concredat* of MSS., which has been already implied in 346; the reading in the text agrees with the next line and states what has not been already urged.

351. **equidem**: a lengthened form of *quidem*, like *ehem eheu eho enim*, and not a contraction of *ego quidem*; for it is found (i) with *ego*, as in Am. 764, Bac. 437, Mer. 264, etc., (ii) with all persons of the singular or plural, e.g. Persius v. 45 *non equidem hoc dubites*, Propert. II. 31. 5 *hic equidem Phœbo uisus mihi pulcrior ipso*, Sall. Cat. 52, 11 *iam pridem equidem nos uera uocabula rerum amisimus*, 58, 4 *scitis equidem milites...*, Pl. Ep. 603 *ádulescentem equidém dicebant émisse.*

352. **Quam citissume...tam**: for this archaic construction cf. Mer. 121 *quam restito tam maxume res in periclo uortitur*, Ter. Heaut. 997 *quam maxume huic uana haec suspitio erit, tam facillume...*, Sall. Jug. 31, 14 *quam quisque pessume fecit, tam maxume tutus est*. So also with comparatives, where classical writers would use *quo*; e.g. Bac. 1091 *quam magis id*

reputo, tam magis uror, Poen. 348 *quam magis adspecto, tam magis est nimbata*, Trin. 861 *quam magis specto, minus placet.*

hoc cedere ad factum: a very strange expression. Brix explains *uolo* (*istum*, Phil.) *cedere ad hoc factum*, comparing Cic. Rosc. Am. 30, 84 *ad maleficium accedere*, but the order of the words is against this. Ussing takes *hoc* as the subject of *cedere*, rendering *hoc ad effectum perduci*. Uss. and Sch. both consider the passage corrupt, the latter reading HE. *Quam c. p. tam hoc iter eat.* TY. *Factum uolo.* If the distribution of the line is not to be altered, I think one might read *quam c. p. tam hoc te dare effectum uolo*, cf. Cas. 439, Cist. 328, Ps. 530, Curc. 385, Ter. Eun. 212, all quoted on 345.

353. **Num quae causast quin**: a legal formula employed in making an agreement, *conuentio* (cf. 378 *conuenit*). Similar phrases are *num quid causae est, num quid causam dicis*; cf. 625, Am. 852 *num quid causam dicis quin te hoc multem matrimonio?* ALC. *si deliqui, nulla causa est.* AM. *conuenit*, Aul. 261 *nuptias hodie quin faciamus num quae causast?* EV. *immo hercle optuma*, Ps. 533 *num quid causae est ilico quin te in pistrinum condam?* PS. *non unum in diem, uerum hercle in omnes, quantumst.*

uiginti minas: 1 talent = 60 minae, 1 mina = 100 drachmae, 1 dr. = 6 oboli; the talent and mina were of course not coins but sums of money. Comparing the quantities of silver in a drachma and a shilling we find the ratio to be about 9·75 : 12, and we therefore call the drachma equal to 9¾*d.*, the mina to about £4, the talent to about £240. But it must be borne in mind that these sums represent their *present* value, i.e. the amount of our money into which they might be re-coined; they give us no information as to prices (i.e. relative values of goods) in Greece; an Athenian could buy with a drachma much more of one commodity and much less of another than a Frenchman can buy with a franc.

354. **Optuma immo**: 'on the contrary, there is the best reason why I *should* do so.' For this affirmative answer to a question with *num* cf. Aul. 261, Ps. 533, quoted on the last line. *Immo* corrects the form of Hegio's expression but agrees with and strengthens the substance of it; see on 287. It stands second in Aul. 765 *pernego immo*; not apparently in classical Latin until Livy (xxxv. 49).

355. **Atque**, 'and indeed,' substitutes a stronger or wider expression for that which one has just used; cf. 811, As. 716 *Fortunam atque obsequentem*, Cic. Tusc. v. 15 *hebeti ingenio atque nullo*, Or. 16, 32 *rem difficilem, di immortales, atque omnium difficillimam.* Often with *adeo*, e.g. Cic. Cat. I. 2

intra moenia atque adeo in senatu, Verr. III. 29 *si damnatus eris, atque adeo cum damnatus eris* (*nam dubitatio damnationis, illis recuperatoribus, quae poterat esse?*) *uirgis te ad necem caedi necesse erit.*

omnes omnia opt. off. Alliteration and repetition, cf. Ter. Ad. 978 *di tibi, Demea, omnia omnes semper optata offerant.*

356. **honore honestas**: repetition. For the mood, see on 923.

357. **haud molestumst**: litotes, 'not bad' for 'very good.'

collus collari caret: assonance and alliteration. For the masculine form *collus,* see on 902.

358. **gratia ea**=*gratia eius beneficii,* 'gratitude for it is pregnant with good results'; cf. Pers. 672 *si quid bonis boni fit, esse idem et graue et gratum solet,* Rud. 939 *bonis quod bene fit, haud perit.* For *ea*=*eius rei,* see on 934; notice the repetition and double alliteration here.

359. **dice monstra praecipe**: asyndeton, see on 406, 658. 'In the verbs *duco, fero* (and their compounds), *facio* (with compounds which retain the radical *a*), and *dico,* the final *e* of the singular present imperative was always dropped after Terence's time,' R. 582.

360. **uin**=**uisne**: cf. *po(s)no, ae(s)num* and see Int. § 95.

361. **Quae res bene uortat**: used like *di bene uortant,* when saying or hearing something important: so Trin. 502 *di bene uortant, spondeo,* Ps. 645 *res agitur apud iudicem.* HA. *Di bene uortant,* Aul. 218 *quoniam tu me et ego te, qualis sis, scio, quae res recte uortat mihique tibique tuaeque filiae, filiam tuam mihi uxorem posco,* Cur. 729 *hodie fient nuptiae.* TH. *Quae res bene uortat mi et uobis,* 273 *ibo atque orabo* (to Aesculapius). CO. *Quae res male uortat tibi.*

362. **nouos erus**: i.e. Hegio himself.

363. **quod**: for the omission of the antecedent, see on 217.

366. **redimat**: i.e. from Menarchus.

mutatio: *muto,* like *moto,* is a contraction of *mouito*; its original meaning is shewn in Am. 274 *neque se luna quoquam mutat.*

367. **ut fiat**: final clause, depending on another final clause *ut redimat*; cf. 1027 and on 260.

filiis: probably dative of the indirect object, with *fiat* 'may happen for our sons,' but it is also possible to take it with *mutatio* as an abl. of price, cf. 28 *quo mutet suom. Mutare hoc illum* is 'to give or get that man in exchange for this,' and the process would be *mutatio hoc illius*; in the present reciprocal case the full expression would be *mutatio inter nos filiorum filiis*, and possibly, as one is implied in the other, the genitive is omitted.

368. **rectum**: participle, 'directed,' cf. Bac. 412 *ego illum haberem rectum ad ingenium bonum.*

369. **rota**: Brix says 'a child's hoop,' but cf. Ep. 371 *uorsutior es quam rota figularis.*

371. **tuopte**: for the termination see R. 389. Notice alliteration and repetition in this line.

373. **em**=**en**, cf. 540, 859, Trin. 3 *em, illae sunt aedes; i intro.* The ejaculation *hem*, for which the MSS. sometimes read *em*, is the natural sound made in clearing the throat.

374. **Quom facis**: see on 923.

copiam istam=*copiam istius rei*, see on 934.

376. **Qui me quid agitem perferat**=*qui quid ego agitem perferat*; the stock instance of this idiom, by which the logical subject of the dependent clause is made the object of the principal verb, is Coel. ap. Cic. Fam. VIII. 10 *nosti Marcellum quam tardus sit.* Cf. also 557, 609, Am. 508 *te experior quanti facias uxorem tuam*, Aul. 696 *sed seruom meum Strobilum miror ubi sit*, Trin. 698 *scio equidem te, animatus ut sis*, 992 *si te flocci facio, an periisses prius*, Ter. Heaut. 84 *fac me ut sciam*, Eun. 1035 *scin me in quibus sim gaudiis?* Here the construction is complicated by the insertion of a second object (*omnem rem*) to the principal verb, grammatically in apposition to the relative clauses.

quid rerum: this partitive gen. after adverbs, neuter pronouns and adjectives is a favourite construction with Pl. and Ter. Cf. 125, 193, 267, 385, 585, 660, 669, 698, 776, 869, 958, 1028, Am. 769 *quid hoc sit hominis*, Men. 457 *adfatimst hominum*, Ter. Hec. 643 *quid mulieris uxorem habes?* etc.

379. **patrem** without any possessive pronoun properly means '*my* father,' as in 239; but both Tynd. and Phil. use it so with reference to the same person, the father of Phil. In the following conversation it occurs 7 times, each time without the pronoun, 382, 384, 389, 395, 400, 406, 440; the ambiguity is of course intentional, for Hegio understands Tynd. to mean 'my father' and Phil. 'your father.'

380. **rebitas**: *bito* 'to go' (whence *arbiter*, 211) is anteclassical: Pl. uses the compounds *adbito* (604), *rebito* (409, 696, 747), *abito ebito inbito interbito perbito* and *praeterbito.*

382. **aliquem** 'some one else,' cf. Cic. Cat. I. 8 *dubitas, si emori aequo animo non potes, abire in aliquas terras?* Liv. XXXIV. 38 *aut ipse occurrebat aut aliquos mittebat.*

383. **ergo** 'that is why,' giving a conclusion drawn from another person's remark; cf. 423, 721, 1020.

385. **adhuc locorum**: for the partitive gen. see on 376, R. 1296; similar pleonastic expressions with *locus* (in the sense of 'time') are Cist. 523 *postidea loci*, Cas. 120 *postid locorum*, Ter. Eun. 255 *interea loci*, Lucr. v. 443 *inde loci*, Sall. Iug. 102 *postea loci*.

faciam ut...petam: for this periphrasis cf. 439, Cic. Att. III. 15 *non faciam ut...angam*, Sen. 12 *inuitus feci ut Flaminium e senatu eicerem*; so Fam. v. 9 *non committam ut...uidear*, Fin. v. 9 *omne animal id agit ut se conseruet*, and cf. on 268.

386. **in rem conducat tuam**: cf. Cist. 367 *quod in tuam rem bene conducat*; so often with *esse*, e.g. 398, Trin. 628 *si in rem tuam esse uideatur*; cf. *ex re* 296, *ab re* 338.

387. **uiribus**: this, the reading of J, is adopted by most edd. Sch. however reads *animo, ore atque auribus.*

389. **salutem dicito**: S. D. (=*salutem dicit*) was the usual way of beginning a letter.

390. **si quem alium**: i.e. 'any other friend of mine you may come across'; so Trin. 1183 *ego ducam, pater, et eam et si quam aliam iubebis.*

391. **seruitutem seruire**: cognate accusative, R. 1100, K. 212; sometimes the words are cognate only in sense, as in Verg. Aen. VI. 122 *itque reditque uiam*, XII. 753 *mille fugit refugitque uias*, sometimes they are cognate both in sense and etymology, as here. The latter use, which is a form of the repetition noticed on 247, 250, 840, is common in Pl., cf. Cur. 24 *facinus facere*, Mil. 628 *uitam uiuere*, Poen. 759 *calidum prandisti prandium*, Ps. 524 *istam pugnam pugnabo*, Trin. 32 *metere messem maxumam*, etc.

392. **Honore honestiorem fecit**: *Honor* is personified, according to Tyrrell (on Mil. 620); cf. Cist. 376 *O Salute mea salus salubrior!* As. 268 *illos lubentiores faciam quam Lubentiast.* The ordinary reading *honore hon. f.* is taken to mean *nimio honore honestauit*, 'has treated me with more consideration than I deserve.' Notice the repetition.

393. **ne praecipias**: the subjunctive is jussive (R. 1596), not final.

tamen 'all the same,' see on 187.

396. **mora mera** 'mere waste of time,' cf. 906. Notice the assonance and alliteration.

monerier: sc. *me*. For the termination see on 438.

397. **Vt**: the construction is carried on from 394 *conuenerit*.

398. **utrique**: here and in Aul. 129 *quod in rem esse utrique arbitremur*, Ter. And. 546 *si in remst utrique*, we must take *utrique* as gen. Cf. Pers. 341 *in uentris rem*, Ter. Hec. 102 *in remst Bacchidis*, and *in rem meam, tuam* (385); for similar genitives cf. Truc. 292 (quoted on 647), Sti. 729 *uni animi sumus*, Ter. And. 608 *nulli consili sum*, Varr. L. L. IX. 38 *maris et feminae et neutri*. Prisc. VI. p. 694 (Put.) quotes *illi soli* from Cato, *ipsi toti* (fem.) from Afranius.

399. **uidere**: sc. *cupere*, see on 302. Notice the chiasmus *tuom tu...ille suom*.

401. **Me hic ualere**: repeated from 391. As the line stands, *tute...Tyndare* must be taken as a parenthesis ('slave tho' you are, you have my leave to say,' alluding to the tone of the following lines), and *inter nos fuisse* must stand for *nos inter n. f.*, which is not impossible. The ingenious emendation of Sch., *me hic pol et te tute*, avoids both the repetition and the difficulty of construction. Fl. and Uss. bracket *Me... inter*; which may have been interpolated to explain or lessen the strangeness of the remarks that follow.

403. **te aduorsatum mihi**: so Madvig (Advers. II. p. 6), Sch., Brix, Uss., for MSS. *me adu. tibi*, which would be a curious expression from a master to a slave and would involve an awkward change of subject in the next line.

404. **gessisse morem**: see on 198.

tamen: elliptical, the concessive sentence being represented by *in tantis aerumnis*; see on 187.

405. **med**: the ablative singular originally ended in *-d* (R. 362); thus *med* and *ted* are properly ablatives and *sed*, the conjunction, was originally the ablative of *se* ('by itself'). Owing however to the identity of the accusative and ablative forms in these pronouns, *med* and *ted* came also to be used, as here, for accusatives (R. 385).

med deseruisse te: the ambiguity is probably intentional, as in the answer of the oracle to Pyrrhus, *aio te, Aeacida, Romanos uincere posse*; cf. Shaksp. Hen. VI., Act 1, Sc. 4, 'the duke yet lives that Henry shall depose.'

406. **dubiis, egenis**: asyndeton. Pl. uses asyndeton (cf. Ballas, Gram. Pl.) chiefly (i) where more than two proper names come together, see on 864, (ii) in long lists, see on 771,

(iii) in lively and terse narratives of consecutive incidents, see on 505, (iv) in personal descriptions, see on 647, (v) where the same word is repeated at the beginning of different clauses, see on 903 and cf. on 939, (vi) to mark a contrast, see on 575, and (vii) between words of similar meaning, viz. (a) verbs, see on 658, 791, (b) substantives, as in 199, Am. 196 *ductu imperio auspicio suo*, 898 *stupri dedecoris*, 991 *eius dicto imperio*, As. 824 *turbas lites*, Aul. 399 *congrum muraenam*, Bac. 732 *morbum mortem*, Cas. 664 *sub arcis sub lectis*, Cist. 381 *pessulis repagulis*, Cur. 647 *uentus turbo*, Ep. 450 *armis arte duellica*, 523 *fictor conditor*, Men. 1133 *miseriis laboribus*, Merc. 832 *usus fructus uictus cultus*, Mil. 288 *forte fortuna*, 647 *sputator screator*, Ps. 327 *hostias uictimas*, 580 *dolos perfidias*, Rud. 23 *donis hostiis*, 839 *ui uiolentia*, Sti. 280 *gloriam laudem decus*, Trin. 835 *turbines uenti*, Tru. 318 *blandimentis ornamentis*. (c) adjectives and participles, as in the text, 99, 502, 640, 722, As. 223 *oratione uinnula uenustula*, Aul. 318 *plorans eiulans*, 786 *infelix miser*, Bac. 935 *obsignatas consignatas*, Cist. 302 *plorans obsecrans*, Ep. 256 *calidi conducibilis consili*, Men. 863 *indomitos feroces*, Mil. 202 *curans cogitans*, 663 *aduocato tristi iracundo*, 952 *condicio noua luculenta*, Most. 143 *totae perpetuae*, 716 *piscatu probo electili*, Pers. 169 *indoctae inmemori insipienti*, Ps. 677 *instituta ornata cuncta...certa deformata*, 697 *hominem strenuom beneuolentem*, Sti. 304 *insperato opportuno bono*, Trin. 821 *laetus lubens*, Tru. 435 *unanimantis fidentis*. (d) adverbs, as in Aul. 264 *propere strenue*, Bac. 374 *continuo protinam*, Cas. 744 *propere cito*, Cist. 371 *propere ocius*, Mil. 177 *repente subito*, Poen. 662 *clam furtim*, Ps. 382 *simulter itidem*, 1191 *uero serio*, Rud. 1323 *propere celeriter*.

egenis: cf. Poen. 130 *res...dubias egenas inopiosas consili*, Verg. Aen. VI. 91 *supplex in rebus egenis*.

407. **haec...ut**: a colloquial construction; *haec* refers to the preceding lines and the *ut*- clause is added in loose apposition to it; cf. 442.

408. **Numquam**: Donatus, on Ter. And. 384, says '*numquam* plus habet negationis quam *non*'; cf. 542, 657, As. 630 *numquam ad uesperum uiuam*, Aul. 555 *quos si Argus seruet... numquam seruet*, Ter. Heaut. 559 *numquam commodius umquam erum audiui loqui*. So in Eng. 'you never mean to say...,' etc.

tam auarus quin: in negative consecutive sentences, if the principal sentence is affirmative, *ut non*, *qui non* are used; if the principal sentence is negative or quasi-negative, *quin*. R. 1680, 1696, K. 422.

gratus 'thankful' 'in gratitude,' cf. Merc. 105 *eius pro meritis gratum me et munem fore*, Cic. Agr. II. 8 *ut grati ac* *memores benefici esse uideantur.* I have retained the reading of BDVE; most edd. emend *gratiis* (MSS. often have *u* for *ii*), but *gratiis*, though the MSS. sometimes write it *gratis*, is always trisyllabic in Pl.

emittat manu: the original method of liberating a slave was by a collusive action at law, called *vindicta*; the master and slave appeared before one of the higher magistrates (usually the Praetor), and a third party, the *assertor*, claimed the slave's freedom in set form, *hunc ego hominem liberum esse aio.* The master having hold of the slave turned him round, gave him a slight slap on the cheek, replied *hunc ego hominem liberum esse uolo*, and let him go (*emittebat e manu* or *manu*). The magistrate gave judgment for the *assertor* and the slave was free.

411. **redire denuo**, 'return back again,' pleonasm: cf. 767, Mil. 386 *perge porro*, 592 *redeo rursum*, 701 *rursum restitues*, Trin. 182 *redemi rursum*, Ter. Hec. 38 *refero denuo*, etc.

412. **Quom** 'in that,' R. 1729.

418. **fuisti**, where we should have expected *fuisses*, a sort of anacoluthon, 'if you had been my slave, with just the same deference have you acted,' instead of 'would you have acted.' Sonnenschein points out that the indicative is the more appropriate, as Tynd. had of course actually been as deferential as a slave. Fl., Brix, Böthe read *sis*, but cf. Mil. 1207 *nam si possem ullo modo impetrare ut abiret nec te abduceret, operam dedi*, and conversely Rud. 744 *iam tanta esset, si uiuit, scio.*

Di uostram fidem: sc. *obsecro*, cf. Cist. 396 *Di, obsecro uostram fidem*, but the phrase is a mere exclamation, not an invocation, R. 1129.

420. **Videas**: see on 202.

quibus et quantis laudibus: for this use of the rel. (*qui*= 'such'), cf. Cic. Fam. XIII. 78 *quae tua natura est*, XI. 13 *qua enim prudentia es*, IV. 5 *qui illius in te amor fuit...non uolt*, R. 1715. But Sch., reading *quantis laudauit* with MSS., marks a *lacuna*, to be filled up thus:

quantis laudauit *suom*
seruolum hic modo laudibus, tum quam sincere suam uicem
suom erum seruos conlaudauit,

and is thus enabled to give the next speech to Phil. with the MSS. On the other hand Hegio's next speech, *Ergo quom optume fecisti...*, requires a preceding remark in praise of Phil., which must be made by Tynd.

421. **centensumam partem**: an adverbial accusative, like *uicem* (see on 526) and *cetera* (R. 1102, K. 213); cf. Mil. 763 *haud centensumam partem dixi atque possum expromere*. Similarly *meam partem, magnam maiorem maxumam minumam partem, bonam partem* (Lucr. VI. 1249), etc. For the form *centensumam*, see on 980.

422. **quam**: for the construction *haud cent. partem quam*, cf. Mil. 763 quoted above (where *atque*=*quam*, comparative). It is a compound of two constructions, (1) *haud cent. partem laudat* (*laudum*) *quibus ipse* etc., where *cent. pars*=$\frac{1}{100}$, R. App. D. VI. 1, (2) *centum partibus minus laudat quam ipse* etc., where *centum partibus minus*='100 times less,' cf. Cic. Acad. II. 36 *multis partibus sol maior est quam terra*, and R. 1204. Cf. the use of *quam* after *dimidium, multiplex*, etc., e.g. Liv. XXXV. 1 *praetor uix dimidium militum, quam quod acceperat, successori tradidit*.

423. **quom** 'since,' see on 923.

424. **cumulare**: epexegetical infinitive standing in place of a genitive, cf. Cur. 60 *occasiost subripere se*; the regular construction is also found, e.g. Ep. 271 *occasio faciundi*, and both are combined in Ter. Ph. 885 *occasio eludendi senes et Phaedriae curam adimere*. The inf. is rare except after verbal substantives and phrases equivalent to a verb (R. 1360); cf. however Men. 244 *operam sumam quaerere*, 233 *numquid modi futurumst illum quaerere?* Ps. 1076 *periclumst stipularier*, Cic. Att. X. 8 *tempus est cogitare*, etc. *Cumulare* is 'to complete the heap,' 'to crown,' cp. Cic. Att. IV. 1 *unum ad cumulandum gaudium...mihi defuisse*.

ut geras 'by carrying out,' lit. '(namely) that you should carry out'; the simplest construction after *occasio* would be a genitive, *beneficii* or *bene faciendi*, and for this may be substituted an infinitive, *bene facere* (see last note), or an *ut*-clause, *ut bene facias* (cf. Ps. 285 *fuit occasio ut daret*, Rud. 927, etc.). So with *causa* we have *appellationis* (Caes. B. C. II. 28), *obiurgandi* (Ter. And. 158), *consurgere in arma* (Verg. Aen. X. 90) and *ut seruem* (supra 257). In the text two of these constructions are combined, *occasio cumulare* and *occasio ut geras*, and the *ut*-clause, being added as an equivalent for the infinitive, really amounts to an explanation of it; hence we translate '*by* carrying out.' So in 485 *canem uoluit imitarier...dentis ut restringerent*='by shewing their teeth,' lit. '(namely) that they should shew,' only there the infinitive and the *ut*-clause stand for accusatives, not as here for genitives. Cf. Mil. 188 *ut ne abstineat disciplinam colere*. PE. *Quem ad modum?* PA. *ut eum uerbis uincat* (where *ut uincat* is substituted for *colere* and = 'by convincing him'), Pers. 36 *facere amicum me potis es.* SA. *Quem ad modum?* TO. *ut mihi des...*

425. **Magis non**, etc., i.e. 'my wishes for that cannot be more earnest than my exertions will be.'

factum uelle: see on 345.

426. **testem laudo**: the MSS. have *testem do*, which will not scan: the true reading is given by Nonius, p. 335 *laudare etiam significat nominare...Plautus Captiuis: id ut scias, Iouem supremum testem laudo, Egio.* Cf. Gell. II. 6 *laudare significat prisca lingua nominare appellareque; sic in actionibus ciuilibus auctor laudari dicitur, quod est nominari.* This latter phrase occurs several times in Cicero, e.g. de Or. III. 49 *quod eo saepius testificor ut auctoribus laudandis ineptiarum crimen effugiam.*

428. **quam memet mihi**: sc. *facturum*, attraction of a short relative clause into the infinitive, cf. Cic. Sen. 1 *te suspicor eisdem rebus, quibus me ipsum, commoueri* (for *quibus ipse commoueor*, as in the text *quam memet* = *quam egomet faciam*), Fam. II. 16 *affirmaui quiduis me potius perpessurum quam ex Italia exiturum.*

429. **expedire**: so Fl., Uss., Brix; cf. on 40. Schoell reads *dicta tua experiri re et opera.*

operis: for the plur. cf. Bac. 45 *dederit operas*, Rud. 321, etc., and on 522.

430 may be taken in two ways: (1) 'and I wish you to take heed of something which I have not yet mentioned concerning you,' lit. 'by which' (*quo* abl. of difference, with *minus*) 'I have said less than I wanted to about you'; cf. Ter. And. 655 *immo etiam, quo tu minus scis aerumnas meas, haec nuptiae non adparabantur mihi*, and the phrases *uno minus, multis partibus maior*, etc., R. 1204; (2) more simply, *quo minus dixi* (*eo magis*), *an. ad. uolo* (*quo minus* = 'in proportion as...less'), cf. Cic. Quint. 1 *quo minus ingenio possum, subsidium mihi diligentiam comparaui*, R. 1643.

431. **horunc uerborum**: i.e. the lines which follow. The sequence of thought is not clear; he means 'listen to what I am going to say about yourself—and don't take offence at it, but reflect upon it—namely, that you are being sent...'; that is, *atque...fuas* is logically a parenthesis and *cogitato* resumes and repeats *an. ad. uolo.* But grammatically 432 is connected, not with 430 but with the parenthesis.

iratus fuas: so in 237 Tynd. after appealing to Phil. not to be ungrateful, deprecates any offence. For *fuas* see on 260.

433. **pigneri**=*pignori*, the spelling of MSS. here and in 655. The difference is said to be *pignera sunt rerum, pignora filiorum et affectuum.* The dat. is predicative, see on 259 and cf. 655, Ps. 87 *me opponam pigneri*, Ter. Ph. 661 *ager oppositust pigneri.*

434. **Ne ignores**: the subjunctive may be final, of the class noticed on 290, but is more probably jussive. In prohibitions to a definite person Cicero uses the present subj. act. once only (in a proverb, *actum ne agas*, Att. IX. 18) and the present deponent once only (Att. XIV. 1), R. 1600; but both are common in the comic poets, e.g. 247, 331, 349, 393.

quom extemplo=*extemplo quom* (559 *extemplo ubi*), *extemplo* belonging in sense to *ignores* not *abscesseris*; so 786, Ps. 804, etc.

435. **pro te** is to be taken closely with *seruom*, 'me in slavery instead of you,' at least that is how Hegio is meant to understand it. Notice the repetition *seruom in seruitute.*

436. **ducas...deseras...neque des**: *ne* is to be supplied from 434 before each of these verbs; thus *neque des*=*et* (*ne*) *non des*, 'nor omit to give.'

438. Brix considers this line a gloss on 432 interpolated here: it is certainly superfluous, as Phil. had been informed of the fact by Hegio in 364 and by Tynd. in 379, and again reminded of it in 432.

mittier: this old form of the infinitive passive arose, according to R. 614, 615, by the addition of the ordinary passive suffix *r* (which originally=*se*, the reflexive pronoun) in the form *-er* to the active infinitive, whose final *e* was dissimilated to *i* before *er*. The final *r* was then dropped because of its ill sound after another *r* (R. 185), and *ie* contracted into *i*. Thus *censēre-ĕr*, *censerier*, *censerie*, *censeri*. If the same course had been followed in consonant and *-i* verbs, the syllable *-ĕr* would have recurred (e.g. *mittĕriĕr*); the Romans therefore preferred to omit the first (R. 28), i.e. to append *-ier* immediately to the final consonant of the stem (e.g. *mittier*). Analogy afterwards reduced *mittier*, etc. to *mitti*. Before about 220 B.C. the longer form was in use; from then to about 120 B.C. was the period of transition, and after that the longer form was used only as an intentional archaism.

439. **Fac sis**: see on 385.

fidelis sis fideli: notice repetition and alliteration. Fl. reads *fidele sis fidelis*, from Non. p. 512 *fidele pro fideliter Plautus Captiuis 'fac fidele caue fidem fluxam feras.'* Cf. Aul. 314 *parce parcum*, Cas. 522 *scite scitus*, Ps. 13 *misere miser.*

geras: Sch. reads *feras* with Nonius; *caue* 'beware' sometimes takes the subjunctive without *ne*; in Poen. 117 the subjunctive is plural, *caue dirumpatis*.

441. **inuentu** 'by finding his son'; so Sch., who refers to Merc. 847 *eorum inuentu*. The MSS. reading, *inuentum*, is taken to mean '(on your return) find a friend in this man, in whom we have already found one'; in support of it Brix quotes Men. 452 *homines occupatos occupat*, Cur. 540 *subiges redditum ut reddam tibi*, Cic. Fam. XIV. 1 *uide ne puerum perditum perdamus*.

440. Brix puts this line before 439, Sch. brackets it. I have put it after 441, taking the connection to be 'and make Hegio your friend by finding his son; for my father, I know, will do his part,' i.e. by redeeming Philopolemus and sending him back with you.

442. **Haec...ne fuas**: cf. on 407.

dextera retinens manu: 'the person interested took his friend by the right hand and told him that he placed in his hand the trust he was anxious to have discharged; the trust or commission itself was hence called *mandatum* (*manu datum*),' Sandars on Justin. Inst. 3 XXVI. pr.

444. **Hoc age**: see on 930. For the asyndeton *tu...tu...tu*, see on 903 and 406.

patronus: the correlative of *patronus* is *cliens* (334); the relation is *clientela*, which under the empire was the connection between advocates and their clients, but in earlier times was a much wider institution, in some respects similar to mediæval vassalage, involving services on the one side and protection on the other. It descended from father to son, but besides his hereditary clients a man was also *patronus* to his *liberti* and to those strangers who had sought his protection (see on 335). The ties of this relation were very sacred; on the one hand the duties of the *patronus* were most imperative and neglect of them made him accursed (cf. the law of the XII. Tables, *patronus si clienti fraudem fecerit, sacer esto*, Caes. ap. Gell. v. 13 *neque clientes sine summa infamia deseri possunt; quibus etiam a propinquis nostris opem ferre instituimus*, Hor. Od. II. 18. 25, Verg. Aen. VI. 608), and on the other hand greater respect was due to the *patronus* than to anyone except the *pater* (cf. passages quoted on 238 *patrem nominem*).

446. **Satin**=*satisne*, see on 360; **tua ex sententia**, on 347.

448. **Numquid aliud**: a common form of leave-taking; the full phrase occurs in Mil. 575 *numquid nunc aliud me uis?* and

there are various abbreviations, e.g. Aul. 175 *numquid me uis?* Ter. Eun. 363 *numquid me aliud?* 191 *numquid uis aliud?* supra 191 *numquid uis?* and that in the text.

449. **a trapezita**=*ab argentario*, see on 193. *Ab argentario scribere* or *soluere* is to pay from one's account at a bank, as opposed to *de domo* from money at home; cf. Cur. 618 *solui a trapezita meo*, 682 *decem minas dum soluit, omnes mensas transiit; postquam nihil fit...reddit argentum domo*, Hor. Sat. II. 3. 69 *scribe decem a Nerio*, Dig. XII. 1. 40 *L. Titius scripsi me accepisse a P. Maeuio quindecim mutua numerata mihi de domo*. The order on the banker was given either personally (as here) or in writing (as in Cur. 429).

450. **Eadem opera**: see on 344. Notice the Roman allusion in *praetore*.

syngraphum: properly a 'written agreement,' as in As. 746, but here used for a 'writing,' a 'document,' as συγγραφή sometimes is (e.g. Plato Legg. 953 E).

Quem syngraphum: see on 574.

451. **Quem** etc., i.e. a passport.

ad legionem: *legio* ('the gathering' or 'levy,' from *lego*) originally meant the whole army; it consisted, the state being tripartite, of three 'hundreds' (*centuriae*) of horsemen, and three 'thousands' of infantry (*milites* from *mille*). As the state grew this number came to form only one brigade or division of the army, but the word was still sometimes used in its original meaning, as here, Ep. 56 *quotidie ad me ab legione epistulas mittebat*, 203 quoted on 153, and generally in Pl. in the singular.

hic...huic: for the repetition see on 593.

452. **Bene ambulato**: see on 900.

454. **Expediui**: see on 40; the remark is true in a sense he does not intend, with reference to Tynd.

si dis placet 'please God,' here used εὐφημίας ἕνεκα, but often ironically, e.g. Ter. Ad. 476 *ille bonus uir nobis psaltriam, si dis placet, parauit quicum uiuat.*

456. **sultis**=*si uoltis*, see on 110. Notice the double alliteration here.

458. **Ad fratrem**: see on 497.

modo inuiso: so the MSS. The two objections are *modō* (but see Int. § 120) and the present tense, *inuiso*, between two futures; but *inuiso*='I am going to see,' and so is not out of place with the future, cf. Sti. 66 *iam ego domi adero: ad meam maiorem filiam inuiso modo*; following which, Brix here reads *modo ad c.*, Uss. has *ibo dum* for *modo*, Sch. *modo eo c. a. inuisum*.

459. **Eadem**: sc. *opera*. **hunc**: Tyndarus.

460. **praeuorti**, 'to turn one's first attention to,' is constructed in Pl. either with a substantive in the dative, as here, Merc. 113 *pigritiae*, 379 *rei mandatae*, Mil. 765 *huic rei*, Pers. 796 *litibus*, or with a neuter pronoun in the accusative, as in 1026, Am. 921 *id te serio praeuortier*, Ps. 602 *hoc praeuortar*, see on 542.

ACT III. Scene I.

In the heading of this scene B has DV, i.e. *diuerbium*, meaning (if it is not a mistake) that, contrary to the usual custom, these trochaic septenarii are to be spoken, not sung.

461. **edit**: for this old form of the subjunctive, see on 331.

463. **se rupit**: i.e. by running after it; so Sch., for *esse cupit* of MSS., which will not scan and merely repeats the previous line. For the phrase cf. Merc. 151 *me rupi causa currendo tua*, and Poen. 540, and see on 14.

464. **Nam**: elliptical, '(I say this) because.' *Nam* (*namque*) has two uses: I. explanatory, II. in emphatic interrogations (see on 799). The explanatory use is two-fold: (A) *causal*, giving the reason or cause for what is mentioned in the preceding sentence, (B) *corroborative*, giving the grounds upon which the preceding statement was made or is to be believed; thus 'he fell asleep for he was very tired' (causal), 'he was very tired for he fell asleep' (corroborative). A. The causal use (i) is common, e.g. 103, 239, 275; (ii) the reason may be put as an argument, not as a fact, e.g. 711; (iii) sometimes *nam* is used elliptically to give the reason for mentioning the previous facts, as in the text, (but in these cases of ellipse it is evidently impossible to be quite sure whether they belong here or under B), or it may give a reason for having omitted a statement or a consideration, thus meeting an objection, as in 440, 906; (iv) the preceding sentence may be a command or wish and *nam* may give the reason for uttering or obeying it, e.g. 167, 232, 263. B. The corroborative use (i) is found in 169, 580, 981, etc.; (ii) the corroboration may consist in giving a particular instance of a general assertion, e.g. 295, 1002, (iii) or the *nam*-clause may refer to and explain the use of a single word in the previous sentence, e.g. 94, 185; (iv) to this head are probably

to be referred the instances of ellipse in which one speaker gives a confirmation or approval of a previous remark by another, the ellipse being '(you are right) for,' e.g. 229, 604, 896. For *enim*, see on 568.

diei oculos: a comically incongruous metaphor, like Sti. 191 *ei hercle uerbo lumbos defractos uelim.*

465. **malignitate onerauit**: oxymoron, *malignus* being the opposite of *benignus* or *largus*, cf. Bac. 401 *iustus iniustus, malignus largus, comis incommodus*, Verg. G. II. 179 *collesque maligni*, Aen. VI. 270 *lunae sub luce maligna.* Notice the double alliteration here.

466. **ieiuniosiorem**: sc. *quam me*, probably; Brix however takes it of the 'day,' which has just been personified. The word is a Pl. coinage from *ieiunium*, on the analogy of *ingeniosus, odiosus, uitiosus*, etc.

ecfertum fame: oxymoron, cf. Aul. 84 *aedes inaniis oppletae*, Merc. 574 *ieiunitatis plenus* and Horace's *strenua inertia* and *concordia discors.*

467. **quoi minus procedat**: for the phrase cf. Sall. Iug. 85 *benefacta mea reipublicae procedunt*, Cato R. R. 148 *totidem dies emptori procedent.*

468. **resident esurialis ferias**: *residere* (=*quiescere*) is constructed with a (cognate) accusative on the analogy of *ferias agere*; cf. Cic. Leg. II. 22, 55 *denicales feriae, quae a nece appellatae sunt quia residentur mortuis. Esurialis* (which does not occur elsewhere) is coined in imitation of *feriae nouendiales, denicales*, etc.

469. **Ilicet**=*ire licet* (hence *arti* constructed with *licet* and *malam crucem* with *ire*), so *scilicet* (*scire l.*) *uidelicet* (*uidere l.*); the *-re-* dropped out owing to its similarity to the following syllable *-li*; cf. *homi(ni)cidium, uene(ni)ficium*, R. 28 and cf. on 438, 980.

malam crucem: crucifixion was the capital punishment specially reserved for slaves; in Mil. 372 the slave says *scio crucem futuram mihi sepulcrum: ibi mei sunt maiores siti, pater, auos, proauos, abauos.* Like our 'go and be hanged,' *i in crucem* was an imprecation and *malam* intensified it (cf. on 531); then *malam crucem*, being regarded as one word, was again intensified, as here and Men. 328 *ut eas max. m. c.*; for a similar phrase see 636. *Crucem* is acc. of the goal of motion, R. 1108, cf. Poen. 496 *malam crucem ibo potius*, Ter. Eun. 536 *malam rem hinc ibis?*

471. **Lacones** is generally explained of the Spartan fortitude with which the parasites stood being knocked about (see on 88; Uss. quotes Petron. Sat. 105 *tres plagas Spartana nobilitate concoxi*), but it is more naturally taken with the following words as referring to the absence of luxury in the *subsellium*; cf. Sti. 698 *potiusne in subsellio Cynice hic accipimur quam in lectis?* Cic. Mur. 35, 74 *neque tamen Lacedaemonii...qui cotidianis epulis in robore accumbunt, neque uero Cretes, quorum nemo gustauit umquam cubans...*

imi subselli uiros: the MSS. here and in Sti. 489 have *uni*, which does not make sense. In the latter passage the Parasite is begging to be asked to dinner, but his patron objects on the ground that there were already nine in company and that there was therefore no room (for at a Roman dinner three couches, *lecti*, were placed so as to form three sides of a square with the table in the middle, the fourth side being left open for the waiters, and on each couch not more than three persons reclined). To this the Parasite replies *haud postulo me in lecto accumbere; scis tu me esse imi* (MSS. *uni*) *subselli uirum*. The phrase must mean an inferior who, while the other guests reclined together on the *lecti*, sat on a stool or bench apart at the bottom, or open side, of the table.

472. **Plagipatidas**: = *qui plagas patiuntur*, see on 88; the word is hybrid, having a Greek patronymic termination after the style of *Romulidae*, *Memmiadae*, *Scipiadae*. It implies that the *Plagipati* were an equally noble family; so Aul. 370 *Rapacidae*, Trin. 1022 *Collicrepidae*, *Crurícrepidae*.

uerba 'witticisms,' cf. 482 and Sti. 221, where a parasite out of work holds an auction of his effects: *logos ridiculos uendo, age licemini,... cauillationes, adsentatiunculas ac periuratiunculas parasiticas*.

473. **reddant**: sc. *idem*.

474. **obsonant**, ὀψωνοῦσι. Cf. Mil. 667 *primarium parasitum atque obsonatorem optumum*. In Ter. Eun. 255 sqq. the parasite Gnatho describes his marketing, and Theophrastus, Char. II., mentions the Flatterer running errands to the market, ἀμέλει δὲ καὶ τὰ ἐκ γυναικείας ἀγορᾶς διακονῆσαι δυνατὸς ἀπνευστί.

475. **aperto capite**: we say 'bare-faced.' Ordinarily the Roman wore nothing on his head in town: in bad weather, or for purposes of concealment, he wrapped his toga over it (*capite inuoluto*, Cic. Ph. II. 31, 77). In the country or on a journey he either wore a hat or a hood (*cucullus*) attached to the *paenula*.

476. **in tribu**: i.e. in the Comitia Tributa, which tried offences against the commonalty and was a court of appeal from magistrates' decisions. Notice the Roman allusion.

477. **terrunci**: all the MSS. here have *rr*, which is also the spelling in an inscription given by Th. Mommsen in Hermes XXII. 485, and of A in Cic. Fin. III. 14, 45.

faciunt 'esteem,' 'value,' as in 616, 986; similarly *facere nihili, nauci, flocci, pili, huius* (see on 267), *tanti* and *quanti.*

478. **dudum**, 'just now,' viz. at v. 191. Notice alliteration in this line.

foro: the Forum Vetus was the only forum at this time. In the forenoon it would be crowded; in Hdt. (IV. 181, etc.) ἀγορῆς πληθυούσης = the period before noon; about mid-day people took lunch (*prandium*, called *cibus meridianus* in Suet. Aug. 78).

479. **atque** 'and behold,' used in noticing or mentioning some fresh incident, especially (with *eccum*) a sudden arrival: cf. Am. 954 *mirum quid...secreto ille agat—Atque aperiuntur aedes*, Poen. 1075 *aperi, si audes; atque adest.* We should generally use 'but.'

480. **hoc** = *huc*; cf. Corp. Inscr. L. I. 1431 *heus tu, uiator lasse, qui me praetereis, cum diu ambulareis, tamen hoc ueniendum est tibi*, Bac. 1150 *hosce intro inlicere hoc*, Truc. 531 *adduce hoc tu istas*, Ter. Eun. 501 *si Chremes hoc forte aduenerit*; so, according to Serv., in Verg. Aen. VIII. 423, and perhaps even in Cic. Fam. VIII. 6 *hoc sic nuntiatum est.* Pl. also uses *illoc, istoc* = *illuc, istuc.*

profitetur: the technical term for applying for a privilege or offering oneself for an office; e.g. for an allotment of land, Cic. Verr. II. 3. 48 *in Leontino iugerum subscriptio ac professio non est plus* XXX *milium*, for Roman citizenship Arch. 4 *professus est apud praetorem*, and for the consulship Sall. Cat. 18 *Catilina prohibitus erat petere consulatum quod intra legitumos dies profiteri nequiuerit.*

481. **me rident**: *ridere aliquem* is usually 'to laugh *at* a man,' 'to ridicule him,' but here it means to laugh at his witticisms: so in Ter. Eun. 249 *hisce ego non paro me ut rideant*, Petron. 61 *satius est rideri quam derideri.*

482. **unum** seems sometimes to have been used colloquially as an indefinite article, just as it came to be afterwards in the Romance languages; cf. 862, Most. 664 *ad unum saxum me fluctus ferunt*, Ps. 948 *lepida ibidem una aderit mulier*, Truc.

251 *est huic unus seruos uiolentissumus*, Cic. Ph. II. 3, 7 *tanquam mihi cum M. Crasso contentio erat, non cum uno gladiatore nequissimo.*

de dictis melioribus: in Sti. 400 the parasite says *ibo intro ad libros et discam de dictis melioribus.* Notice the cognate accusative *dictum*, and the repetition and alliteration.

483. **menstrualis** 'for a whole month.'

484. **de conpecto**: for this meaning of *de*, see on 48. *Conpecto* is also used without *de* in the same sense, e.g. 488, Cic. Scaur. 5, 7, Liv. v. 11. The stem is *pag*, whence *pango* and *paciscor* (for these formations, see R. 632, 634, K. 149). *Compingo* is used of literal fixing together, *compeciscor* metaphorically, of bargains; the former makes *compactus*, the latter *compectus.*

485. **canem inritatam**: perhaps *canem* (fem.) = the mother with puppies, but the feminine is generally used of the species. On *inritatam* cf. Lucr. v. 1063 *inritata canum cum primum magna Molossum mollia ricta fremunt duros nudantia dentes, longe alio sonitu rabie restricta minantur*, on which Munro quotes Donat. ad Ter. And. 597 '*inritatus: ducitur autem uerbum a canibus qui restrictis dentibus hanc litteram* r *imitantur.*'

486. **dentis ut restringerent**: see on 424. The order of the words is *ut, si non adr., saltem r. d.*

487. **postquam uideo**: for the historic present with *quom*, see on 282; it is also found in Pl. with *postquam, ut, ubi, quoniam.* Cf. 24, Cur. 683 *postquam nil fit, posco*, Mil. 124 *postquam occasiost, conqueritur*, Men. 24 *postquam septuennes sunt, pater onerauit*, Ter. Hec. 826 *postquam uideo, coepi*, Pl. Mil. 114 *ut scio, paro*, 178 *ubi abit, conclamo*, Aul. 9 *quoniam moritur..., uoluit.*

ludificarier: see on 613.

489. **Velabro**: another Roman allusion. The Velabrum and the Vicus Tuscus comprised the low-lying district between the Tiber and the Palatine (Liv. XXVII. 37 *in foro pompa constitit...Inde Vico Tusco Velabroque per Forum Boarium in Cliuum Publicium atque Aedem Iunonis Reginae perrectum*). It was originally a swampy lake, cf. Ov. Fast. VI. 405 *qua Velabra solent in Circum ducere pompas, nil praeter salices cassaque canna fuit*, Propert. IV. 9. 5, Tibull. II. 5. 33, but was drained by the building of the Cloaca Maxima and became noted for its provision markets; cf. Cur. 482 *in Velabro uel pistorem uel lanium uel haruspicem*, and Hor. Sat. II. 3. 227.

olearii: the makers and sellers of olive oil, which was used for anointing and for burning as well as in cookery; there seems to have been a 'ring' or combination among the dealers to keep up the price.

490 is clearly an interpolation, made up from 487. Sch. brackets the next line also, as interrupting the narrative.

492. **barbarica lege**: i.e. *Romana lege* (see on 884), referring either to its general principles, or to some special provision, such as the *Lex Iulia de Annona* (which may have been as early as this).

493. **consilium iniere**: cf. Nep. Lysand. 3 *consilium init reges Lacedaemoniorum tollere.* The MSS. have *concilium*, which would require a different verb.

494. **Is**=*eis.* Pl. has *i*, *ei*, *is*, *eis*, not *ii*, *iis* (Brix on Trin. 17).

diem dicam, inrogabo multam: Erg. implies that this is a matter of general importance, a fit subject for a public prosecution, and then he goes on to assume the functions of a high magistrate. A criminal prosecution before the Comitia could only be undertaken by a magistrate who had the right of holding such Comitia; he gave public notice that on a certain day he would summon the Comitia to try the charge (*diem dixit*), and on the day appointed he presided at the meeting and, after stating the charge and after evidence had been heard, brought in a bill (*rogatio*) inflicting certain penalties on the accused; the Comitia Tributa could only impose a fine (*multa*), so that in a prosecution before the Tribes the presiding magistrate would be said *irrogare multam.* This bill was discussed and voted on just like any ordinary piece of legislation.

495. **egero**: *agere* is the technical term for carrying on an action at law. For the tense see on 194.

496. **portum**: Erg. suddenly drops his Roman allusions and returns to the seaport town in Aetolia in which the scene of the play is laid; having tried everyone in the market-place he thinks his only chance is to meet with some new arrival at the harbour.

497. **ad senem**: after a verb of motion *ad me* often='to my house': cf. 126, 458, 505, 831, 855, Ter. Eun. 612 *eamus ad me*, Cic. Fam. III. 8 *neque domum unquam ad me litteras mittam.*

ACT III. SCENE II.

499. **Bono publico**: abl. of attendant circumstances, R. 1240; so Am. 366 *malo tuo*, Liv. II. 1 *pessimo publico.* Hegio means that he has benefited himself by getting someone to exchange for his son, while he has also benefited the state by paying a good price (258).

500. **quisque uident**: a construction κατὰ σύνεσιν, according to the sense, R. 1434, K. App. III., the singular *quisque* implying the plural *omnes;* examples are frequent, e.g. Cur. 180 *sibi quisque habeant quod suomst*, Ep. 212 *filios suos quisque uisunt*, Verg. Aen. VI. 741 *quisque suos patimur manes*, Pl. Trin. 35 *faciunt pars hominum*, Most. 111 *magna pars morem hunc induxerunt*, Am. 1071 *neque nostrum quisquam sensimus*, and often *aperite aliquis, euocate aliquis.* So Men. 779 *loquere, uter meruistis culpam?* 785 *ut cauetis, neuter ad me iretis*, Bac. 755 *uterque adcubitum eatis.* The construction is less harsh in instances like the following, Men. 522 *satin, ut quemque conspicor, ita me ludificant?* Pers. 56 *numquam quisquam maiorum fuit, quin pauerint.*

501. **gratulantur eam rem**: we find in Pl. *gratulor tibi* (Trin. 581), *tibi quom* (Rud. 1270), *tibi hanc rem* (Sti. 567), *quom* (Truc. 516), *hanc rem* (as here), *hoc ita esse* (Sti. 386). Classical writers use a *quod*-clause and sometimes an abl. (with *de*, *in*, *pro*, or alone) of the thing.

502. **retinendo**: most editors omit *-que* of MSS. *metri gratia;* the whole scene is written in a jerky style without conjunctions (cf. on 505) to express Hegio's excitement; for similar asyndeta see on 406 and cf. Poen. 223 *lauando eluendo*, Merc. 192 *armamentis complicandis componendis.*

504. **eminebam**=*ut eminerem*, "instead of a consecutive sentence with *ut*, the consequence is sometimes stated absolutely in the indicative," R. 1699, either as a colloquialism (like the English 'there was such a noise I couldn't hear') or for emphasis; cf. 227, 779, 801, Men. 101 *ita mensas exstruit, standumst in lecto*, Mil. 1047 *ita me occursant multae, meminisse haud possum*, Most. 142 *ita tigna umide haec putent, non uideor mihi sarcire posse aedes meas*, Poen. 499 *ita res diuina mihi fuit, res serias omnes extollo*, Sti. 525 *ita rem uxor curauit meam, me fecit...*, Cic. Brut. 80 *tantum abfuit ut inflammares nostros animos, somnum isto loco uix tenebamus.*

505. **ad praetorem**; *ad* 'to the house of' (cf. *ibi*), see on 497; for *praetorem* cf. 450. Notice asyndeton in 505 sqq., as

generally in terse and vivid narratives of consecutive events; cf. Truc. 407 *haec, ut operast, circuit per familias, puerum uestigat, clanculum ad me detulit, datum sibi esse dixit*, Cur. 329 sqq., Merc. 937 sqq., Mil. 205 sqq., and see on 406.

506. **ilico**: probably from *i*(=*eo*) *loco;* the cases of *is* are from two stems, *i-* and *eo-* (R. 377); from the former come the nominative masc. and neut., the locative *ibi*, an old accusative *im* in the XII Tables, and a dat. and abl. plur. *ibus* in the comic poets and Lucr.; probably *i* was an old abl. from this stem, as *qui* (101) from *quis*. For the change of ŏ (in *loco*) to ĭ cf. *hominis* (*homŏn*), *cardinis* (*cardŏn*), *inquilinus* (*incola*), etc. R. 213.

508. **reuortor domum**: not 'return home' but 'turn back homewards,' according to Brix; for instead of coming straight home, he goes right on (*protinus*) past his own neighbourhood to his brother's, cf. 457.

510. **inde abii**: the objection to these words is obvious and they have been generally omitted; Brix and Sch. read *inde, ubi mei.*

511. **ex Alide**=*Alidensem;* cf. Ter. Eun. 165 *ex Aethiopia ancillulam*, Caes. B. G. v. 27 *Q. Iunius ex Hispania quidam*, Cic. Verr. I. 5 *Herennium, negotiatorem ex Africa.*

ecquis hominum: so Hermann, Sch. for *omnium* of MSS., which does not occur in this or any similar phrase elsewhere in Pl. Cf. 540 and on 828.

513. **Hic...hunc**: see on 593. *Sibi* may have been inserted from *eum sibi* in 512.

515. **quod orauisti**: a relative definition (see on 207 *agitis*); hence the indicative although dependent upon a subjunctive.

uti conuenias: a substantival clause in apposition to *id* understood, which is the antecedent of *quod.*

ACT III. SCENE III.

516. **illud est quom**: Brix quotes Rud. 664 *nunc id est quom* and Ter. Ad. 299 where, however, the MSS. have *nunc illud est quod.* Cf. also Aul. 4 *multos annos est quom*, Ps. 1325 *erit ubi te ulciscar*, and similar phrases; see on 303, 980.

fuisse: i.e. to be dead, R. 1477, K. 399; cf. 243, Ps. 312 *ilico uixit amator ubi supplicat*, Verg. Aen. II. 325 *fuimus Troes, fuit Ilium*, and Cicero's '*fuerunt*' when announcing the execution of Lentulus and the other conspirators to the crowd outside the prison.

517. **spernuntque se**: in a physical sense, cf. Mil. 1232 *ille illas spernit segregat ab se*, Enn. ap. Non. 399 *ius atque aequom se a malis spernit procul.*

518. **Hic illest dies quom**: cf. Enn. Ann. 383 *nunc est ille dies quom gloria maxuma sese nobis ostendat*, and on 516.

519. **exitium exitio**: so Brix, Sch., Tyrrell on Mil. 1432, for *exilium exitio* of MSS. *Exitio* is a verbal noun from *exire*, found also in Truc. 511 *quid illi ex utero exitiost?* When the verbs from which they are formed take an acc., Pl. sometimes uses these verbal nouns in *-tio* with an acc., as Truc. 622 *quid tibi hanc aditiost? Quid tibi hanc notiost, inquam, amicam meam?* Poen. 1308 *quid tibi hanc digito tactiost?* As. 920 *quid tibi hunc receptio ad te est meum uirum?* Now *exire* is so used with an acc. by Pl., Mil. 1432 *postquam portam exierunt*, and Ter., Hec. 378 *ut limen exirem.* Such a pun is quite in Plautus' style.

520 does not scan and is obviously copied from 521.

521. **sycophantiis** = συκοφαντίαις: in Greek the word means 'false accusations' 'slanders,' having been first used of public informers, but in Pl. it is always used of trickery and deception without either the Greek notion of 'slandering' or the modern one of 'flattering.'

mantellum = *integumentum*: such nouns can be followed by either a genitive or a dative, cf. Cic. Cael. 20 *integumentum flagitiorum*, Pl. Trin. 313 *aetati integumentum meae*, Cur. 441 *factis monimentum suis*, etc.

obuiamst = *in promptu est*, cf. Aul. 344 (*a furto*) *te scio facile abstinere posse, si nihil obuiamst.*

522. **perfidiis**: the plural of abstract substantives is not uncommon to express the exhibition of the quality in several instances or several people, cf. Sti. 300 *secundas fortunas decent superbiae*, Most. 340 *summis industriis*, Trin. 490 *deos decent opulentiae*, 1028 *ueteres parsimoniae.* The datives in this line and the next are due to *perfidiae malefacta* etc. being personified, 'my acts of perfidy can't beg themselves off, there is no way of escape open to my evil deeds,' etc.

523. **confidentiae hospitium**: cf. Most. 342 *nusquam stabulumst confidentiae. Hospitium* and *deuorticulum* are synonymous, cf. Mil. 741 *in amici hospitium deuorti potest.*

525—528 are considered spurious by Ussing on metrical grounds (see metr. notes); *negotium de hac re* is scarcely Latin and *meamque* (527) is nonsense. 529 comes better, both in metre and in sense, after 524 than after 528.

526. **oppetam pestem**: i.e. *mortem*, cf. As. 22 *ut pestem oppetas*, Accius in Cic. Tusc. II. 16, 32 *priusque oppeto malam pestem.*

uicem 'instead of,' adverbial acc., of the part concerned, R. 1102, used with a gen. or a possessive pronoun, as Truc. 158 *et nostram et illorum uicem.* The MSS. reading *meamque* has no meaning; Bosscha substitutes *malam* (cf. Accius quoted above), Sch. reads *pestem mortemque eri uicem.*

528. **Philocrati**: dative, not genitive; the classical construction with *sodalis* would be a genitive and *Philocrati* might be a gen. in Pl. (see on 562), but on the other hand a dat. is required with *cognatus* and is always found in Pl. with *sodalis est*, except in (I believe) only one passage, Merc. 995 *sodalis eius es.*

529. **Salus seruare**: apparently a proverbial expression, cf. Most. 343 *nec Salus nobis saluti iam esse, si cupiat, potest*, Ter. Ad. 761 *ipsa si cupiat Salus seruare prorsus non potest*, Cic. Verr. III. 57, 131 *quo ex iudicio te nulla Salus seruare posset.*

copiast 'is there a chance' (of safety).

531. **malum** 'confound it'; Rud. 492 *quo, malum, properas?* Am. 604 *quas, malum, nugas?* Men. 390 *quoi, malum, parasito?* etc. Notice double alliteration here.

532. **Nugas**: sc. *ago*, cf. 628; the words *nugae*, *nugari*, etc. have two distinct meanings, (i) that of 'trifling' 'nonsense,' (ii) that of 'trickery' 'deception' (not in Cic. or later writers). Pl. very seldom uses *nugae* in the second sense or *nugari*, *nugator* in the first.

incipisso: see on 168, and cf. 214, 802.

ACT III. Scene IV.

533. **se proripuisse dicam**: see on 268.

537. **perderent**: in Latin the imperfect of the (jussive) subjunctive is used, as well as the pluperfect, of advice no

longer applicable, where in English we use only the pluperfect, R. 1604, e.g. Poen. 387 *sic enim diceres*, 'you should have said,' Trin. 133 *non ego illum argentum redderem?* ME. *Non redderes*, 'you ought not to have handed over,' Cic. Verr. v. 65 *civem Romanum in crucem egisti: asseruasses hominem, clausum habuisses...aliquid de summo supplicio remitteres.* And similarly, but more rarely, the imperfect is used in wishes, the fulfilment of which is no longer possible, as here and in Rud. 494 *utinam te prius quam oculis uidissem meis, malo cruciatu in Sicilia perbiteres!* CH. *Utinam, quom in aedis me ad te adduxisti tuas, in carcere illo potius cubuissem die!*

periisti 'disappeared,' cf. Poen. 86 *periere eae Magaribus*, 989 *periere Carthagine*, Rud. 1111 *Athenis periit.* There is a play on the two meanings of *perdere* ('lose' 'destroy') and of *perire* ('be lost' 'be destroyed'). Notice the alliteration.

539. **Occisast haec res** 'the game is up,' as in Men. 512, Ps. 423, *res* being used indefinitely, as 284 *salua res est*, 488 *una res*, 778 *certa res est;* similarly in 217, 377, 460, 525 we have *res* (instead of a neuter pronoun) with a substantival clause in apposition to it, and in 264 *quarum rerum* follows *quae.*

atrocem 'outrageous'; so we say 'an atrocious pun' 'awfully hot' 'dreadfully wet,' and the Roman said *insanum magnum* (Bac. 761), *insanum bonum*, etc.

541. **Quid istuc est quod** = *quid*, as *nunc illud est quom* = *nunc* (516).

542. **aspernari** 'turn yourself away from,' as Brix points out, governing the accusative *me. Spernor* = *sperno me* (517), as *cingor* = 'I gird myself,' see on 592; then, *spernor* being compounded with a preposition, the compound gains a transitive force and takes an accusative, as often in Latin (see R. 1121). In just the same way *auersor aliquem* = 'I turn myself away from a person,' and so Verg. G. III. 499 *equus fontes auertitur*, and infra 1026, *id praeuortor.*

544. **a puero** = *a pueritia:* cf. 644, 720, 991 with Ter. Heaut. 183 *iam inde a pueritia fuit semper familiaritas;* see on 757.

546. **qui appelles** 'inasmuch as you call'; for the subj. see R. 1714, K. 454, and cf. 258.

548. **istic** after *hic*, 547; such variations are not uncommon in Pl., cf. 2, where the MSS. have *hos...illi...hi*, 112 *istos ...his*, 733 *istum...huic*, 1014 *illic...hunc*, Mil. 22 *hoc...illic.* Also more naturally, Mil. 131 *illum...is*, 348 *illi...eae*, Most. 1135 *is...illum*, Rud. 810 *illic...istunc.*

auris inmittas: the acc. *auris* is governed by the *in* of *inmittas*, which is repeated in Ep. 335 *id in auris inmitto meas;* cf. 149 *istuc animum induxis*, Tru. 762 *te manum iniciam*, Lucr. I. 117 *pecudes alias diuinitus insinuat se*, Cic. Off. III. 16 *arbitrum illum adegit*, R. 1118, etc. The subjunctive *inmittas* may be final, of the kind noticed on 290, but more probably is jussive; see on 434.

550. **qui insputatur morbus**: i.e. the epilepsy, *comitialis morbus* (so called, according to Festus, because its occurrence was ominous and stopped the *comitia*). Theophrastus says of the superstitious man (Char. 16) μαινόμενόν τε ἰδὼν ἢ ἐπίληπτον εἰς κόλπον πτύσαι. So Plin. 28. 4. 7 *despuimus comitialem morbum, hoc est, contagia regerimus.* But here the sufferer was to be spat upon, which was supposed to have a remedial effect; e.g. Pliny, ubi sup., *terna despuere deprecatione in omni medicina mos est atque ita effectus adiuuare*; also to avert the evil eye, Persius II. 32 *frontemque atque uda labella infami digito et lustralibus ante saliuis expiat urentes oculos inhibere perita*; and the practice of spitting 'for luck' upon money still prevails among the lowest class.

551. **ab istoc**: J has *abstoc*, probably by accident, but even Cic. and Verg. sometimes wrote *stic*, *stuc*, etc., see Lachm. Lucr. p. 197.

Vltro istum: *ultro=apage*, which takes an acc., as if it were an imperative; Cas. 459 *ultro te, amator, apage te*, Trin. 537 *apage a me istum agrum*, and so *en* and *ecce* in *eccum*, *ellum*, etc.

553. **utqui**: see on 243.

554. **Ne uerere**: in 58, 349 and generally in Pl., this means 'don't be afraid,' here it apparently means 'don't be ashamed' (of having the disease), as in Bac. 158 *hic uereri perdidit*, Mil. 1285. Notice the alliteration.

555. **Quibus**, with *fuit*; *saluti*, predicative dative, 'a cause of safety,' cf. 259.

is (*=eis*, see on 494): for this substitution of a demonstrative for a relative pronoun in the second of two relative clauses, cf. Lucr. II. 87 *durissima quae sint neque quicquam a tergo ibus obstet*, Cic. Or. 9 *quam intuens in eaque defixus* (cf. R. 1432). It is common in Greek, e.g. ἐκεῖνοι τοίνυν, οἷς οὐκ ἐχαρίζονθ' οἱ λέγοντες οὐδ' ἐφίλουν αὐτούς (Dem.). For the pleonasm *saluti fuit atque profuit*, cf. As. 636 *quid pollent quidue possunt*, Mil. 452 *nec noui neque scio*, 1348 *metuoque et timeo*, Poen. 1326 *gaudeo et uolup est mihi.*

556. **etiam**: often in incredulous questions, 'do you mean to say that?' As. 677 *etiam me delusisti?* Merc. 202 *etiam rogas?* 'are you serious in asking?' 763 *etiam negas?* 'do you mean to deny?' So *at etiam* in 563.

credam: for the subjunctive see on 139.

557. **intuitur**: so Böthe for *intuetur* of MSS., to improve the rhythm of the line. Both conjugations are found in Pl., the second in Rud. 449, Most. 825, etc., the third in Most. 821 (A), 823, etc. For the ind. in a dependent question, see on 207.

concedi=*concedere*, but Pl. prefers the passive, even when the verb is intransitive and so must be impersonal in the passive; cf. Mil. 737 *istis rebus desisti decet*, Most. 941 *triduom unum est haud intermissum hic esse et bibi, scorta duci, pergraecari, fidicinas tibicinas ducere.*

560. **Quin** 'why,' in emphatic statements; this use is derived from that noticed on 592, *quin fugis?* See R. 1617, and cf. 589, 643, 975, 990, 1017, Most. 445 *cur non tangerem* (*has aedes*)? *Quin pultando, inquam, paene confregi fores*, Trin. 932 *lubet audire, nisi molestumst.* SY. *Quin discupio dicere.*

561. **Haud uidi magis**=*haud uidi, magis qui sodalis sit*, always ironically, Am. 679 *expectatun aduenio?* S. *Haud uidi magis*, Merc. 723 *Haeres.* LY. *Haud u. m.*, Poen. 141 *ignoscere id te mihi aequomst.* M. *Haud u. m.*

562. **Et quidem** 'aye, and,' cf. 307.

Alcumeus, etc.: he names three of the most celebrated madmen in Greek story. *Alcumeus*=Ἀλκμέων, the Attic form of Ἀλκμαίων; for the insertion of *u* see on 974. Similar changes of declension are seen in the genitives *Electri* (Am. 99) *Titani* (Pers. 26), and the acc. *Adoneum* (Men. 144); sometimes a name has the Greek nom. but inflexions are found belonging to a different Latin declension: thus *Harpage* (Ps. 665) is voc. of *Harpax*, *Tranium* (Most. 549) acc. of *Tranio*, and *Achilli* (Bac. 938), *Euripidi* (Rud. 86), *Charmidi* (Trin. 744, A) are genitives.

563. **Vna opera** 'just as much' 'just as well,' see on 344. Sometimes the correlative sentence is understood, as in Most. 253 *una opera ebur atramento candefacere postules*, sometimes it is expressed, as here and (more fully) in Ps. 319 *qua opera credam tibi, una opera...*

furcifer: the *furca* in question was a sort of hod or frame for carrying burdens, having two handles which came over the shoulders, so that the burden was at the back of the neck.

Slaves were sometimes punished by having the *furca* tied on them, their hands being fastened to the handles.

565 is considered spurious by Fl.; *non nouisse* comes in awkwardly and may have been a gloss to clear up the ambiguity of *id;* the rest of the line is repeated from 546.

566. A good example of chiasmus; cf. 567 and on 151.

568. **enim**: with ellipse, '(of course,) for'; according to Langen (Beitr. p. 261—271) *enim* in Pl. is always corroborative, never causal (see on 464). Here the corroboration is ironical. *Enim* is also used simply as an affirmative particle, without any reference to what has gone before; see on 592.

repertu's qui superes: *esse* must be supplied, 'you have been found to be a person who can surpass'; cf. 610, 625, Bac. 541 *reperiuntur falsi*, etc.; so with *inuentu's* in the next line and Ps. 631 *tu inuentu's uero meam qui furcilles fidem.*

ueriuerbio: coined on the analogy of *priuilegium*, *aequinoctium*, etc.

569. **uanitudine** 'lying'; so *uanidicus*, *uaniloquos*, etc.; *uanus* often=*mendax*.

570. **conuincas uera**: cf. Lucr. IV. 764 *falsum ueris conuincere rebus.*

aspice ad and *aspice contra* are ante-classical: Pacuv. ap. Gell. I. 24 *adulescens, tametsi properas, hoc te saxum rogat ut ad se aspicias*, Most. 1086 *aspice dum contra me.*

572. *aut mihi* seems meaningless and may have been an alternative suggestion in the margin for *tibi*. Langen (Beitr. p. 220) omits the words, inserting *aio* to fill up; so Brix, Uss. It might easily have fallen out after *ais*, but the line could be scanned without it, as *ăis* is sometimes found; and in Am. 725 we have *tu me heri hic uidisti?* AL. *Ego, inquam.*

573. **Alidem**: so in 330 *Alide*, for Elis was the name of the town as well as the country, cf. Cic. Fam. XIII. 26.

574. **Quem patrem**: in these short questions the case in which the word was used originally is adopted; cf. 450, Ep. 571 *ut matrem tuam uideas.* FI. *Quam meam matrem?* Ter. Eun. 823 *iste Chaerea.* TH. *Qui Chaerea?*

qui seruos est: *qui*=*nam is*, R. 1026 (b). The union of slaves (*contubernium*) was not in Roman law considered a legal marriage; the children were therefore *nullius patris*, i.e.

were considered to have no known father. This followed from the ancient idea of *patria potestas;* as much obedience was due from the son as from the slave (see on 20), and thus if the slave were considered to have a father as well as a master, he would be subject to two possibly conflicting dominions at the same time.

575. **Seruos es, liber fuisti**: asyndeton, to express contrast; cf. 615, 989, Cur. 219 *ualetudo decrescit, adcrescit labor*, Truc. 50 *ipsus gaudet, res perit.* See on 406.

fore: sc. *liberum.* Tynd. pretends not to see the force of A.'s remark, and quibbles.

576. **reconciliasso**; for the form see on 124, for the meaning on 33.

577. **gnatum**: with emphasis, for A. sees through the quibble and asks if Tynd. was *born* free. Tynd. then tries to pass it off with a joke, 'he never said his name was Liber.'

579. **te ludos facit**: Ramsay, Most. Exc. 16, distinguishes between *ludos facio hunc* and *ludos facio huic. Ludi* are 'Public Games' and *facere ludos* is to exhibit such games. So *hunc ludos* (never *ludum*) *facio*='I make an exhibition of this man,' i.e. make a fool of him, as in Ps. 1167 *exploratorem hunc faciamus ludos suppositicium adeo donicum ipsus sese ludos fieri senserit,* and often. On the other hand *ludos facio alicui* is properly 'I exhibit public games in honour of one deceased,' and so ironically, in honour of one who, though not dead, is just as helpless in my hands as if he were; cf. Most. 418 *ludos ego hodie uiuo praesenti hic seni faciam, quod credo mortuo numquam fore*, Truc. 759 *ego tibi, inlecebra, ludos faciam clamore in uia*, 'will make an exhibition in honour of you by creating a disturbance in front of your house.'

580. **se** is used because Tynd. is logically, although not grammatically, the subject of the sentence, *erat ei=is habebat* (R. 2265); Brix quotes Cist. 102 *ei nunc alia ducendast domum, sua cognata*, Rud. 49 *ei erat hospes par sui.*

581. **qui**: see on 101. Tynd. again pretends to misunderstand; as if A. had accused him of being too poor at home in Elis to keep a slave.

582. **similis tibi**: Ritschl (Opusc. II. 570, 579) says that *similis* and its compounds always in early Latin take a gen. (as in 116), never a dative; but a few examples occur in the MSS. of Pl., viz. Men. 1089 *neque lacte est lacti, crede mihi, usquam*

similius quam hic tui est tuque huius autem, Am. 601 *neque lac lacti magis est simile quam ille ego similest mei*, Truc. 505 *ecquid mihi similist*, and in Ter., Eun. 468 *nostris similia*, Heaut. 381 *isti formae ut mores consimiles forent*. In later writers the dat. is of course common, R. 1142.

583. **Est miserorum** 'it is characteristic of' etc.; so Cic. Ph. XII. 2 *cuiusuis hominis est errare; nullius, nisi insipientis, in errore perseuerare* (R. 1282). In classical Latin an infinitive follows, here we have *ut inuideant;* Brix quotes As. 190 *non meumst...ut mittam*, Pers. 47 *hoc meumst ut faciam sedulo* (*est meum*, etc., is always used, not *est mei*). For the sentiment cf. Sall. Cat. 37 *semper in ciuitate, quibus opes nullae sunt, inuident bonis*, where *boni* (as in the text and often)='the well-to-do classes'; Cic. Att. VIII. 1 *bonorum, id est lautorum et locupletium.*

584. **sis**=*si uis*, 110.

585. **aliquid pugnae edidit**: *pugnare* is a slang expression in the comic writers for 'to trick,' as in Ep. 492 *frugi es, pugnasti; homo es, qui me emunxisti.* And *pugnam dare* is an equivalent phrase, Ps. 525 *priusquam istam pugnam pugnabo, ego etiam prius dabo aliam pugnam*, Bac. 273, etc. *Pugnas edere* is found in Cic. Att. I. 16.

586. **quod ait** 'his saying' 'the fact that he says,' R. 1701. *Id* of course refers to *quod ait*, but Tynd. purposely takes it as referring to *se redimere tuom filium.*

ne utiquam: *ne* was the original negative, of which traces exist in composition (*neque nescio nullus neuter necopinatus*, etc.) and in its use with *quidem;* in the old language it was used to negative a single word, e.g. in the SC de Bacc. *haice utei in couentinoid exdeicatis ne minus trium noundinum.*

589. **amisi**: see on 36. Tynd. wants to let A. know the truth without arousing Hegio's suspicions.

592. **Enim**: asseverative, simply strengthening the assertion, an use confined to *enimuero* in later writers; only the comic writers place it first in the sentence: cf. Ep. 700 *ni matris filiast...pignus da.* PE. *Enim istaec captiost*, Pers. 236 *quid id ad te adtinet?* PA. *Enim non ibis nunc*, 317 *sine ire pastum.* SA. *Enim metuo ut possim reicere in bubile*, Mil. 429 *quid metuis?* SC. *Enim ne nos nosmet perdiderimus uspiam.* Cf. 884 *quia enim.* In the text the MSS. have *enimuero*, which makes the line too long and was probably due to later copyists not understanding this use of *enim*. Sch. reads *enim uero hau queo.*

contineri=*continere me*, cf. Rud. 1172 *contineri quin complectar non queo*, Ter. Eun. 859 *vix me contineo quin inuolem.* For this reflexive use of the passive see R. 1417 and cf. Mil. 1368 *uix reprimor quin te manere iubeam*, Trin. 641 *retineri nequeo quin dicam.*

ait: indicative in dependent question, see on 207.

quin fugis 'why don't you run away?' *Quin=qui ne*, 'why not?' R. 1613; cf. 636, Merc. 190 *quin, sceleste, abstrudebas ne eam conspiceret pater?* Trin. 291 *quin prius me ad pluris penetraui?* 118 *quin eum restituis? quin ad frugem corrigis?* Men. 638 *quid id est? quid taces? quin dicis quid sit?* This interrogative use with the second person is equivalent to a command, hence the use of *quin* (i) with the imperative, as Most. 168 *quin me aspice et contempla*, (ii) with the indicative in startling statements (see on 560).

593. **illic...illunc**: similar repetitions in 451, 513, 638, 737 and often.

insectabit: usually deponent, but the active is also found in Cic. Div. II. 70. Pl. uses active forms of the following verbs which are deponents in later writers: *arbitro, aucupo, auspico* (766), *contemplo, crimino, cuncto, fabulo, fluctuo, frustro, indipisco, ludifico* (on 613), *minito* (743), *moro, munero* (935), *opino, pacisco, perscruto, sciscito, sortio, tumultuo, uago, uenero;* and the following deponents in passive sense, *philosophari obsequi suspicari uadari*, besides many others which are so used by later writers also. See Brix on Mil. 172, R. 734. The passive use of deponent perfect participles is fairly common.

595. **maculari**: a sign of madness, cf. Men. 829 *ut uiridis exoritur colos ex temporibus atque fronte, ut oculi scintillant, uide.* ME. *Hei mihi, insanire me aiunt.* Uss. quotes also Verg. Aen. IV. 643 *effera Dido, sanguineam uoluens aciem, maculisque trementes interfusa genas.* Notice repetition in this line.

596. **Atra bilis**=μελαγχολία, a diseased state of the bile which the ancients considered the cause of madness. Cf. Am. 727 *delirat uxor.* SO. *Atra bili percitast; nulla res tam delirantis homines concinnat cito*, Cic. Tusc. III. 5, 11 *quem nos furorem μελαγχολίαν illi uocant*, Sen. Ep. 94. 17 *bilis nigra curanda est et ipsa furoris causa remouenda.* For the connection between madness and epilepsy cf. Hippocr. Epidem. VI. 8. 95 οἱ μελαγχολικοὶ καὶ ἐπιληπτικοὶ εἰώθασι γένεσθαι (Uss.).

597. **Atra pix**: Lucr. III. 1017, mentions this among other tortures, *uerbera carnifices robur pix lammina taedae.*

598. **deliramenta**: the metaphor is from ploughing (*lira* = 'a furrow').

laruae: ghosts of those who had done evil in their lives, condemned to wander upon earth and supposed to torment and frighten mankind. Cf. Am. 777 *haec quidem edepol laruarum plena est*, Aul. 642 *laruae hunc atque intemperiae insaniaeque agitant senem*, Men. 890 *num laruatus aut cerritust?*

599. **quid si iusserim**: the verb of the apodosis is omitted, perhaps not distinctly conceived; *quid si* is found with both subjunctive and indicative, R. 1578, 1579. Cf. 613, Curc. 351 *quid si abeamus, decumbamus?* Cas. 345 *quid si sors aliter euenerit?* Men. 844 *quid si cito?* Most. 571 *quid si hic manebo?* Rud. 721 *quid si attigero?*

magis sapias: for this elliptical use, cf. Bac. 408 *leniter qui saeuiunt, sapiunt magis*, Mil. 1422 *dabitur*. CA. *Magis sapis.*

600. **Crucior** = *aegre fero*, hence it is constructed (κατὰ σύνεσιν) with an acc., as Mil. 1321 *istuc crucior*, Trin. 1170 *id crucior*, or, as here, with an infinitive clause, as in Bac. 435 *haec nunc meo sodali dici discrucior*, Ter. Heaut. 673 *crucior bolum mihi tantum ereptum.*

mastigiae: μαστιγίας = *uerbero* (551).

601. **concinnat**: a colloquialism for *reddit*, cf. Am. 727 (quoted on 596), 529 *lacrumantem concinnas uxorem*, Trin. 684 *se concinnat leuem*, Sti. 286 *tranquillam concinna uiam.*

602. **te uolo**: sc. *conloqui*, which is sometimes expressed, e.g. Am. 898 *te uolo, uxor, conloqui.*

603. **tamen**: see on 187.

604. **namque**: with ellipse, 'you are right, for'; see on 464.

os denasabit: one of Pl.'s coinages, not found elsewhere; similar phrases are Am. 318 *exossatum os esse oportet*, Rud. 662 *uelim improbissumo homini malas edentauerint*, 731 *ni ei caput exoculassitis.*

605. **creduis**: see on 331.

609. **te faciam ut reperiare**: see on 376.

610. **False** 'counterfeit': so Verg. Aen. III. 302 *falsi Simoentis ad undam.*

611. **mi abnutas** 'shake your head at me,' to make him be silent; cf. Men. 612 M. *Non taces?* P. *Non hercle uero taceo;* (to M.'s wife) *nutat ne loquar.*

612. **Quid agat,** etc.: i.e. if he is making signs to me in your presence to hold my tongue, you can judge why he wants you to go away. Lessing first gave these words to A.

613. **Quid ais** 'look here' 'I say,' as in Am. 364, 418, 620, 848 and generally (but in literal meaning Curc. 190, Men. 602); so *quid ais tu* generally = 'look here, you,' e.g. Bac. 1155 *quid ais tu, homo?* NI. *Quid me uis?* (but sometimes, as in Aul. 717, Bac. 600, it = *quid tu ais*, see on 289).

ludificabitur: deponent here, but frequently passive, as in 487; Pl. also uses the active form, e.g. in Am. 1041, Cist. 215.

614. **neque pes neque caput** 'neither head nor tail'; cf. As. 729 *neque caput nec pes sermoni adparet*, Cic. Fam. VII. 31 *res ita contractas ut, quemadmodum scribis, nec caput nec pedes.*

615. **Ornamenta** 'theatrical costume'; cf. Cist. fin. *ubi id erit factum ornamenta ponent (histriones)*, Curc. 464 (Choragus loq.) *ornamenta quae locaui metui ut possim recipere*, Pers. 160 *πόθεν ornamenta?* T. *Abs chorago sumito*, Trin. 858 *ipse ornamenta a chorago haec sumpsit suo periculo.*

Aiacem: son of Telamon. The story of the *Armorum Iudicium* (the contest for the arms of Achilles), and the defeat and consequent madness of Ajax, formed the subject of tragedies by Aeschylus, Sophocles, Astydamas, Theodectes, Livius Andronicus, Ennius, Pacuvius and Accius. Notice the adversative asyndeton (see on 575).

617. **inter sacrum saxumque** 'between the altar and the flint-knife,' the position of a victim about to be sacrificed; the phrase occurs also in Cas. 970 *nunc ego inter sacrum saxumque sum*, Appul. Met. XI. 28 *quod ait uetus prouerbium, inter sacrum et saxum positus cruciabar.* (Uss.) For *sacrum* in the sense of altar, cf. Curc. 471 *Cloacinae sacrum;* for the stone sacrificial knife (a survival from a very early age), cf. Liv. I. 24 *porcum saxo silice percussit.*

619. **audibis**: for this old form of the future see on 265.

620. **me expurigare**: *me* is the object of the verb, cf. Aul. 791 *pudeat quin purget sese*, Mil. 497 *expurigare uolo me.* P. *Tun te expuriges?* Am. 909, Cas. 944, etc. For the old form *expurigare* see Int. § 108.

me insaniam tenere: *me* is the object of *tenere*, cf. Men. 891 *num eum ueternus aut aqua intercus tenet?*

622. **faxit**: see on 124; here it may be either indicative or subjunctive, see on 877.

623. **Eho**: used either in commands (with imperatives, as here and Ps. 348, or jussive subjunctives, as in Bac. 445), or in surprised questions with *an*, as Trin. 934 *eho, an etiam Arabiast in Ponto?* 986 *eho, quaeso, an tu is es?*

625. **secus reperies**: sc. *esse*, see on 568; for *esse secus*, see on 120.

causam dico quin: cf. passages quoted on 353.

626. **deliquio** = *deliquium;* it does not occur elsewhere. Pl. also has *excidionem* (Cur. 534) for *excidium;* cf. *obliuio obliuium, obsidio obsidium, contagio contagium.*

627. **Quid tu ais**, 'what do *you* say,' as in 990, Men. 823, etc. In Men. 648 *tu quid ais* in same sense; see on 289.

629. **Qui**: see on 101.

631. **maior**: strictly means more than 25 years old. Notice the repetition in this line and the last.

632. **num**: properly 'now' (*nunc* = *num-ce*), used as in English with questions expecting the answer 'no'; thus it came to be the regular particle for introducing such questions.

635. **Peroe probe** 'I am jolly well done for'; see on 269.

636. **Quin quiescis**: to his beating heart. For *quin* see on 592.

dierectum: the other passages in which the word occurs are given in Int. § 153; all editors insert *i* here, as in the MSS. reading there is no imperative to precede *ac suspende te* and no verb of motion to go with *dierectum.* According to the general view the word is derived from *di* (*dis*), *erectus*, i.e. 'crucified,' cf. Mil. 360 *dispessis manibus patibulum quom habebis;* others consider that it represents διάρρηκτος, an adjective formed (but not found) from διαρρήγνυμι, so that *i dierectus* = διαρραγείης—which may be the sense but is certainly not the derivation. Nettleship thinks the word a *vox nihili* due to confusion between *directum* 'crucified' and *derectum* 'straight.'

suspende te: cf. Cas. 424 (quoted on 344), Poen. 794 (quoted on 180), etc.

637. **subsultas**: notice the frequentative; *sub*='up from under,' as in *sur(ri)go*, *sufferre*, *sustollere*; for the phrase, cf. Cas. 414 *cor lienosum, opinor, habeo; iamdudum salit.* So Aesch. Cho. 161 ὀρχεῖται δὲ καρδία φόβῳ, Anaxandrides in Ath. xv. 688 b ὦ πονηρὰ καρδία, ἐπιχαιρέκακον ὡς εἶ μόνον τοῦ σώματος· ὀρχεῖ γὰρ εὐθὺς ἢν ἴδῃς δεδοικότα.

adsto 'stand up,' as in *assurgo, ascendo, attollo;* cf. Men. 395 *haec mulier cantharino ritu adstans somniat*, Verg. G. III. 545 *adtoniti squamis adstantibus hydri.*

638. **hunc...hunc**: see on 593.

639. **Tam satis quam...inuenies** seems a mixture of two constructions, (i) comparative, *tam satis quam quod maxime* and (ii) consecutive, *tam satis ut non inuenias.*

640. **deruncinatus**: introduced from Mil. 1142, *lepide deruncinauit militem*, instead of *aerumnatus* of MSS. which is not Latin. The metaphor is from carpentry, the victim of the cheat being compared to a log which the workman shapes with plane or adze (*deasciari*, Mil. 884). For similar metaphors, cf. Mil. 1174 *meum opus ita dabo expolitum ut...*, 938 *hunc dolum dolamus.*

deartuatus: another metaphor for cheating, the swindler being compared to a butcher cutting up a carcase, cf. Ep. 488 *istic homo articulatim te concidit.* For the asyndeton, see on 406.

641. **techinis**=τέχναις, 'wiles'; for the insertion of *i* see on 974.

642. **prouisum**: so Cic. Verr. III. 6 *ratio explorata atque prouisa.*

643. **magis certius**: double comparative, a colloquialism not uncommon in Pl. e.g. Aul. 422 *sum mollior magis quam ullus*, Bac. 500 *inimiciorem magis*, Merc. 898 *nequest quoi magis me uelle aequom melius siet*, Poen. 460 *dei deaeque ceteri contentiores mage erunt atque auidi minus;* cf. on 323. So Shakspere has 'for the more better assurance,' 'the most unkindest cut of all,' even 'less happier lands.'

645 comes after 639 in the MSS.; inserted here by Schoell, as *Tum igitur* (640) must be the beginning of an answer. It might have been accidentally omitted here (646 also begins with *Sed*), then written at the top or bottom of the page with a mark in the margin (subsequently omitted) to shew where it belonged.

647. **corpore** 'complexion,' as in Truc. 292 *erubuisti? quasi uero corpori reliqueris tuo potestatem coloris ulli capiendi.* The ablatives are descriptive, R. 1232, K. 234. The MSS. have *et oculis*, which will not scan; moreover in these terse and graphic personal descriptions Pl. does not use conjunctions; cf. Ballas, Gr. Plaut., who quotes As. 400 *macilentis malis, rufulus aliquantum, uentriosus, truculentis oculis, commoda statura, tristi fronte*, Merc. 639 *canum, uarum, uentriosum, bucculentum, breuiculum, subnigris oculis, oblongis malis, pansam aliquantulum*, Ps. 1219 *rufus quidam, uentriosus, crassis suris, subniger, magno capite, acutis oculis, ore rubicundo, admodum magnis pedibus.* Cf. on 406.

648. **Subrufus** 'reddish'; the meaning of *sub-* (R. 986) is emphasized by *aliquantum*, cf. Ter. And. 447 *subtristis uisus est esse aliquantum mihi.*

crispus refers to short natural curls about the head, *cincinnatus* to long ringlets (κίκιννοι) hanging down the back; the latter was not a Roman fashion.

Conuenit 'it tallies,' i.e. the description fits Phil.; but Tynd. takes it as meaning 'it is generally agreed' (cf. Liv. IX. 19 *conuenit iam inde per consules reliqua belli perfecta*), and then fills up the sentence with *ut quidem processerim.* Cf. Aul. 154 *in rem hoc* (marriage) *tuamst.* M. *ut quidem emoriar prius*, Cas. 300 *mihi obtinget sors.* S. *ut quidem pol pereas*, 390 *deos quaeso...mihi ut sortitio eueniat.* C. *ut quidem hercle pedibus pendeas*, Trin. 429 *factum.* S. *ut quidem illud perierit.*

649. **in medium processerim**: lit. 'came forth in public,' i.e. 'began my day's work'; for *in medium*, cf. Ter. Ad. 479 *mater uirginis in mediost*, Cic. Fam. XV. 2 *se tamen eam rem numquam in medium protulisse;* for *procedere*, cf. Men. 964 *nimis prouentumst nequiter*, Sti. 398 *prouenisti futile*, Cas. 564 *ad forum procedere.*

pessume: i.e. *pessumo auspicio;* the ancient Roman was always on the watch for omens, even when performing the ordinary actions of everyday life, e.g. when leaving home in the morning for the Forum; Brix quotes Sti. 459 *auspicio hercle hodie ego optumo exiui foras*, Ep. 183 *liquido exeo auspicio foras, aui sinistra*, Ter. Ad. 979 *processisti hodie pulcre*, 'you left home with a good omen.'

650. **Vae uirgis**: he pretends to pity, not his own back, but the rods that will be broken over it. In Am. 1029 *ulmorum Acheruns* = one upon whose back elm rods are destroyed.

651. **Verba mihi data**: one of the commonest of the numerous phrases for 'deception' which occur in Pl.; so in Cic. Fam. xv. 16 A *uel uerba mihi dari facile patior in hoc meque libenter praebeo credulum*, and Hor. S. I. 3. 22 *dare nobis uerba putas?*

652. **ut uos custodiam**: a comic inversion of their respective positions, cf. As. 297 *quid agis, custos carceris?*

653. **Satine** (=*satisne*) is often used colloquially instead of an interrogative particle; e.g. Cas. 598 *satin propter te pereo ego?* Mil. 393 *satin eadem uigilanti expetunt?* Most. 73 *satin abiit?* Poen. 919 *satine, prius quam unumst iniectum telum, iam instat alterum?*

capti ceperunt: for the antithesis, cf. Hor. Ep. II. 1. 156 *Graecia capta ferum uictorem cepit.* *Capti*=*captiui*, and *ceperunt*=*deceperunt* as in 256, Verg. Aen. II. 196 *captique dolis*, Cic. Acad. II. 20 *cauere ne capiatur, ne fallatur uidere*, Off. III. 17 *captus fraudatusue sim.*

655. **Nuculeum**: dimin. of *nux*, cf. *aculeus hinnuleus* etc. The contracted form, *nucleus*, is classical (Int. § 108).

retinui: so Donatus on Ter. Ad. 796. Nonius (317, 29) and the MSS. have *reliqui.*

putamina, lit. 'offscourings,' Non. (l.c.) *putamina non solum arborum sunt uerum omnium rerum purgamenta. Puto* originally meant to cleanse, esp. trees by pruning, from the root *pu*, whence *punio*, *po(u)ena*, *purus*.

656. **sursum uorsum** or *-sus* is elsewhere used as an adverb, = 'upwards,' cf. Cato R. R. 33. 1 *uineam sursum uorsum semper ducite*, but it makes better sense here to take *uorsum* as a participle agreeing with *os*, 'upturned face.' The phrase is tautologous, for *sursum* is a contraction of *subuersum*.

os subleuere: the reference is to the practical joke of painting a man's face while he is asleep, Non. 45 *subleuit significat inlusit et pro ridiculo habuit, tractum a genere ludi quo dormientibus ora pinguntur.* Cf. Verg. Ecl. VI. 22 *frontem moris et tempora pingunt; ille dolum ridens...*, and inf. 783. Notice the alliteration in this line.

657. **Colaphe, Cordalio, Corax**: from κόλαφος 'a slap,' κορδύλη 'a club,' and κόραξ 'a door-knocker.'

658. **Ite istinc**: the MSS. have *ite istinc atque* which does not scan; moreover *i*, *ite*, are used ἀσυνδέτως with a following

imperative, cf. 184, 950, Men. 435 *ei* (=*i*), *quantum potest abduc istos*, Mil. 812 *ei, face*, Poen. 1319 *ite istinc serui, foras ecferte fustis.* So generally in the case of imperatives which are similar in meaning, e.g. 359, Bac. 693 *conpara fabricare finge*, Men. 352 *para cura uide*, Poen. 357 *exora blandire palpa*, Trin. 289 *rape trahe fuge late.* Cf. on 406.

lora: for binding Tynd., cf. Ep. 683 *uincire uis? em, ostendo manus; tu habes lora*; Colaphus however pretends to think they are to be used for binding faggots, perhaps with a sly allusion to the rods which await Tynd., 'are we to go for sticks?'; cf. Aul. 411 *fustibus male contuderunt, neque ligna ego usquam gentium praeberi uidi pulcrius.*

ACT III. SCENE V.

660. **quid deliqui?** so Am. 816 *quid deliqueris?* Bac. 418 *nequid delinquat*; the acc. expresses the extent of the action denoted by the verb, R. 1094.

661. **sartor**: from *sario* (*sarrio*) which properly makes *sarrītor*; Non. 7 *sartores dicti non solum a sarciendo uerum etiam a sariendo* (MSS. *serendo*).

662. **audebas**=*uolebas*; see on 238.

663. **occant** 'break up the clods with a harrow' before sowing; Merc. 71 *tibi aras, tibi occas, tibi seris, tibi item metes.*

664—666 have most probably been taken from Ps. 459 *bene confidenterque astitisse intellego.* PS. *Decet innocentem, qui sit, atque innoxium seruom superbum esse apud erum potissimum.* Ussing, however, refers to other parallelisms, e.g. As. 186 and Truc. 416, 932, Merc. 225 and Rud. 593.

664. **At ut**: cf. Aul. 52 *at ut scelesta sola secum murmurat!*

contra: with *adstitit*, constructed with a dat. like *contradicere*, *contraponere*; cf. Curc. 163 *sisto ego tibi me et mihi contra itidem ut sistas suadeo*, Am. 339 *certumst confidenter hominem contra conloqui.*

666. **Confidentem**: cf. Am. 836 *quae non deliquit, decet audacem esse, confidenter pro se et proterue loqui.*

669. **quam...rem**, after *quid*; see on 264.

670. **quod**=*quoad*, 'as far as,' cf. 173, Aul. 260 *pactum non pactumst, non pactum pactumst, quod uobis lubet*, Mil. 1160 *impetrabis, quod ego potero, quod uoles*, Ter. Ad. 511 *istam, quod potes, fac consolere*. Pl. sometimes has *quoad*, e.g. As. 296, Men. 769, Ps. 624.

680. **id suscenses mihi**: for the acc., cf. Most. 1143 *neque illi sum iratus neque quicquam suscenseo*, Pers. 430 *id tibi suscensui, quia negabas*. The word is generally derived from *succensus* 'incensed' (*succendere* 'to light up'); others consider it a compound of *sub* and *censeo* 'to take secret counsel against' and so 'to bear ill-will to,' which seems to be putting the cart before the horse. For the spelling *susc-* (almost invariable in the best MSS.) cf. *susque deque, suscitare, suscipere* (sometimes *succipere* according to Serv. ad Aen. I. 148); it arose from the dropping of the *b* in *subs*, while in *succendere*, etc., the *s* is dropped and the *b* assimilated.

681. **cum**: of accompanying circumstances, cf. 802, Bac. 503 *ne illa illud hercle cum malo fecit suo*, Ter. And. 131 *ad flammam accessit satis cum periclo*, Cic. Rosc. Am. 4, 9 *ut attente bonaque cum uenia audiatis*. Often the simple ablative is found, e.g. Am. 366 *ne tu istic hodie malo tuo aduenisti*, Ter. Ph. 377 *abs te hoc bona uenia peto*.

683. **ast**: this old particle occurs in Merc. 246 and is found in later poets and in Cicero's letters; logically the clause *ast ille non redit* should come first. Brix reads *si* for *ast*, making the clause depend on the previous *si*-clause, as in 260.

684. **At** is often found in the apodosis of a conditional sentence, R. 2212; cf. Verg. Aen. I. 543 *si genus humanum et mortalia temnitis arma, at sperate deos*.

687. **potius praeoptauisse**: pleonasm, see on 323.

caput 'life,' the head being regarded as the seat of life; so we speak of 'capital' offences, trials, punishments, etc., meaning those which affect the life of the offender; cf. Trin. 962 *si capitis res sit*, Ter. And. 677 *capitis periculum adire*. Cf. on 229.

periculo ponere: *ponere* is apparently for *exponere*, of which I know no other instance; the phrase is similar to *offerre uilitati* (230). *Periculo* cannot be a predicative dative, like *pigneri ponere*, for then the phrase would mean 'to place as a source of danger.' *Pono*=*posno* (cf. on 360)=*possino* (cf. *sur(ri)go, per(ri)go, pur(i)go*, etc.)=*porsino* (cf. *por-tendere, pos-sidere*=*por-sedere*, etc.). *Sino* is probably another form of *sero* 'to put'; *sero* came to mean 'to put in order,' *sino* 'to put down,' 'leave alone,' 'let.'

689. **Acherunti**: locative, see on 998.

clueas: properly 'to hear' (κλύω), so 'to hear oneself spoken of as,' 'to be considered' (in good sense), and so absol. 'to be esteemed,' 'renowned'; cf. Am. 647 *ut meus uictor uir belli clueat*, Trin. 309 *uictor uictorum cluet*, once in passive, Ps. 918 *ego, stratioticus homo qui cluear.* So *audio* (*bene* or *male*) = 'to be spoken of,' cf. Ter. Ph. 20 *benedictis si certasset, audisset bene*, and the pun in Cic. Tusc. v. 40 *erat surdaster M. Crassus; sed aliud molestius, quod male audiebat.* κλύω and ἀκούω are used in the same sense, e.g. Soph. Tr. 721 ζῆν γὰρ κακῶς κλύουσαν οὐκ ἀνασχετόν, Hdt. II. 173 καὶ οὕτω ἄμεινον σὺ ἂν ἤκουες· νῦν δὲ ποιέεις οὐδαμῶς βασιλικά.

690. **per** 'by reason of,' a rare meaning; cf. Aul. 131 *per metum mussari.*

perit: this is Goetz' emendation to complete the sense and the metre, but it is open to the objection that it involves an anapaest after a dactyl (*-tem pĕrĭt, perit át*), which is very rare; (cf. 39 62 157 and see Int. § 46, v). I should prefer *qui périt per uirtutém perit at non ínterit*, in spite of the ictus on *uirtutém*. Fl. has *perit at non is interit*, Brix (after Spengel) *perbitit, non interit*, and Sch. *perit, abit non interit* (but from 693 it is clear that the antithesis is between *interire* and *perire*, not *abire*).

perit at non interit: i.e. his memory survives. The words are usually synonymous, but perhaps, as Non. says (p. 442), *interire* is the stronger term. Doederlein, Syn. III. 177, says that *perire* is used of the body, *interire* of the reputation. For the sentiment, cf. the epigram of Simonides on the Spartans who died at Thermopylae,

οὐδὲ τεθνᾶσι θανόντες, ἐπεί σφ' ἀρετὴ καθύπερθε
κυδαίνουσ' ἀνάγει δώματος ἐξ 'Αΐδεω,

and, with reference to literary immortality, the epitaph of Ennius, *nemo me lacrumis decoret nec funera fletu faxit. Quor? Volito uiuos per ora uirum*, and Hor. Od. III. 30. 6 *non omnis moriar multaque pars mei uitabit Libitinam.*

691. **exemplis** = *modis*, as often, e.g. Truc. 26 *quot amans exemplis ludificetur, quot modis pereat...*, Rud. 593 *miris modis ludos faciunt hominibus mirisque exemplis somnia in somnis danunt. Exemplum* (from *eximere*) is something picked out as a model, as in Most. 100 *inde exemplum expetunt*; the transi-

tion of meaning appears in such phrases as As. 389 *istoc exemplo* 'after that model,' i.e. in that manner. So that *pessumis exemplis cruciare, interficere*, etc., is 'to torture or kill after the most painful models,' i.e. in the most painful way.

692. **sutelas**: the metaphor is from patching or stitching up a garment, cf. Am. 367 *aduenisti, audaciae columen, consutis dolis.* SO. *Immo equidem tunicis consutis huc aduenio, non dolis.*

Morti seems to be personified, = *Orco*; cf. Verg. Aen. x. 662 *obuia multa uirum demittit corpora Morti*, Hor. S. II. 5, 49 *si quis casus puerum egerit Orco*, and "Αϊδι προΐαψεν in Hom. Il. I. 3, etc.

694. **aiant**: for the omission of *ne*, cf. the construction of *sino uolo facio* noticed on 858. *Aiant* is Fl.'s emendation, met. gr. Brix and Uss. read *interdo dicant*, quoting Rud. 580 *eluas tu an exunguare ciccum non interduim*, Trin. 994 *qui sis, qui non sis, floccum non interduim*, which are scarcely parallel in construction.

695. **faxis**: see on 124; *faxis* and *feceris* are probably both indicative, cf. Ps. 376 *si tu argentum attuleris, cum illo perdidero fidem*, and R. 1533 (bb).

696. **rebitet**: see on 380. The MSS. reading *redibit et*, which makes nonsense and will not scan, arose from the syllable *bi* being repeated, *rebibitet*.

sicut confido adfore, sc. *eum*; in English it would sound awkward to use the adverb of comparison where the comparative clause is completed; thus where Cicero says (Or. I. 53) *quamuis scelerati illi fuissent, sicuti fuerunt pestiferi ciues supplicioque digni, tamen...*, we should say 'however guilty they may have been, as indeed they were, yet...' or 'however guilty they may have been (and they were dangerous, etc.) yet....'

698. **Quid sit hoc**: Brix points out that the usual order is *quid hoc sit* and so reads.

699. **ad patrem**: see on 49.

bene est: adverbs are often used as predicates, especially with the verb *sum*; cf. 129 273 307 639 701 706 754 and on 120.

700. **quisquam homo**: I have inserted *homo* to fill up the line, as in 772, As. 779, Aul. 810, Bac. 617, Mil. 538, Poen. 1202, Rud. 206, Truc. 307, Ter. Ad. 38, etc. It might easily have fallen out, *quisquamomost* becoming *quisquamost*, then *quisquam est*; Fl. inserts **alius** before *aeque*, Brix reads *quis-*

quam sit, Sch. begins this line with *Benest*, adding *domo* at the end of 699.

aeque melius: a confusion of two expressions, 'to whom I wish equally well' and 'to whom I wish better'; cf. 828 and Cas. 860 *nec fallaciam astutiorem ullus fecit poeta aeque ut haec est fabre facta*, Mil. 551 *nam ex uno puteo similior numquam potis aqua aeque sumi.*

701. **dedisse operam malam**: see on 344.

703. **Votuin**=*uetuine*: this old spelling is preserved by the MSS. in several other passages, but *ueto* is also found (as in 856). Similar forms are *uorto uoster* (common), *uocare*=*uacare* (Cas. 527), *uorrere*=*uerrere* (Sti. 389).

te: this is a slip, as it was Philocrates to whom Hegio said (264) *quarum rerum te falsilocum mihi esse nolo.*

704. **mentiri** in Pl. is generally used absolutely, but is also constructed as in the following instances: Am. 468 *ille adeo illum mentiri sibi credet*, Aul. 690 *egone ut te aduorsum mentiar?* Poen. 152 *cur ego apud te mentiar?* Mil. 779 *te de isto multi cupiunt non mentirier*, Cas. 38 *ne quid mentiar.*

707. **seruatum**: sc. *esse*, see on 345 and cf. Cist. 20 *uentum gaudeo ad te*, Most. 1128 *bene hercle factum, et factum gaudeo.* In Curc. 314 this construction gives occasion for a pun, CV. *Facite, uentum ut gaudeam* (by standing me a dinner on your arrival). PH. *Maxume* (fans him). CV. *Quid facitis, quaeso?* PH. *Ventum.* Plautus also constructs *gaudeo* with inf. (Mil. 899), acc. and inf. (Bac. 456), *quom* and indic. (Am. 681), *quia* (Am. 958), *si* and indic. (Trin. 53), acc. neut. pronoun (inf. 842) and abl. (Poen. 197).

quem...quoi: notice the asyndeton and cf. 939, 987.

708. **custodem addiderat**: the usual verb, cf. Mil. 550 *quoi me custodem erus addidit*, Aul. 556 *Ioui Iuno custodem addidit*, Verg. Aen. VI. 777 *auo comitem sese Mauortius addet Romulus.*

709. **id factum arbitrare**: see on 345.

710. **sorsum**=*seorsum*=*se-uorsum*; the opposite phrase is Most. 910 *tecum sentio.*

712. **haberes si faxit**: where *si fecisset* would be regular, and Pl. might have written *si faceret*; but he is careless in such matters, cf. 27 and Am. 745 *ex te audiui ut urbem maxumam expugnauisses regemque Pterelam tute occideris.* Here,

perhaps, *si faxit* is first written as a condition of *cogitato* (cf. Bac. 712 *si id capso, geritote*), and the proper apodosis, *qualem haberes*, is then added as if *si fecisset* had preceded. In Cist. 417, *nam si nemo hac praeteriit, postquam intro abii, cistella hic iaceret*, the metre (bac. tetr.) requires *praeterierit*, an exact parallel to the text.

714. **Essetne** would be *nonne esset* in later writers; *nonne* arose from the insertion of *non*, as in English, in questions expecting the answer 'yes.' It is rare in Pl., but occurs in Am. 404 405 539, Tru. 257, etc.

717. **Quid tu?** see on 270. For *postulauisti*, see on 739.

718. **Recens**: adverb, as in Cist. 139 *recens natum*.

nuperum does not occur elsewhere; it is formed from *nuper* on the analogy of *super superus*. Notice the pleonasm.

719. **Te perdocere**: for the insertion of the pronoun see on 739. *Per* in composition = 'thoroughly,' as in *perficere, peruenire, peruincere*.

consulerem: after *hominem* we should have expected the third person; for the phrase *consulere bene alicui* cf. Bac. 565 *et mi ires consultum male*, Ter. Ph. 153 *ut qui mihi consultum optume uelit esse*.

721. **Ergo**: see on 383.

istam gratiam 'thanks for that,' i.e. *quod melius illi consuluisti*; see on 934.

723. **latomias**: λατομία (from λᾶας, *lapis*, and τέμνω) is the Greek for *lapicidina* (736); the adj. *lapidarias* seems tautologous, but is added, according to Uss., to prevent any confusion with the district of Rome called Lautumiae, formerly stone-quarries, but at this time probably built over.

725. **Cottidiano**: adv., = *quotidie*, see on 855.

sesquiopus 'half as much work again,' cf. *sesquipes, sesquimensis, sesquimodius*.

726. **Sescentoplago**: for the dative see on 69. In Latin 600 is generally used for an indefinitely large number, cf. Aul. 320 *sescenta sunt quae memorem*, Trin. 791 *sescentae ad eam rem causae possunt conligi*. Pl. also uses *ducenti, trecenti, quingenti* in the same sense, as Brix points out. For an indefinitely small number 3 is generally taken, as in *tribus uerbis* (Mil. 1020), *triduom seruire*, etc., and for a small sum *triobolum* (Rud. 1330).

728. **perduis**: for this old form see on 331.

Curabitur 'he shall be taken care of,' personal, as in 737, Men. 895 *illum curari uolo.* Hegio ironically takes *perduis* in the sense of 'lose' (cf. 537). *Curo* is sometimes used with an acc. pers., e.g. Sti. 96 *numquam enim nimis curare possunt suom parentem filiae*, 682 *amicos meos curabo.*

729. **noctu**: originally ablative of a stem in *-u*, whence *nocturnus.* For the form *custodibitur* see on 265.

730. **eximet**: the original meaning of *emo*, 'to take' (cf. Fest. '*emere* antiqui dicebant pro *accipere*') is only found in compounds, such as *demo*, *eximo*, *peremo*, *interemo.*

731. **absoluam**: metaphor from paying off a creditor; cf. Ep. 631 *age age, absolue me atque argentum numera*, Ter. Ad. 277 *ego ad forum ibo ut hunc absoluam*, and note on 449.

732. **moriri** and *aggrediri* occur often in Pl.; he also uses *arcessiri exfodiri congrediri.*

734. **huic** after *istum*: see on 548.

735. **extra portam in lapicidinas**: this does not refer to the quarter of Rome called Lautumiae, which lay within the walls; cf. Liv. xxxix. 44 (quoted on 815).

736. **deductus siet**: for the construction see on 858; for the archaic form *siet*, on 193.

737. **ita curarier, ne sit**: the rule in classical Latin is that *ne* is used with final sentences, *ut non* with consecutive, R. 1680; but here *ne sit* must be consecutive; (if it were final it would mean 'I wish him to be treated in the way I have mentioned *in order that*' etc., which makes nonsense). Similar instances are not uncommon in Pl.; cf. 795, Most. 381 *satin habes si ego aduenientem ita patrem faciam tuom, non modo ne intro eat, uerum etiam ut fugiat longe ab aedibus?* and Brix on Mil. 149 *eum ita faciemus ut, quod uiderit, ne uiderit.* Cf. the use of *ne* for *non* in the early language, noticed on 586.

738. **qui**: old abl. of *quis*, indefinite, 'in any thing'; see on 101. For *hunc...huic*, see on 593.

739. **me esse postulem**: *postulare* often means 'to expect,' as in 186, and with an infinitive 'to expect to be able' to do a thing; and the subject of the infinitive, although the same as that of *postulo*, is often expressed. Cf. 339, 719, Rud. 990 *et uitorem et piscatorem te esse postulas*, 1385 (quoted on 57), Trin. 237 *numquam Amor quemquam nisi cupidum postulat se*

hominem in plagas conicere, 1020 *inter eosne homines condalium te redipisci postulas?* On the other hand, Trin. 972 *nugari nugatori postulas.*

740. **tuo stat periculo** 'costs (i.e. is only to be bought by) a risk to yourself,' the risk, that is, of killing a slave worth a lot of money (238), or perhaps the risk of not recovering his son. For *stare* with an ablative of price, cf. Sti. 223 *logos ridiculos uendo; age licemini. Quis cena poscit? Ecqui poscit prandio? Herculeo stabunt prandio*, Verg. Aen. x. 494 *haud illi stabunt Aeneia paruo hospitia*, Hor. S. I. 2. 122 *magno stet pretio*, Liv. II. 36 *magno illi ea cunctatio stetit.*

741. **in morte** 'in the state after death,' cf. Bac. 1195 *neque, si hoc hodie amiseris, post in morte id euenturum esse umquam.*

742. **ad summam aetatem**: cf. Cic. Rep. I. 1 *ad summam senectutem iactari. summus*='last' 'latest,' as in Verg. Aen. II. 324 *uenit summa dies*; in this sense *supremus* is commoner. For *aetas*='old age,' cf. Most. 825 *aetate non quis obtuerier*, Sall. J. 9 *ipse morbo atque aetate confectus.*

743. **spatium perferundi**: the dative is found also, and the two are combined in Ter. Ph. 701 *spatium quidem tandem adparandis nuptiis, uocandi, sacruficandi dabitur paullulum*; cf. on 212.

minitas: 'pro minitaris,' Non. 473, who quotes Am. frag. *quid minitabis te facturum*; see on 593.

744. **salue**: usually a salutation, but cf. As. 592 A. *Vale.* P. *Aliquanto amplius ualerem, si hic maneres.* A. *Salue.* P. *Saluere me iubes, cui tu abiens adfers morbum?* Cic. Fam. XVI. 9 *uale, salue.*

749. **Periistis**: the perfect ('you are dead men') is more forcible than the future; it is used with either a present or a future, cf. Mil. 828 *periisti nisi uerum scio*, Men. 416 *periisti si intrassis.*

751. **recta**: sc. *uia*, see on 293.

phylacam=φυλακήν: the word is ἅπαξ εἰρημένον, but *phylacistae* occurs in Aul. 518.

754. **Quod absque hoc esset** 'but if it had not been for this man'; see R. 1556 and cf. Bac. 412 *nam absque te esset... haberem*, Men. 1022 *nam absque te esset...numquam uiuerem*, Pers. 833 *nam hercle absque me foret et meo praesidio...faceret,*

Trin. 832 *nam absque foret te...distraxissent*, 1127 *nam exaedificauisset, absque te foret*, Ter. Ph. 188 *nam absque eo esset... uidissem*, Hec. 601 *quam fortunatus ceteris sum rebus, absque una hac foret.* These seem to be the only instances of the phrase; the last is noticeable as having the indicative in the apodosis. *Absque hoc esset=si hic abesset* or *non esset:* consequently *quod* 'but' precedes, R. 2214.

755. **Vsque** 'straight on,' 'to the end of the story.'

offrenatum ductarent: another metaphor for cheating, the victim being compared to a horse, or an ass, bridled and 'led by the nose,' cf. 641; *offrenatum* does not seem to occur again before Appuleius.

757. **Satis sum semel deceptus**: an instance of the Latin tendency to directness and concreteness of expression. Cf. *a puero* (544) 'from boyhood,' *occisus Caesar teterrimum facinus uidebatur* 'the murder of C.,' *Sempronius iratus mihi perridiculus uidetur* 'the anger of S.,' *ante me consulem, ab urbe condita, ereptae uirginis ira*, etc.

761. **repperi**: the double letter in *repperi reppuli rettudi rettuli* is due perhaps to the loss of the reduplication, perhaps to the *d* of *re(d)*, seen before vowels, e.g. *red-eo*, perhaps to both causes. Cf. 764.

762. **Maior**: sc. *filius.*

scelus here='misfortune' (cf. 'wretch' and 'wretched'), as in Men. 322 *quod te urget scelus?* Ter. Eun. 326 *quid hoc est sceleris? perii*, and so the adjective often, e.g. Cist. 419 *me infelicem et scelestam*, and (with a play on the double meaning) As. 476 *sceleste, non audes mihi scelesto subuenire?*

763. **Quasi produxerim** 'as if I had begotten,' cf. Truc. 292 (quoted on 647), Ter. Ad. 271 *age, inepte; quasi nunc non norimus nos inter nos*, Cic. Fam. III. 7 *quasi uero ad cognoscendum ego ad illos, non illi ad me uenire debuerint.* There is a double ellipse in these instances, '(the case stands) as (it would stand) if,' '(you speak) as (you would speak) if,' '(you write) as (you would write) if.'

in orbitatem 'with a view to childlessness'; this sense of *in* (of the effect intended) is rare except in late writers; cf. however Cic. Att. XV. 1 *uenerat enim in funus, cui funeri ego quoque operam dedi*, Rab. Post. 12 *rex scripsit nullam pecuniam Gabinio, nisi in rem militarem, datam.* It is possible also to refer *in orb.* to the children, taking it with *produxerim*, 'as if I had begotten children into a state of orphanhood.'

764. **redducam**: the usual spelling in Lucretius (Munro on I. 228). Cf. 923, 1014.

neminis: replaced by *nullius* in, and after, Cicero; R. 372.

765. **Misereri**: Spengel, Brix and Sch. read *miserere*, but the deponent form occurs also in Ps. 378, Truc. 223, and impersonally in Trin. 430, etc.

766. **Exauspicaui** does not occur elsewhere; for the active form, see on 593. The Romans, at any rate in early times, never began any important business without consulting the will of the Gods (cf. on 649); hence *auspicor*='I make a beginning.' So here A. says 'I have laid aside my chains and begun a life of freedom.'

767. **Redauspicandum** (=*redeundum*) is coined after the pattern of *exauspicaui*; cf. 289, 900 and 791.

denuo is pleonastic after *redauspicandum*; cf. on 411.

ACT IV. Scene I.

769. **opimitatis**: see on 522. The word occurs in As. 282, not elsewhere in classical Latin. Notice the alliteration in this and the two following lines.

770. **ferias**: *festus* is probably from *ferire* (whence *infestus manufestus confestim*), and *fēriae* has been derived *a fĕriendis uictimis*. Key however connects it with χαίρειν (cf. *fatisco* χατίζω, *frenum* χαλινός, *funis* σχοῖνος, etc.).

771. **Pompam**: πομπή is primarily a sacred procession, and then the offerings carried in it. Uss. quotes Pind. Ol. VII. 80 μήλων κνισάεσσα πομπά. In the Latin dramatists it is used of a train of provisions and other requisites for a banquet. Notice the asyndeton in this line and the last; it is the rule in long lists like the present, see on 406 and cf. Aul. 167 *istas magnas factiones animos dotis dapsilis clamores imperia eburna uehicla pallas purpuram nil moror*, Men. 120 *quando ego tibi ancillas penum lanam aurum uestem purpurum bene praebeo*, 1158 *uenibunt serui supellex fundis aedis omnia*, etc.

772. **quoiquam homini**: see on 700, but *homini* may be added here to shew that he does not refer to the Gods.

supplicare, 'to go begging from,' cf. Rud. 1335 *id quod domist numquam ulli supplicabo*. *Supplicare* is properly to bend the knees (*sub-plico*); the Romans usually prayed standing.

773. Notice alliteration and chiasmus (note on 151).

774. **amoenitate onerauit**: cf. 465, 827. For the triple repetition cf. 825 and Am. 278 *optumo optume optumam operam des*, Cist. 376 *O salute mea salus salubrior* (Brix).

amoenus dies: a comic contrast to his previous abuse, 464—468.

775. **Sine sacris hereditatem**: cf. Trin. 484 *cena hac annona est sine sacris hereditas.* Most Roman families had private religious rites, the performance of which entailed considerable expense and was obligatory upon the *heres* of the family property; so that an inheritance free from such an incumbrance was the Roman equivalent for a rose without a thorn. Cicero, commenting upon the Law of the XII. Tables, *sacra priuata perpetua manento*, says (Leg. ii. 19) *de sacris autem haec fit una sententia ut conseruentur semper et deinceps familiis prodantur et, ut in lege posui, perpetua sint sacra. Hoc uno posito, haec iura Pontificum auctoritate consecuta sunt ut, ne morte patrisfamilias sacrorum memoria occideret, iis essent ea adiuncta ad quos eiusdem morte pecunia uenerit.*

aptus: *adeptus* is the more usual word.

777. **a dis**: i.e. only from the Gods, not from a mortal.

amplius: alluding to the return of Stalagmus.

778. **certa res est**=*certumst*, see on 539 and cf. Sti. 473 G. *Promitte.* E. *Certumst.* G. *Sic face, inquam.* E. *Certa res est.*

eodem pacto ut: *ut* is a colloquialism for *quo*. Brix quotes Merc. 263 *eodem pacto ut insani solent*, Rud. 316 *istac facie ut praedicas*, Trin. 827 *eo modo ut uolui*, etc.

comici serui 'slaves in comedy'; the *currens seruos* (Ter. Eun. 36), who is in such a hurry that he has to explain in detail what he will do to anyone who doesn't get out of his way, is a stock character in Roman comedy. It was considered undignified for a free man to run in the streets, cf. Poen. 522 *liberos homines per urbem modico magis par est gradu ire; seruile esse duco, festinantem currere.*

779. **Coniciam**: future, after *certa res est*, an example of co-ordinate for subordinate construction; cf. note on 504 and Am. 1048 *certumst intro rumpam in aedis*, As. 248 *si mutuas non potero, certumst sumam fenore*, Merc. 546 *certumst antiqua recolam et seruibo mihi.*

pallium: the outer garment of the Greeks, answering to the Roman *toga*, cf. Cur. 288 *isti Graeci palliati*; hence the comedies of Pl. and Ter. (in which the scene and costume were Greek) were called *palliatae*, as opposed to the *togatae comoediae*, in which the Roman dress was worn. The *pallium* was a sort of square blanket which the wearer when running folded and threw over his shoulders to keep it out of his way; cf. Ep. 194 *age nunciam, orna te et palliolum in collum conice*, Ter. Ph. 844 *humerum hunc onero pallio atque hominem propero inuenire.*

780. **aeternum cibum**: his expectation is realised, infra 897.

ACT IV. SCENE II.

783. **Ad** 'in accordance with'; cf. 1029, Cic. Tusc. II. 3 *ad hunc modum institutus est*, Or. 8 *ad eorum arbitrium et nutum totos se fingunt*, Am. 5 *ad istorum normam fuisse sapientes.*

sublitum os esse: see on 656. For the exclamatory infinitive, cf. 946 and see R. 1358, who says it is rare except in the comic poets and Cicero; it answers in verbal nouns to the exclamatory accusative in substantives, R. 1128.

784. **id**: i.e. that I was being deceived; see on 196.

785. **scibitur**: for this old form of the future see on 265.

786. **Quom extemplo** = ἐπεὶ τάχιστα, see on 434.

787. **Hic ille est**: as in 518, Trin. 43, etc. *hic* = 'this present,' *ille* 'that well-known.'

doctus 'wily,' as often in the comic poets, cf. 40, 226.

788. **procul**: for the size of the Roman stage, see on 252.

790. **age hanc rem**: see on 930.

791. **Eminor interminor**: *eminor* is formed on the analogy of *edico* just as *interminor* is used, as a stronger word, for *interdico*; cf. Ter. And. 495 *edixi tibi, interminatus sum, ne faceres.* The MSS. have *interminorque*, but Bentley and Brix omit *que*; it is against the metre, it is frequently inserted in MSS., and asyndeton would be appropriate here, either as intended to give a legal tone (R. 2204), or as being very common in Pl. between verbs of similar meaning; Ballas quotes As. 784 *nutet nictet adnuat*, Bac. 931 *cepi expugnaui*, Ep. 118 *diffatigor differor*, Merc. 360 *abdidi abscondidi*, 681 *disperii perii*, Pers. 332 *scis tenes intellegis*, Tru. 253 *absterret abigit*, etc. Cf. also Ter. Eun. 962 *dico edico uobis*, and see on 406, 658.

792. **Nisi qui arbitrabitur** is an exception, not a condition; hence the indicative, R. 1569.

793. **ore sistet** 'shall stand on his head,' i.e. shall be knocked over; for the phrase cf. Curc. 287 *nec quisquamst... cum tanta gloria quin capite sistat in uia de semita*, Mil. 850 *capite sistebant cadi.*

794. **itinera insistant sua**: so As. 54 *rectam instas uiam*, Cist. 412 *utrum hac an illac iter institerit?* Liv. XXXVII. 7 *iter quod insistis.*

795. **ita...ne conferat**: for *ne* in consecutive sentences, see on 737. *conferat*=*adferat*, as in *conferre se*; cf. As. 258 *quo hanc celocem conferam?* Bac. 797 *pulcre haec confertur ratis*, Colum. I. 5 *quae nisi submouentur pecudibus hominibusque conferunt pestem.* Hence the accusative, *in hanc plateam*, is required; the ablative, which is found in the MSS., would require the plural verb, *ne qui conferant*, in the sense of 'discuss' (cf. Cic. Fam. VI. 21, Att. I. 20). *Platĕa* (whence 'place') is the Greek πλατεῖα, as *balinĕum gunaecĕum* (Most. 740)= βαλανεῖον, γυναικεῖον.

796. **ballista, catapulta, aries**: the *ballista* (βάλλω) was a machine for throwing large stones, while the *catapulta* (καταπέλτης) threw darts; the names are also applied to the missiles, as in Trin. 668 *itast amor, ballista ut iacitur: nil sic celerest neque uolat*, Pers. 28 *uide modo, ulmeae catapultae tuom ne transfigunt latus*; hence Erg. compares his fist to the stone, his lower arm to the dart. The *aries* or ram was a heavy beam suspended from a frame, so that it could be swung backwards and forwards, and is therefore compared by Erg. to the upper arm, which hangs from the shoulder. Notice the chiasmus in this line.

797. **ut quemque icero**: so most editors, as in Mil. 1264 *omnes mulieres te amant ut quaeque aspexit*, As. 246 *exobsecrabo ut quemque amicum uidero*, Cic. Verr. Act. I. 7, 19 *ut quisque me uiderat, narrabat*, etc. Cf. 500, R. 1717. Sch. reads *ad quem adiecero.*

798. **Dentilegos**: coined by Pl. 'I'll make them pick up their teeth,' i.e. by knocking them out; for *legere* in this sense, cf. *sacrilegus* 'a stealer of sacred things,' *sortilegus* 'one who draws lots,' *spicilegium* 'gleaning,' etc.

omnis mortalis, quemque offendero: so in Mil. 1391 *qui omnes se amare credit, quemque aspexerit.* In the older writers *quisque* is sometimes a relative, =*quicunque* (R. 2290), as here, As. 404 *quisque obuiam huic occesserit irato, uapulabit*, Merc.

20 *quemque attigit magno multat infortunio*, Mil. 156 *ni hercle diffregeritis talos posthac, quemque in tegulis uideritis*, 160 *quemque uideritis hominem, huc deturbatote*, 460 *quemque uidero eum ego obtruncabo.* But when used with *ut* or *ubi* (as in 500, 797), *quisque* has its usual sense.

799. **nam**: an interrogative particle, seen in *quisnam* (789) etc.; for its position in the sentence, cf. Bac. 1114 *quid tibi ex filio nam, obsecro, aegrest?* Tru. 938 *tria.* S. *Quae tria nam?*

800 occurs again (with *memineris*) in Ter. Eun. 801. Sch. brackets 800—802 as a spurious repetition of 791—799; in 801 he marks a lacuna.

801. **faxo opstiterit**: possibly *opstiterit* is subjunctive, like *meminerit opstiterit* just above (cf. on 858), but more probably it is indicative (Parataxis for Syntaxis) as in 1010, Am. 355 *familiaris accipiere faxo haud familiariter*, Men. 950 *helleborum potabis faxo aliquos uiginti dies*, Mil. 463 *iam faxo hic erit.* So Aul. 578 *faxo et operam et uinum perdiderit simul*, Trin. 64 *faxo haud tantillum dederis uerborum mihi.* Cf. note on 779 and R. 1605.

802. **cum minis**: for *cum* of attendant circumstances see on 681. Notice the repetition *tantum tantis*.

803. **edico**: Erg. is assuming one of the functions of the aediles (cf. 823) who had the *ius edicendi* and made bye-laws for the streets and markets; cf. Rud. 374 *quamuis fastidiosus aedilis est: si quae improbae sunt merces, iactat omnis*, and Persius I. 130 (quoted on 61).

propter culpam capiatur: in Roman law *culpa* = negligence without evil intention; so that Erg. means 'in order that no one may get into trouble through unintentional disobedience,' i.e. disobedience due to ignorance. *Capiatur* is a final subjunctive, giving the purpose of his making the proclamation (see on 290): the proclamation itself is in the imperative, *continete...prohibete; capere* here = 'to convict,' αἱρεῖν, as in Am. 821 *tu si me impudicitiai captas, capere non potes.*

805. **Mira sunt** = *mirum est* (824); cf. Am. 431 *mira sunt nisi latuit intus*, Poen. 839 *omnia edepol mira sunt nisi erus hunc heredem facit*, Cas. 191 *mira sunt, uera si praedicas*, Men. 1046 *quid sit, mira sunt*, 361 *mira uidentur te hic stare foras.* Distinguish between *mirum est ni*, 'it's a wonder if... not,' and *mirum est quin* 'it's a pity that...not' (generally ironical).

in uentrem: he would say *in animum* of anyone but a parasite.

807. **pistores** 'millers,' see on 160; the antecedent *pistores* is attracted into the case of the relative *qui* (see on 1), then *eorum* (809) is inserted in the proper case; cf. 813, 818. The compound *scrofipascus* does not seem to occur elsewhere.

furfuribus: so Brix Sch. for the MSS. *furfure;* Luchs, in Studemund, Stud. I. 56, shews that *furfur*='a husk,' *furfures* ='bran.'

808. **odore**: abl. of efficient cause (K. 241, R. 1228); cf. 135, Most. 825 *aetate non quis obtuerier*, etc. Notice alliteration here.

810. **Ex ipsis dominis**; instead of from the sows.

exculcabo (from *calx*) is of course the wrong word with *pugnis*; he uses it for *excutiam* by way of a joke, cf. on 109. For the weakening of the vowel in *calco exculco*, see on 8.

812. **profecto**: he is now certain of it: in 805 he only said *mira sunt ni.*

813. **piscatores, qui..., eis**; see on 807. Notice the marked alliteration here.

814. **Qui**: referring to the fish, which are brought to market (*aduehuntur*) in baskets or panniers (*surpiculis*) slung across the back of a screw. For *aduehuntur* cf. Cic. Verr. III. 74 *ex iisdem agris frumentum Romae aduexissent.*

crucianti: i.e. jolting its rider with its rough paces.

cantherio is a 'gelding' (cf. Varr. R. R. II. 7. 15, Festus p. 46); from Aul. 494 *muli...uiliores Gallicis cantheriis*, as well as from the text, they seem to have been little valued. But in Greek κανθήλιος apparently='pack-ass.' Notice alliteration and assonance in this line.

815. **subbasilicanos** 'loungers in the basilica,' cf. Curc. 472 *ditis damnosos maritos sub basilica quaerito,... sumbolarum conlatores apud forum piscarium.* The *basilicae* at Rome were covered spaces adjoining the Forum, and the one in question was evidently between the Fish-market and the Forum Romanum, being separated from the latter by the Via Sacra. The name is derived from the βασιλικὴ στοὰ at Athens in which the Ἄρχων βασιλεύς held his court. The genuineness of these lines has been doubted on the ground that the Porcia Basilica (erected by Cato the Censor in 184, the year that Pl. died) was

the first one built at Rome; but all that Livy says is (xxvi. 27) that in 210 there was no basilica in Rome, and (xxxix. 44) that in 184 Cato *atria duo in Lautumiis et quattuor tabernas in publicum emit basilicamque ibi fecit quae Porcia appellata est.* The fact of its being called Porcia goes to prove the existence of an earlier one which, as being the first, would be called simply '*the* basilica,' and which would be the one referred to in the text.

811 stands in MSS. before 812 where it is obviously out of place; perhaps both lines are interpolated, but if they are retained Sch. seems right in inserting 811 here, if only on the ground of symmetry.

atque imperiosas: *atque* lays the greater stress upon the second word, see on 355. The Roman would naturally consider the *imperium*, or authority of the higher magistrates of Rome, as something superior to the power of foreign kings.

edictiones habet: *edictio* for *edictum* occurs also in Ps. 142; *habere* is used on the analogy of *habere orationem, disputationem*, etc.

818. **lanii, qui...eorum**: see on 807. Their dishonesty is noticed also in Ps. 196 *lenonum aemulos lanios, qui...iure iurando male quaerunt rem.* The word seems to be connected with √*lac*, whence *lacer, lacero, -lacio* (*allicio*) and perhaps *lassus* (*lag-sus*, cf. *la-n-gueo*).

819. **locant caedundos**: for this form of the gerundive, see on 117. *Locator* and *conductor* are the two parties to a contract which consists in the *locator* handing over goods, with which or to which the *conductor* is to do something; which of them pays the other depends on who benefits by what the *conductor* does. Thus if A hands over a horse for B to ride, B would pay A; but if A hands it over for B to shoe, A would pay B; in either case, however the contract would be *locatio-conductio*. So if A hands over a sheep for B to slaughter and return, A would pay B, but if A hands it over for B to sacrifice and eat, B would pay A. The latter case would of course amount to a sale and purchase, but the Romans spoke of it as a *locatio-conductio*; cf. Aul. 567, where Euclio is complaining of the emaciated state of a sheep which Meg. had presented to him for a dinner party: *ossa atque pellis totus est...* MEG. *Caedundum illum ego conduxi.* EV. *Tum tu idem optumumst loces ecferundum; nam iam credo mortuos est*, 'I got him for killing' (i.e. as being fit for killing). 'Then you had better give him (to someone) for burial; for I believe he is dead by now.' The phrase *caedundos agnos*, as is evident from

this passage, implies that the lambs are fat and fit for killing; and *locare c. agnos* apparently means to contract to hand over such lambs, the *conductor* intending to sacrifice them first and eat them afterwards (see on 862).

duplam agninam: this, the MSS. reading, must be taken to mean that the purchaser finds, when the animal arrives, that he has twice as much lamb (*agnina* sc. *caro*) as he bargained for, i.e. that it is a full grown sheep. This at any rate agrees with the next line and would make good sense if the sale were by weight. Most editors however adopt Rost's emendation *dupla* (sc. *pecunia*), 'at double the proper price'; but the repetition *agnos...agnina* would be very awkward, while the parasite would naturally care about the quality but not about the price.

danunt=*dant*: for this old form of the verb (not found in or after Ter.) see R. 630, K. 149, and cf. *nequinont* (=*nequeunt*) in Liv. And., *obinunt* (=*obeunt*) mentioned by Festus, as well as forms like *tem-n-o* (perf. *tempsi*), *cer-n-o* (*cre-ui*), *li-n-o* (*li-ui*, *le-ui*), *si-n-o* (*si-ui*), etc.

820. **petroni**: said to mean an old ram whose flesh is as hard as a stone (πέτρα); more probably one that was tough and lean from living in stony places (cf. *petronius canis* in Grat. Cyneg. 202).

sectario: formed from *seco* (cf. Mart. IX. 7), not, as Festus says, from *sequor*; for the case, see on 69.

821. **Eorum** is Brix's emendation of MSS. *eum*; cf. 809, 815.

822. **mortalis**: he includes the *petro* by way of a joke.

824. **agoranomum**: the ἀγορανόμοι were magistrates at Athens and elsewhere who regulated the markets, saw that false weights were not used and that fair prices were charged; cf. Mil. 727 *sicut merci pretium statuit, qui est probus agoranomus.*

825. **parasitus**: παράσιτος, 'one who dines at another's table,' is first found in a fragment of Ararus, a writer of the middle comedy and son of Aristophanes; originally the word was used of a class of priests who took their meals in common.

regum rex regalior: for the triple repetition, cf. 774: for *rex* 'patron,' see on 92. *Regum* is genitive after *rex*, R. 1312; *regalior*=*nimis regalis*, see on 102.

826. **conmeatus cibus**: sometimes taken as if *conmeatus uentri* were in apposition to *cibus* and formed part of the predicate, 'is come into harbour as provision for my stomach,' but the order of the words renders this a stiff construction, out of place in such conversational Latin: more probably *cibus* is genitive, as *lectus* in Am. 513 *prius abis quam lectus ubi cubuisti concaluit locus.*

827. **hunc Hegionem senem**: the usual order. Uss. quotes Am. 1077 *tua Bromia ancilla*, Bac. 346 *meus Mnesilochus filius*, Cas. 762 *nostro Olympioni uillico*, Cist. 279 *mei Lampadisci serui*, Cic. Clu. 8, 25 *eius Lucium filium*, etc.

828. **Qui**=*quo*, see on 101.

hominum nemo: so in Ter. Eun. 561, 756; cf. sup. 540, Ter. Hec. 262 *ut unus hominum homo te uiuat numquam quisquam blandior.*

adaeque fortunatior: see on 700.

830. **ecquis** *hic est? ecquis*: Böthe supplies the words in italics, after the model of Am. 1020 *aperite hoc: heus, ecquis hic est? ecquis hoc aperit ostium?* Bac. 582 *heus, ecquis hic est? ecquis hoc aperit ostium?* The *ostium* was the inner door, so that Erg. has now passed the *ianua* and entered the *prothyrum*; see on 108.

831. **ad cenam ad me**: this seems inconsistent with 805, 812, 837; it is evidently the same dinner to which Erg. had invited himself in 175; consequently the action of the play occupies but one day although the journey from Aetolia to Elis and back, which Phil. performs, would be at least 80 miles. *Ad me*='to my house,' see on 497.

ambas foris: the *ostium* had folding doors (*ualuae*), of which one leaf only would usually be opened; hence the singular is sometimes used, e.g. in Aul. 657. But Erg. considers it due to his importance to have both thrown wide.

832. **assulatim**: the reading of the MSS., *uel assultatim*, doubtless arose from some copyist writing an alternative suggestion above the line thus:—*assulatim* (with *uel assultatim* written above); see the critical note. For *assulatim*, which Nonius reads (72. 22), cf. Men. 859 *dedolabo assulatim* and Merc. 129 *foribus facere hisce assulas.* It is quoted by Non. from Naevius, but does not occur elsewhere.

833. **hominem conloqui**: Pl. when he does not use the verb absolutely, always (except in Per. 725 *cum lenone conloqui*) constructs it with the acc., other writers never.

qui uocat? for the substantival use of *qui* interrogative, see R. 380.

834. **Respice**: Erg. pretends to take this in the sense in which it was used of the gods, 'to look favourably upon' 'to help'; cf. Rud. 1316 *di homines respiciunt*, Poen. 408 *respice! respexit; itidem edepol Venerem credo facturam tibi*, Ter. And. 642 *et me et te imprudens, nisi quod di respiciunt, perdidi*, Cic. Att. VIII. 1 *nisi idem deus respexit rem publicam*, Hor. Od. I. 2. 36 *siue neglectum genus et nepotes respicis, Auctor.*

hoc me iubes: the double acc. is uncommon and is only found where the 'thing' is expressed by a neut. pronoun, as in Ps. 1328 *fac quod te iubeo*, Cic. Fam. XIII. 26 *litteras, non quae te aliquid iuberent.*

837. **nescio...fastidis**: this cannot stand after 836, where Erg. certainly does not shew *fastidium*. If retained, it seems to come in most naturally after 834.

ubi=*apud quem*; cf. As. 767 *ne illi sit cera, ubi facere possit litteras*, Mil. 118 (quoted on 7), Ter. And. 637 *'ubi fides?' roges*, Cic. Quint. 9 *neque nobis adhuc praeter te quisquam fuit, ubi nostrum ius contra eos obtineremus*, Liv. IV. 13 *dixit se dictatorem L. Quinctium dicturum; ibi animum parem tantae potestati esse.*

835. **mihi**: with *optume*, but *omnium* or *O omnium* would be a probable emendation, cf. Ter. Ph. 853, quoted on 836.

836. **Quantumst hominum**=*omnium hominum* (but *omnis* is sometimes added); cf. Aul. 785 *di immortales omnes deaeque quantumst*, Bac. 1170 *senex optume quantumst in terra*, Ps. 37 *di deaeque quantumst*, 351 *quantum terram tetigit hominum periurissume*, 533 (quoted on 353), Rud. 706 *natum quantumst hominum sacrilegissume*, Ter. Heaut. 810 *di deaeque omnes quantumst*, Ph. 853 *O omnium quantumst, qui uiuont, hominum homo ornatissume.*

838. **Cedo manum**: in congratulation, cf. 859, Merc. 965 *uxor tibi placata et placida est; cette dextras nunciam*, Ps. 1065 *O fortunate, fortunato cedo manum.*

839. **gaudeam**: for the subjunctive see on 139.

840. **maestissumi maerores**: the MSS. have at the end of the line ER. *Noli irascier*, which is taken from 845 and does not scan or make sense here. Uss. substitutes *gaude modo*, Geppert *noli angier*. Sch. gives the whole line to Heg. reading *maerores familiares* to complete the verse. With the same

object I have inserted *maestissumi* which might have fallen out before *maerores mi.* Similar cognate adjectives are 773 *amoenitate amoena*, Cas. 217 *nitoribus nitidis*, Cist. 376 *salus salubrior*, Ep. 120 *pretio pretioso*, Most. 157 *Venus uenusta*, Mil. 959 *pulcram pulcritudinem*, As. 266 *falsae fallaciae*, etc.

841. **ex corpore**: by way of a joke, instead of *ex animo*, 'I'll clear your body of every spot of sorrow.'

842. **quod** is acc. neuter pronoun, cf. Am. 1100 *iam istuc gaudeo*, and note on 707.

843. **Bene facis**, 'thank you'; Donatus on Ter. Eun. 186 says 'non iudicantis est sed gratis agentis'; cf. Curc. 271 *pacem ab Aesculapio petas*...CA. *Bene facis, ibo atque orabo.* Similarly *facis benigne* (949), *lepide facitis*, etc. But *recte facis* (cf. 1028) is the expression of an opinion.

iubeam: for the subjunctive, see on 139.

Ignem ingentem: for cooking, the natural way for a Parasite to express his joy. The assonance is emphatic.

844. **uolturi**: a type of greediness, cf. Trin. 101 *te uolturium uocant: hostesne an ciues comedis, parui pendere.* For the form of the vocative see R. 352, K. 35.

846. **Iuben an non iubes**: a forcible form of expression, in which we should use the future, 'will you or will you not'; so Trin. 983 *properas an non properas ire?* Mil. 449 *mittin me an non mittis?* Pers. 531 *tacen an non taces?* Tru. 755 *redin an non redis?*

astitui: sc. *igni*, which Geppert inserts to avoid hiatus. Notice the chiasmus in this line.

847. **pernas**: so Sch. for the MSS. *epulas*; the general word would be out of place among so many particulars, and *pernae* and *laridum* are mentioned together in 903.

foueri: in its original sense 'to be warmed'; this use of the word, without any notion of 'cherishing,' is very rare.

foculis: *fōculum* only occurs here and in Pers. 105 *iam intus uentris fumant focula; calefieri iussi reliquias.* It is a contraction of *fouiculum* (from *foueo*, as *terricula* 'bugbears' from *terreo*, etc.; for the contraction see Int. § 113) which would properly mean 'that which warms,' and seems to be here used for a stewpan or something of that sort. In the Persa it is used figuratively, *uentris focula* = that which warms the stomach, i.e. food. Fl. and others read *foculis in fer.*, from *fŏculus*, diminutive of *focus*, but this scarcely agrees with *ignem ingentem*, 843. Notice the alliteration.

848. **praestinatum**: for this so-called supine in *-um*, really the acc. (of the goal of motion) of a verbal substantive, see R. 1114. *Praestino* is a Plautine word, not found in subsequent writers until Appuleius. On the analogy of *de-stino ob-stino*, it appears connected with *stano*, a form of *sto* (cf. *danunt*, 819).

uigilans somniat: a proverbial expression for day-dreaming; cf. Am. 697 *quaene uigilans somniat*, Ps. 386 *qui imperata ecfecta reddat, non qui uigilans dormiat*, Lucr. III. 1048 *et uigilans stertis nec somnia cernere cessas*.

849. **pullos gallinaceos** is not tautology, for *pullus* is used for the young of any animal, even of frogs (Hor. S. II. 3. 314).

850. **Scis bene esse**: *scire* with infin. = 'to know how'; *esse* is from *sum* not *edo*, cf. Men. 485 *minore nusquam bene fui dispendio*, Merc. 582 *quin ergo imus atque obsonium curamus, pulcre ut simus*, Tru. 741 *de eo (argento) nunc bene sunt*.

unde: sc. *bene sis* 'the wherewithal,' cf. the last quotation.

Pectinem: I have substituted this (partly to avoid the hiatus) for the MSS. *pernam*, which in its ordinary meaning is obviously out of place here among the fish; *perna* occurs however in Plin. XXXII. 11. 54 as the name of a shell-fish belonging to the same order as the *pinna* (Cic. Nat. D. II. 48) and the *pecten*. These latter attain a large size in the Mediterranean; according to Tryon the shell of the *pinna* sometimes measures 2 feet in length, and Pliny, XXXII. 53. 6 speaks of *pectines maximi et nigerrimi aestate laudatissimi*. Appuleius (Apol.) quotes Ennius *Mitylenae est pecten*, and Horace, S. II. 4. 34, says *pectinibus patulis iactat se molle Tarentum*. Fl. reads *muraenam*; Brix suggests *percamque*, but (according to Ballas) Pl. does not use *que...atque* or *et...atque*.

ophthalmiam: ὀφθαλμίας (Lat. *oculata*) is the river lamprey, called in German Neunauge, 'nine-eye.'

851. **Horaeum scombrum**: σκόμβρος is the generic name for the tunny fish: ὡραῖος applied to fish properly means 'in season' (Soph. Fr. 446) and ὡρ. τάριχος = 'fish pickled in season,' i.e. when at their best. In Latin the word does not occur elsewhere; its proper meaning 'in season' is out of place here and it is generally translated 'pickled' but there seems to be no instance of its meaning this in Greek. Ussing takes it to mean 'qui uere, τῆς ὥρας, uenit' i.e. 'spring-mackerel,' but the epithet would be superfluous if the season were spring and

absurd if it were not. Possibly it means 'young,' cf. Ar. Eq. 1008 περὶ σκόμβρων νέων.

trugonum et cetum: *trugōnum*=τρυγόνα 'sting-ray,' a fish with a sting or prickle in its tail; *cetum*=κῆτος (neuter), a name for any large fish, esp. the larger kind of tunny (tunny weighing 1000 lbs. are not rare in the Mediterranean). This was pickled or salted, so *cetarii*=sellers of salt-fish, ταριχοπῶλαι. For the difference in declension of the Latin and Greek forms, cf. *architectus* (ἀρχιτέκτων), *polypus* (πολύπους), *schema* gen. *-ae* (σχῆμα, -ατος), etc.

852. **Nominandi istorum copia**: the genitives of the gerund and gerundive are always dependent on nouns and are used indifferently, R. 1394; thus Cic. Fin. v. 15 *ita nati factique sumus ut et agendi aliquid et diligendi aliquos et referendae gratiae principia in nobis contineremus*, where we might have had *alicuius rei agendae* or *referendi gratiam*. So in the text either *nominandi ista* or *nominandorum istorum* would be regular. The construction in the text is also found in Tru. 370 *tui* (fem.) *uidendi copia*, Ter. Hec. 372 *eius* (*uxoris*) *uidendi cupidus*, Heaut. 29 *date crescendi copiam, nouarum qui spectandi faciunt copiam*, Enn. Med. 207 *neue nauis inchoandi exordium*, Lucr. v. 1225 *poenarum soluendi tempus*, Varro R. R. II. 1 *principium generandi animalium*, Cic. Inv. II. 1 *exemplorum eligendi potestas*, Fin. v. 7 *eorum adipiscendi causa*, and several other passages in Cic. and Gellius. In these passages the gerund is always in the genitive and its object is plural (except in the two first of the above quotations, in which it is a pronoun which might, but for the context, be masculine). Roby says that this construction is an attempt to retain the gerund while putting the dependent substantive into direct relation to the noun which governs the gerund; between which and the dependent substantive there is often a real connection (vol. II. p. lxvii—lxx). But the construction is, no doubt, rendered possible by the fact that the gerund, although mainly verbal (*nominandi ista* being a gen. of *nominare ista*), is also substantival (*nominandi*=*nominationis*), and thus affords an excuse for the attraction. Madvig thinks the construction may also be due to a dislike of the long form of the gen. plural of the gerund.

854. **ne frustra sis**: a colloquialism. The subjunctive is either jussive ('make no mistake about that') or, more probably, final of the kind noticed on 290 ('that you may make no mistake' 'to be plain with you').

855. **cottidiani**: this is the usual spelling of B and is found also in the Lex Julia Municipalis, B.C. 55 (Corp. Inscr. R. I. 206).

uicti: for this gen. of a *-u* stem see R. 399. Pl. also has *senati gemiti quaesti sumpti tumulti; aduenti fructi ornati* occur in Ter.; Sallust and Cicero use *senati*.

ad me 'to my house,' see on 497.

857. **Tu ne**: for *ne*=*ναί* (sometimes written *nae*) see R. 523. It generally comes first in the sentence, but is sometimes placed after a personal pronoun, as here, Sti. 635 *Egone? Tu ne. Mihine? Tibi ne*, etc.

858. **Vin faciam**: so 736 *facite deductus siet*, Am. 981 *haec curata sint fac*, Ps. 922 *uolo tu prior occupes*, Rud. 662 *uelim malas edentauerint*, Cap. 694 *nil interdico aiant*, As. 902 *sine uenias modo domum*, etc. In these constructions the subjunctive is jussive, in quasi-dependence upon the principal verb, R. 1606. Cf. on 801.

859. **Di te adiuuant**: a form of congratulation, as in Ep. 392, etc.

Nil sentio: Hegio pretends to expect some conjuring.

860. **senticeto...sentis**, a pun; for the termination cf. *dum-etum, ros-etum, uin-etum*, etc. As to the *c* in *senti-c-etum*, it is perhaps due to the fact that the usual word is *fruticetum* from *frutex* 'a shrub'; or perhaps the form *sentix*, which is found in late writers, existed also in early times.

861. **Vasa pura**: cf. Am. 1126 *iube uasa pura actutum adornari mihi, ut Iouis supremi multis hostiis pacem expetam.*

ad 'for the purpose of,' as in Aul. 429 *uenimus coctum ad nuptias*, Ter. And. 32 *nil istac opus est arte ad hanc rem*, Hec. 693 *confingis falsas causas ad discordiam*, and frequently with the gerund.

862. **agnum**: calves, lambs, kids and sucking pigs were called *hostiae lactentes.* Cic. Leg. II. 12. At a private sacrifice part of the *exta* were burnt on the altar; the remainder and the flesh were (unless the sacrifice was to one of the *di inferi*) eaten by the family; cf. Sti. 251 *iamne exta cocta sunt? quot agnis fecerat?* CR. *Ille quidem nullum sacruficauit.*

propere unum: Böthe's emendation of the MSS. *proprium*; Sch. reads *propteruom. Unum* is sometimes used almost as an indefinite article, see on 482.

863. **sum summus Iuppiter**: Brix quotes Ps. 327 *accerse hostias uictimas lanios, ut ego huic sacruficem summo Ioui; nam hic mihi nunc est multo potior Iuppiter, quam Iuppiter.*

864. **Salus...Gaudium**: according to Ballas, asyndeton is the invariable rule in Pl. with more than two proper names; he quotes Bac. 115 *Amor Voluptas Venus Venustas Gaudium Iocus Ludus Sermo Suauisauiatio*, 255 *Volcanus Luna Sol Dies*, 892 *ita me Iuppiter Iuno Ceres Minerua Lato Spes Opis Virtus Venus Castor Polluces Mars Mercurius Hercules Summanus Sol Saturnus dique omnes ament*, etc.

866. **mihi**: Erg. pretends to take *mihi* with *esurire* instead of with *uidere*. Uss. compares Cur. 72 *me inferre Veneri uoui iam ientaculum.* PA. *Quid? anteponas Veneri te ientaculo?*

868. **Iuppiter dique**: i.e. 'and the other gods,' cf. 909, 922, Cas. 275 *Hercules dique istum perdant*, Aul. 658 *Iuppiter te dique perdant*, Bac. 892 (quoted on 864), and in Greek Ζεῦ καὶ θεοί.

Te hercle: Erg. is going to retort with another curse but changes his mind and finishes the sentence differently. So in Mil. 286 *di te perdant!* PA. *Te istuc aequomst—quoniam occepisti, eloqui*, Ep. 23 *di te perdant!* EP. *Te uolo—percontari*, Men. 328 *num quid uis?* M. *Ut eas maxumam malam crucem.* C. *Te ire hercle melius est—intro iam atque accumbere*, Cas. 279 *qui illum di omnes deaeque perdant!* CH. *Te uxor aiebat tua—me uocare.*

aequomst: 'would be right,' see on 61.

869. **porto a portu**: paronomasia.

870. **Nunc tu mihi places**: i.e. now your dinner will satisfy me and I shall seek no other *condicio* (180); for you are sure to have a big feast.

stultus: the nom. is sometimes used for the vocative in the poets and in antiquated style (Madv. 299 *b*); so As. 664 *da, meus ocellus, mea rosa, mi anime*, 691 *mi Libane, ocellus aureus*, Sti. 764 *meus oculus, da mi sauium*, Cas. 138 *meus festus dies, meus pullus passer, mea columba, mi lepus.* Brix, Müller read *stultu's*, = *stultus es*.

871. 'You might more reasonably have said that (viz. *abi*) if I had come earlier (before I could have brought you the good news).' *Igitur* (from *is*) was originally an adv. of time and in older writers often introduces the apodosis, as in Am. 209 *sin aliter sient animati...sese igitur oppidum oppugnassere*, Mil. 772 *quando habebo, igitur dabo*, Lucr. II. 678 *cetera peragrans, igitur inuenies* 'if you go through the rest, you will then find'; sometimes pleonastically with *tum*, as here, Most. 127 *ubi unum emeritumst stipendium, igitur tum specimen cernitur*, 676

igitur tum accedam hunc, quando quod agam inuenero; with *deinde*, as Sti. 86 *post id igitur deinde ut animus meus est, id faciam palam*; with *demum*, Rud. 930 *iam ubi liber ero, igitur demum instruam agrum.*

olim, lit. 'at that time' (past or future), from *olle* or *ole*, old form of *ille* (for the termination, cf. *interim istim*, etc.); here it means 'some time ago.'

874. **publica celoce**: according to Nonius *celox* (*κέλης*) is 'breue nauigium, sic dictum a celeritudine'; it is sometimes used for a despatch-boat, as here and in Mil. 986 *haec celox illius est,...internuntia*, sometimes for a privateer, as in As. 258 (quoted on 795), Ps. 1306 *unde onustam celocem agere te praedicem?* Cf. Thuc. IV. 9.

875. **tuom Stalagmum seruom**: for the order, see on 827.

876. **quadrimus**: so *bimus* and *trimus*; 'one year old' is *anniculus*; for the other years Pl. uses compounds of *annus*, *quinquennis sexennis septuennis*, etc.

877. **Ita me amabit**: the combination of the fut. indic. with the pres. subj. (*condecoret*) is noticeable; Pl. uses these tenses indifferently in this phrase, cf. Aul. 496 *ita me di amabunt ut ego hunc ausculto lubens*, Ter. Heaut. 463 *sic me di amabunt ut me miseritumst*, with Most. 177 *ita tu me ames ut uenusta es.* Sometimes the *ut* is omitted, as in Trin. 447 *ita me amabit Iuppiter, neque te derisum uenio neque dignum puto.*

sancta Saturitas, 'St Gorge,' an appropriate patron saint for a parasite; so in Bac. 120 the lover swears by *Suauisauiatio*, and the boor in Truc. 276 by his weeding-hoe, *ita me amabit Sarculum.*

878. **condecoret cognomine**: so that he should be called Saturio (like the parasite in the Persa) or Saturius, which was a Roman surname.

879. **genium**: the parasite's patron, cf. Cur. 301 *ecquis est qui mihi conmonstret Phaedromum genium meum?* Men. 138 *quid agis?* P. *Teneo dextera genium meum*; see on 290.

880. **Μὰ τὸν Ἀπόλλω**: in Attic Greek *μά* is used without *ναί* or *οὐ*, but generally in the sense 'no, by...,' the negative being supplied by the context (so in Most. 955 *triginta talentis?* PH. Μὰ τὸν Ἀπόλλω, *sed minis*); sometimes, however, it is affirmative, as here and in Plat. Gorg. 489 E, Alcib. I. 109 D.

881. **Ναὶ τὰν Κόραν**: the name under which Persephone was worshipped in Attica; but the form τὰν Κόραν is of course Doric, such as would be used in Magna Graecia. Cf. Ar. Vesp. 1438 εἶθ' ἡ Συβαρῖτις εἶπεν "εἰ ναὶ τὰν Κόραν..." Cora was also the name of a town in Latium, now Cori; hence Erg. goes on to swear by other towns in Latium, making them all feminine as if they were goddesses; the towns mentioned are all close to the Via Latina, probably the oldest of the Roman roads.

882. **Iam diu**: this, the MSS. reading, can hardly stand after 873; Sch. reads *iam, diui*,—but the exclamation occurs nowhere else in Pl. Acidalius reads *ain tu?* Bücheler *tuan fide?* Uss. proposes *iam dies*—. I would suggest *itane ais?* (cf. Mil. 62, Ter. Ph. 315) or *ain tandem?* (as in As. 901, Aul. 290, Truc. 599, Ter. And. 875, Ph. 373).

Πραινέστην: Praeneste (the modern Palestrina) stands on a spur of the Apennines (Verg. Aen. VII. 682 *altum Praeneste*) about 20 miles from Rome.

Σιγνίαν: now Segni, said to have been founded by Tarquinius Superbus; fragments of its cyclopean walls and a gateway still remain.

883. **Φρουσινῶνα**: Frusino (the modern Frusinone) on the Via Latina; Alatrium or Aletrium is about five miles off.

884. **barbaricas**: βάρβαρος = non-Greek, and Pl. adopts the word from his originals in this sense. In most cases it means Roman or Italian; thus in 491 *barbarica lege* = Roman law, in Mil. 212 *poeta barbarus* = Naevius, in Most. 813 *pultiphagus opifex barbarus* = *Romanus* (*puls* being the national food of the Roman peasants: see Plin. N. H. XVIII. 8), in Sti. 193 *mores barbaros* refers to a Roman auction, in Bac. 122 *stultior es barbaro Potitio* refers to the family of the Potitii (see Liv. I. 7. 14); so in Trin. 19 *Plautus uortit barbare*, As. 11 *Maccius uortit barbare* means 'translated into Latin'; in Poen. 598 *Barbaria* = *Italia*; in Cur. 150 the word is applied to Italian or Etruscan dancers, but in Rud. 583 to a Sicilian by the slave of an Athenian; in Bac. 119 *es barbarus* means 'you are an ignorant barbarian.'

Quia enim 'why, because,' *enim* being simply asseverative; see on 592.

asperae may mean 'rugged' 'precipitous' in situation, or 'harsh' in dialect, or 'uncultivated' in manner; there was considerable animosity at this time between Rome and the Latin towns (see Mommsen, H. R. II. 333).

885. **autumabas**: in 188, cf. 497.

Vae aetati tuae: a forcible colloquialism for *uae tibi*, cf. Rud. 375 *uae capiti atque aetati tuae*, Poen. 783 *uae uostrae aetati*, Men. 675 *sibi inimicus magis quam aetati tuae.* A similar expression is *uae capiti tuo*, used to express annoyance at an ill-timed joke in Rud. 375, Am. 741, etc., *caput* meaning 'individual' 'person' (see on 229).

886. **Quippe quando**: 'yes, it is 'woe to me' when you don't believe me.' *Nil* is an emphatic *non*, as in 103.

887. **abit**: for the tense see on 282.

888. **Siculus**: during the operations in Sicily in the 1st and 2nd Punic Wars, whole towns were sold into slavery, e.g. Agrigentum in 211 B.C. Notice the Roman allusion.

Boius est—boiam terit: a pun, the latter words meaning both 'wedded to a Boian wife' and 'wearing a *boia*' (a collar of wood or iron, mentioned among other shackles in As. 550 *neruos catenas carceres numellas pedicas boias*); *terere catenas*= 'to wear out chains,' cf. the epithets *ferriteri*, *compedium* or *stimulorum tritor*, *flagitriba*, etc. In the year 225 B.C., which was about the time that Pl. began to exhibit, the Boii, then a powerful tribe south of the Po, and other Celts over-ran Etruria and were defeated at the battle of Telamon, 10,000 of them being taken prisoners. Roman colonies were founded in their territory and they again revolted in 218, but the outbreak of the Punic War saved them for a time. At the end of that war in 201, the Romans at once set about the subjugation of Gallia Cisalpina and finally defeated and destroyed the Boii at Mutina in 193.

890. **bonan fide**: cf. Aul. 772 *dic bona fide, non surrupuisti?* LY. *Bona*, Ter. Heaut. 761 *bonan fide?* SY. *Bona.* So in a double sense Most. 657 *tuos emit aedis filius.* TH. *Bona fide?* TR. *Si quidem es argentum redditurus, tum bona; si redditurus non es, non emit bona.*

891. **iterum gnatus**: so Poen. 1077 *iterum mihi natus uideor quom te repperi.*

895. **cellarium**: properly a superior slave (*ordinarius*) who had charge of the store-room, larder and wine cellar (*cella penaria, uinaria*).

896. **Nam**: with ellipse, 'you are right, for'; see on 464.

mantiscinatus does not occur again and is uncertain both in origin and meaning; the context here requires the meaning to be *sumpsero* or *impendero*, and in Donatus (ad Ter. Eun. 258) we find *de alieno manticinor et impendo.* Most editors read *manticinatus,* deriving it from *μάντις* on the analogy of *uatĭcinor* from *uates*, but against this there is (i) the scansion, (ii) the anomaly of the formation, (iii) the use of *probe*, (iv) the sense of the passage, which evidently refers to Erg.'s preparations for the feast, (v) the phrase in Donatus, given above.

probe 'properly,' a colloquialism: see on 269.

fusti pectito: a slang expression; so Rud. 661 *leno pugnis pectitur.* In the Eng. 'give him a dressing,' which seems analogous, 'dressing' is probably the same word as 'thrashing' (provincial 'drashing').

897. **dapinabo**: coined by Pl. from *daps;* it is not found elsewhere.

898. **id** refers rather vaguely to the preceding sentence; see on 196.

Sponden...spondeo: an instance of *stipulatio*, i.e. the making of a formal contract by question and answer, in the words of the text or other equivalent words. The person who asks the question is called *stipulator*, the other *promissor.* Several instances of a *stipulatio* occur in Pl., e.g. Bac. 881 CH. *roga hunc tu, tu promitte huic.* NI. *promitto, roga.* CL. *ducentos nummos aureos Philippos probos dabin?* CH. *'Dabuntur' inque; responde.* NI. *Dabo.*

899. **respondeo**: here in its etymological meaning 'promise in return,' with allusion to the ordinary sense of 'answer.'

900. **potest**: sc. *curari* or *fieri*, used impersonally as often; cf. 352, Am. 971 *quantum potest, parata fac sint omnia,* Bac. 1031 *abduce me hinc quantum potest,* Men. 835 *concede huc ab istoc quam potest longissume.*

Bene ambula is a form of leave-taking; cf. 452, Most. 837, etc. Cf. the use of *ambulare* for *abire* in 12.

redambula: coined by Pl. to answer to *ambula*, like *ire* (=*abire*) and *redire*; cf. 768, 791.

901. **rem summam cibariam**: instead of *rem summam publicam* (Merc. 986).

902. **collos**: masculine also in 357, Pers. 688 and, according to Non. p. 200, in Accius, Lucilius, Cato and other early writers. Pl. also uses *guttur papauer corius dorsus*, etc., as

masculines, *nasum pane artua* etc., as neuters (see Tyrrell on Mil. 18).

tegoribus: so Turnebus, for the MSS. *tergoribus* which gives a dactyl in the 7th foot (Int. § 66). The form is found in A, inf. 915, and in BC, Ps. 198.

903—905. The alliteration and assonance in these lines express the delight of Erg. The asyndeton is in accordance with Pl.'s usual practice where the same word is repeated at the beginning of several clauses; cf. 114, 444, As. 526 *ultro amas, ultro expetessis, ultro ad te arcessi iubes*, Curc. 178 *sibi sua habeant regna reges, sibi diuitias diuites, sibi honores, sibi uirtutis, sibi pugnas, sibi proelia*, Men. 132 *hoc facinus pulcrumst, hoc probumst, hoc lepidumst, hoc factumst fabre*, and many other instances in Ballas.

904. **sumini absumedo**: a pun. *Sumini* is dative because it is to be taken with *ueniet*, not *absumedo*; the latter word is coined by Pl. on the analogy of *uredo, torpedo, grauedo*, etc.

callo calamitas: another pun. *Callum*=*callum aprugnum*, Poen. 579.

906. **Nam** often introduces a sentence accounting for an omission or meeting an objection; cf. 440 and note on 464.

mora est: '*would be* waste of time,' see on 61.

907. **pro praefectura mea**, 'in virtue of my authority as prefect'; for this meaning of *pro*, cf. note on 244. Erg. likens himself to a *praefectus iuri dicundo*, or deputy judge, appointed by the *praetor urbanus* to administer justice (*ius dicere*) in towns which had the *ciuitas sine suffragio*; their position was inferior to that of *municipia* or *coloniae*, which had their own magistrates. The first instances of this constitution were Caere 351 B.C., Capua 330 B.C. For the metaphorical use of the word cf. Cas. 99 *quin ruri es in praefectura tua*, and *prouincia* in 156, 474. This line is a good instance of the great value of A and of Studemund's life-long work upon it. Before the publication of the Apographon, in which the results of his work have been embodied, only UTPRO—AM (with space for 10 or 11 letters) had been deciphered, and to reconcile this with the reading of BVEJ Geppert had suggested *ut properem in praefecturam*, Schoell *ut pro re agam praeturam.* It is instructive to notice how wide of the truth these suggestions were, and how simple the real solution of the difficulty turns out to be.

908. **pendent indemnatae perneis**, for *causis* or *litibus*, an instance of ἀπροσδόκητον. There is a play on the word *pendeo* which is used of persons or things that are 'in suspense,' as in Verg. Aen. IV. 88 *pendent opera interrupta. Indemnatae causae*='undecided actions,' Cic. Rab. Post. 4 *causa iudicata atque damnata*, Clu. 3 *causa quae conuicta atque damnata sit.*

ACT V. SCENE I.

The division of Latin comedies into Acts was known to Varro and Cic. (Verr. II. 6. 18, Q. F. I. 1. 16) and to Hor. (A. P. 189 *neue minor neu sit quinto productior actu Fabula*) but was probably unknown to Pl. or Ter. The MSS. divide only into scenes, and the plays were probably acted straight on, without any interval. Where, however, a character leaves the stage at the end of a scene and re-enters at the beginning of the next, or where, for any other reason, some space of time must elapse between two consecutive scenes, the interval was filled up by music from the *tibicen*: cf. Ps. 573 *tibicen uos interea hic delectauerit.* Whoever divided the Captiui into Acts would have done better to make the 5th begin with this scene, before which an interval is necessary, rather than with the next, as in the MSS.

909. **Diespiter**=*Dies Pater*, an old name for Jove; cf. *Iuppiter* (=*Iou-pater*). The words *dies diurnus diuos deus* δῖος Ζεύς *Iouis* (old form *Diouis*) are all connected, the common idea being 'brightness.' For *Diespiter dique* see on 868.

911. **modo in**: most editors retain these words and read *clades calamitas*, with Böthe; but this does not seem probable in view of the MSS. readings and the singular verb *aduenit.* For the acc. after *aduenire*, cf. Verg. Aen. I. 388, *Tyriam qui aduenеris urbem*, and note on 548. For *intemperies* cf. Colum. praef. *caeli noxia frugibus intemperies; calamitas* also was originally applied to the destruction of crops by storms, cf. Cat. R. R. 141, Ter. Eun. 79 *nostri fundi calamitas*, Cic. Verr. III. 98 *in calamitate fructuum.*

modo is used of the immediate past, the present and the immediate future; cf. As. 927 *modo odium, non uxor, eram*, Ter. Ad. 289 *modo dolores occipiunt primulum*, And. 594 *domum modo ibo.*

912. **After this verse, parts of a line beginning with** UBIUOLT **and ending with** IMPETUM **have been deciphered in A. The fact of its having ended with the same word as this verse would account for its accidental omission.**

913. **Nimis male formidabam** 'was too horribly frightened of'; for *nimis* see on 102; for *male* with verbs of hating and fearing cf. Aul. 61 *nimisque ego metuo male*, Men. 189 *odi male*, Mil. 128 *peius odisse*, Rud. 920 *nimisque id genus odi ego male*, Ps. 1019 *nimisque ego illunc hominem metuo et formido male*, etc.

915. **glandia**: cf. Plin. N. H. XI. 37, 66, 175 *tonsillae in homine, in sue glandulae.* Notice the double alliteration in this line.

916. **calices**: here 'vegetable dishes' or 'tureens,' cf. Ov. Fast. v. 509 *stant calices; minor inde fabas, olus alter habebant.*

917. **seriae**: large earthenware jars, chiefly used to hold wine or oil; they were smaller than the *dolium* (which would hold a man, Iuv. XIV. 308), but larger than the *amphora* (six gallons); at any rate, much too large for boiling.

918. **Cellas omnis**: e.g. the *cella uinaria, penaria, olearia.*

reclusit: for this force of *re* in composition see R. 2104 and cf. *reserere resignare retegere*, etc.

921. **hic quidem ut adornat**, 'to judge from Ergasilus' preparations.'

aut ei: I have inserted *ei* to complete the line and the sense; most editors insert *in hoc* after *nam.*

ACT V. SCENE II.

922. **Ioui disque**: see on 868.

923. **Quom** 'because' is not used with the indicative after Cic., and in Cic. only after *laudo gratulor*, etc. In the earlier writers this latter is its most frequent use, but it is also found in other phrases. Instances are (i) in Cicero, Fam. IX. 14 *gratulor tibi quom tantum uales*, pro Mil. 36, 99 *te quidem, quom isto animo es, satis laudare non possum*, (ii) in Pl. after similar words, 151 *laudo*, 374 *gratiam habeo*, Am. 681 *gaudeo*, As. 545 *laudes gratiasque habeo*, Trin. 823 *laudes ago*, Rud. 906 *ago gratias*, 1178 *gratulor*, etc., (iii) after words expressing a similar idea, 216, 356, 995, Rud. 1176 *uolup est q.*, 1183 *uoluptati est q.*, 1206 *rem diuinam facio laribus q.*, (iv) after other expressions, As. 80 *quom is me dignum cui concrederet habuit, me habere honorem eius ingenio decet*, Merc. 577 *scio pol te amare*

quom istaec praemonstras, Trin. 617 *quom absenti hic tua res distrahitur tibi, utinam te rediisse saluom uideam.*

reddacem: for the *dd* see on 764.

925. The MSS. reading scans properly, but is rejected by editors on account of (1) *quae* (neut.) after *miseriis*, (2) *carens fui* for *carebam.*

926. **hunc...haec**: δεικτικῶς, cf. 447, 1011, Mil. 377 *haec hinc huc transire potuit.*

927. **haec fides**=*huius fides*, cf. Liv. VII. 35 *quae pars maior erit, eo* (=*eorum*) *stabitur consilio*, and on 934.

re: inserted by Spengel, met. gr.; it might easily have dropped out before the following *re-*, as in Trin. 1015. *Res*= 'action' as opposed to 'words,' cf. on 52.

928. **ex animo** 'from the bottom of my heart,' cf. Ep. 526 *miserescat miser ex animo*, Sti. 1 *miseram fuisse Penelopam suo ex animo*, Trin. 397 *miser ex animo fit.* The usual phrase is *animo* (cf. Cic. Fam. XVI. 14 *angere animo*) or *animi* (locative, cf. Ep. 326 *qui te angas animi*, Cist. 215 *lassus animi*, etc.) which are less emphatic.

ex cura: *ex* denotes the source of the *dolor*; Brix quotes Poen. 69 *conicitur ipse in morbum ex aegritudine.* Cf. also Cic. Fam. XVI. 21 *quoniam igitur tum ex me doluisti, nunc ut duplicetur tuum ex me gaudium praestabo*, Rep. II. 21 *ex uolnere aeger.*

[et] was not in A, and asyndeton in such cases is the rule in Pl., see on 903.

930. **Hoc agamus** 'and now to business,' the usual phrase in recalling a person's attention to the matter in hand; cf. 444, Cas. 401 *hoc age sis, Olympio.* OL. *Si hic literatus me sinat*, Ps. 152 *hoc uide sis, ut alias res agunt. Hoc agite, hoc animum aduortite.* So 790 *age hanc rem*, Mil. 225 *hanc rem age; res subitariast*, Men. 825 *satis iocatu's, nunc hanc rem gere*, Curc. 635 *hanc rem agite atque animum aduortite.*

932. **referre gratiam** or *gratias* is 'to repay a kindness,' *habere gratiam* or *gratias* 'to be grateful'; cf. Cic. Fam. v. 11 *nec enim tu mihi habuisti modo gratiam, uerum etiam cumulatissume retulisti*, Off. II. 20 *commode autem, quicumque dixit, pecuniam qui habeat non reddidisse, qui reddiderit non habere; gratiam autem et qui rettulit habere, et qui habeat rettulisse.*

satis proinde ut: *satis* is redundant, expressing the same idea as the following clause.

934. **et petere id a te ego potero**: the reading of the MSS. *et poteris et ego potero* is open to objection; *poteris* is strange after *potes*, while *potero* (*gratiam referre*) is inapplicable, as Philop. would have nothing to do with the liberation of Tynd. Brix reads *Immo, mi pater et tu poteris et ego potero*, which gets over the first objection but not the second. Sch. reads as in the text without *id*, which however would account for the MSS. *poteris* and would refer forward to 935. The sense of the passage is 'whenever anyone may do us a kindness I shall ask you, and the gods will enable you, to requite him; just as they have put it in your power to requite this man.'

eam potestatem=*potestatem eius rei*, viz. *ut muneres*. So 358 *gratia ea*, (218) 374 *copiam istam*, 721 *istam gratiam*, Cas. 1000 *da uiro hanc ueniam*, Mil. 769 *hanc ecficiamus copiam ut*..., 971 *eam copiam sibi potestatemque facias*, Most. 909 *nec tu eam habebis gratiam*, 1146 *dat istam ueniam*, Liv. x. 13 *hic terror omnes in Q. Fabium conuertit*.

935. **bene merenti nostro** 'one who deserves well of us.' Brix compares Trin. 46 *tui beneuolentis*, 1147 *meus et tuos beneuolens*.

muneres: the verb is elsewhere deponent, except in a quotation from Turpil.; see on 593. Gertz, Brix and Uss. read *munerer*, on the ground that otherwise the next line would be a mere repetition of this. But this line is a general assertion, the next is a particular illustration; see above. *Sicut* (936) is often used loosely in introducing an illustration to explain one's meaning, as in Men. 588 *iuris ubi dicitur dies, simul patronis dicitur. Sicut me hodie nimis sollicitum cluens habuit*, Most. 371 *miserumst opus igitur demum fodere puteum ubi sitis fauces tenet; sicut ego aduentu patris nunc quaero quid faciam miser*, Poen. 504 *tardo amico nihil est quicquam inaequius, praesertim homini amanti...; sicut ego hos duco aduocatos, homines spissigradissumos*. Cf. Ep. 272, Mil. 514, 974 (and Tyrrell's note), Langen Beitr. p. 249. Notice alliteration and repetition in this line and the last.

936. **merito maxume**: *optume* is more usual, but cf. Corp. Inscr. L. 1175 *donu donunt Hercolei maxsume mereto*.

937. **Quid opust uerbis?** 'out with it'; *lingua nullast* is a strong asseveration, not a mere good-humoured concession.

938. **reliqueram**: see on 17.

939. **quem...qui**: we should say 'whom...*and* who'; cf. 707, 987.

941. **Quod bene fecisti**=(*eius*) *q. b. f.*, a relative clause dependent upon *gratia*; cf. on 217.

referetur gratia id: Sch. reads *ref. gratia: aequom postulas*, Brix *ref. gratia; et quod postulas Et si tu aliud quid*...The meaning of the MSS. reading is obvious, 'for your services a requital shall be made to you in the way you ask,' lit. '(namely) that which you ask.' The want of construction is probably due to carelessness, aided perhaps by *refertur gratia* being considered a sort of compound verb meaning 'a requital is made' and so constructed with a subject (*id ref. gr.* 'that requital is made'). Similar constructions are not uncommon in Greek, e.g. Soph. El. 556 μ' ὧδ' ἀεὶ λόγους ἐξῆρχες (=προσεφώνεις), 125 τάκεις οἰμωγὰν Ἀγαμέμνονα (=οἰμώζεις Ἀ.).

943. **suscensere quod**=*susc.* (*id*) *quod*, *quod* being relative, see on 680.

946. **meum caput**=*me*, see on 229.

labores 'troubles,' as Vergil speaks (Aen. IV. 78) of *Iliacos labores*.

euenisse: exclamatory infin., see on 783.

947. **libellam argenti**: a small silver coin of which no specimen exists; it was probably not coined after the first Punic War. *Libella* is dimin. of *libra*; it was equal in value to the copper *as*, which was originally a pound (*libra*) of copper, but was from time to time reduced in value; during the first Punic War it was worth about a penny, at the end of the second about a half-penny. Hence *libella* is used, as here, for a trifling sum; cf. Ps. 629 *tibi libellam argenti numquam credam*, Cic. Verr. II. 10, 26 *ecquis Volcatio unam libellam dedisset?*

949. **Facis benigne**: see on 843.

Licet 'by all means,' an affirmative answer to a question (as Bac. 35 *quid si loquar?* SO. *Lepide; licet*), or command (as Men. 158 *etiam concede huc.* PE. *Licet*), or request (as here, Trin. 372 *istam uolo me rationem edoceas.* LY. *Licet*).

950. **Vbi estis uos?** a way of calling slaves, cf. 830, Ps. 1136 *heus, ubi estis uos? Heus, ubi estis?* Cist. 38 *ubi estis, serui?*

951. **interibi**: a Pl. word for *interea*, as *postibi* (Poen. 108) for *postea*; cf. *inibi*.

statua uerberea 'whipping post,' also in Ps. 911. Stalagmus is called *statua* from his silence and indifference (cf. Hor.

Ep. II. 2. 8 *statua taciturnius exit*); but other statues are of marble or bronze (*marmorea, aerea*), this is of lashes (*uerberea*).

952. **quid sit factum filio**, 'what was done with my son,' cf. Truc. 799 *quid eo fecisti puero?* Mil. 973 *quid illa faciemus concubina?* Cic. Fam. XIV. 4 *quid Tulliola mea fiet?* Att. VI. 1 *quid illo fiet? quid me?* A more usual construction is *de* with the abl., as Ter. Ad. 996 *de patre quid fiet?* If the person is regarded as the indirect object, the dat. is used, as Bac. 360 *quid mihi fiet postea?* Cic. Caec. 11 *quid huic tu homini facias?*

953. **lauate**: after the journey, cf. Am. 802 *adueniens ilico me salutauisti...lauisti...*, Bac. 105 *aqua calet; eamus hinc intro ut laues; nam ut in naui uecta es...* The reflexive use of *lauare*, 'to wash oneself,' is colloquial.

ACT V. SCENE III.

954. **bone uir**: ironically, as in Curc. 610 (quoted on 240), Bac. 775 *bone serue, salue*, Mil. 364 *ubi iste est bonus seruos qui...falso insimulauit...* Stalagmus however pretends to take it seriously.

mancupium (*manu capere*) lit. 'a grasping with the hand,' a name for one of the methods of transferring property recognised by Roman Law; then 'a chattel' so transferred, more frequently used of a slave than of any other chattel.

956. **bellus** = *benulus*, diminutive of *benus* = *bonus*.

957. **ne spem ponas**: this, the MSS. reading, would mean 'do not lay aside hope' (cf. Curc. 536, Cist. 523), which does not make sense. The affirmative *ne* (*nae*, *ναί*) could hardly be used with a jussive subjunctive. Cic. Att. XIV. 21 quotes a line *hoc metuere, alterum in metu non ponere*; and I should be inclined to read *ne in spe ponas* here. The subjunctive is probably jussive, see on 434.

959. Either this v. or 968 must be omitted, and 968 is required by 969, while this v. neither makes sense in itself nor fits in with what follows; it might be emended *tua ex re; rem facies*, but I believe that it has taken the place of some line which formed the protasis to *loquere*, such as *si uis rem tuam nunc fieri ex m. m.*

960. **Recte et uera**: Sch. refers to Ter. Ad. 609 *et recte et uerum dicis*; so in Plato Phaedo 79 D καλῶς καὶ ἀληθῆ λέγεις. Notice the chiasmus.

961. The construction is *pudeat, credisne, (id) quod fatear, quom (id) autumes?* The subjunctive *pudeat* is potential (R. 1536) and *credin* is parenthetical. The antecedent of *quod* is *id* understood, which is the subject of *pudeat; fatear, autumes* are subjunctives because dependent on the subjunctive *pudeat; quom* = 'because.'

962. **in ruborem**, etc. 'will make you redden all over' (by whipping). Uss. quotes As. 426 *iussin in splendorem dari bullas?* Ps. 928 *in timorem dabo.*

963. **credo ego**: ironical parenthesis, to be taken with *inperito.*

964. **istaec aufer** 'stop that,' cf. Aul. 638 *aufer cauillam,* Men. 607 *aufer hinc palpationes,* Trin. 66 *aufer ridicularia,* Ter. Ph. 223 *aufer mi 'oportet,'* 857 *pollicitationes aufer et quod fers cedo.*

quid fers is a dependent question, whereas *quod fers cedo* (in last quotation) is a relative definition; see on 207. *Fers* = 'propose' 'offer,' as in *ferre condicionem* (180); it is probably used for the sake of the repetition *aufer...fers...feras*; and *feras* = *auferas*, as in *ferre palmam*, etc.

965. **fieri dicta conpendi**: *conpendium* 'a saving' is opposed to *expendium* or *dispendium*, 'a squandering.' With *facere* it is used in two phrases, (1) *facere conpendium alicuius rei*, e.g. Sti. 194 *ut faciam praeconis conpendium*, Ps. 605 *conpendium te facere pultandi uolo*, Rud. 180 *errationis fecerit conpendium*, and so (as what is saved is gained) without a gen. in the sense of 'making an acquisition,' Bac. 159 *conpendium edepol haud aetati optabile fecisti, quom...*; (2) *facere compendi aliquid*, e.g. Pers. 470 *conpendi feci binos panes in dies*, Bac. 183 *conpendi uerba multa iam faciam tibi*, and in the passive, as here, As. 307 *uerbi uelitationem fieri conpendi uolo*. For the gen. in this second phrase cf. *lucri facere, damni facere*; these were perhaps book-keeping terms, 'to enter as a gain, loss, or saving,' *nomine* being understood. Cf. R. 1307 and Cas. 517 *ponere ad compendium*, Mil. 781 *confer ad conpendium*. It will be seen that the MSS. reading here, *fieri dictis conpendium*, is unparalleled as well as unmetrical.

968 must be taken to mean *tuas res feceris ex malis meliusculas* (for *ex* in this sense see on 235), perhaps with an allusion to the phrase *e re tua*; but it does not seem Latin. Possibly it was originally *uerax, ex tuast re; tuas res f. m.*, which might have been corrupted into *uerax, ex tuas res*, then altered into *uerax, ex tuis rebus*.

969. **quid dignus siem**: cf. As. 491 *ne id quidem me dignum esse existumat*, Ps. 938 *si exoptem, quantum dignus es, tantum dent*... Ter. Ph. 519 *di tibi omnes id quod dignus es duint*. The acc. expresses the extent of the action, etc., denoted by a phrase which is equivalent to a verb (R. 1094); cf. Cic. Fam. VI. 8 *quid sim tibi auctor*, and *id operam do*, etc. For *siem*, see on 193.

971. **Pauca** is emphasized, 'it is few that I shall escape.'

973. **Theodoromedi Polyplusio**: cf. 277, 288.

974. **Sex minis**: see on 274, 353. Pl. always shews a business-like exactness in money-matters, a characteristic of the early Roman character. *Mina* = μνᾶ; the early Romans found the Greek combinations κλ, κμ, κν, μν difficult to pronounce and so inserted a vowel, *u* before *l* or *m*, *i* before *n*; e.g. *Aesculapius* (Ἀσκληπιός), *Hercules* (Ἡρακλῆς); *Alcumena* (Ἀλκμήνη), *Tecumessa* (Τέκμησσα), *drachuma* (δραχμή); *Procina* (Πρόκνη), *Cucinus* (κύκνος), 641 *techina* (τέχνη); *gyminasium* (γυμνάσιον), and *mina* (μνᾶ).

977. **genium**: see on 290. **te uolo**: see on 602.

ACT V. Scene IV.

980. **Quam diu**, etc. 'how long ago was that?' cf. As. 251 *iam diust factum quom discesti ab ero*, Pers. 818 *diu factumst postquam bibimus*, Most. 466 *scelus inquam factumst iam diu*.

uicensumus: *n* frequently falls away before *s*; thus *formosus* = *formonsus*, *cesor* is found for *censor*, *trimestris* = *trimenstris*; cf. *tostrina*, 266. After Augustan times *uicesimus*, *quoties*, *uicies*, etc. were written (R. 168). The short vowel before *-mus* was written *u* before Augustus' time, *i* after (R. 224). *Viginti* = (*d*)*ui*-(*de*)*cem-ti*; for the omission of the initial *d* see on 68, of the syllable *de* on 469.

983. **Quid nomen**: see on 285. **dum**: see on 160.

984. **Paegnium** = παίγνιον 'plaything,' cf. the Greek proverb quoted on 22; it is the name of a boy in the Persa.

uocitatust: frequentative, of the use of a nickname; the praenomen was not given to boys until the age of 14 (Festus s. v. *pubes*) or 17 (Scaevola ap. Val. Max.).

indidistis: sc. *ei nomen*. For the dat. *Tyndaro* see on 69.

985. **obliuisci neque nouisse**: for the omission of the antecedents see on 217.

hominibus: the genitive is more usual after *mos est*, but the dat. is not uncommon, e.g. Verg. Aen. I. 336 *uirginibus Tyriis mos est gestare pharetram.*

986. **nihili faciunda**: for the locative, see R. 1187, for the phrase see on 477.

987. **isne istic fuit** etc. 'was that boy, whom you sold to my father and who was given to me, Hegio's son?' This must be the meaning, although the reference of *is* is not made very clear; in 979 Hegio tells Phil. that S. has made an assertion which falls into two parts, (1) that he had sold a boy to Phil.'s father, (2) that this boy was Hegio's son. Phil. proceeds by questioning S. to convince himself that he is telling the truth on the first point, that he did sell a boy and that this boy is Tyndarus; he then proceeds to the second point, *isne istic fuit*, was that boy H.'s son? If it had not been suggested who the boy was, he would have asked *quis istic fuit?* As it is, he substitutes *isne* in reference to the suggested answer. Hence S.'s answer *Huius filius*. The passage is usually taken to mean 'was the boy you sold the same boy that was given to me?,' a question the answer to which S. has already given Phil. in 982, and to which his next words *huius filius* give no answer at all. For the asyndeton *quem...qui*, where we should say "whom...*and* who," cf. 707, 939.

989. **Viuitne is homo?** so Hegio calls his son *is homo* in 337. We must suppose that H. is so excited that he did not catch what S. said in 984.

nil curaui ceterum: not 'I cared for nothing else,' but 'I cared nothing about what followed,' *nil* standing for an emphatic *non*, as in 16, 32, 103 etc. For the asyndeton, see on 575.

990. **Quid tu ais?** see on 627.

991. **argumenta loquitur**: cf. Am. 1087 *argumenta eloquar*, Rud. 1180 *argumentis hanc rem magis exquirere. Argumenta* are facts which go to prove something: *argumentum* is also used for the reasoning by which the facts are marshalled and their bearing shewn; cf. Quint. v. 10. 11.

nam: corroborative, see on 464.

995. **Eheu, quom**, 'alas, that,' *quom* giving the reason for the exclamation: cf. on 923 and Poen. 791 *eheu quom ego habui ...*; so *ei mihi, quom* in Men. 303, Mil. 1358, etc.

plus minusque feci quam 'have done and left undone more than'; he means that he has done more in the way of punishment and less in the way of kindness than he ought.

quam me aequom fuit: Brix takes *me* as the subject of *facere* understood. Roby (1201) would take it as abl., on the analogy of *dignus*; cf. Bac. 488 *quam me atque illo aequom foret*, Mil. 619 *neque te decora neque tuis uirtutibus*; so probably Rud. 47 *leno, ut se aequomst, flocci non fecit fidem.*

996. **Quod** is relative not causal, the antecedent *id* being omitted (see on 217); for *crucior id* see on 600.

modo si=*si modo*, Gr. *μόνον εἰ* with optative; the subjunctive is really conditional, with the apodosis suppressed, thus amounting to a wish; see R. 1582.

possiet: see on 193.

997. **eccum** is used with an acc. if no verb follows, e.g. 1015, Bac. 568 *duas hic intus eccas Bacchides*, Most. 549 *Philolachetis eccum seruom Tranium*; if a verb follows its subject is usually in the nom. as in 1005, Bac. 611 *Mnesilochus eccum maestus progreditur foras*, Ter. Eun. 79 *eccam ipsa egreditur*, but is sometimes attracted into the acc., as in Am. 1005 *sed eccum Amphitruonem aduenit*, Mil. 1290 *sed eccum Palaestrionem stat cum milite.*

ornatus: referring to his chains and his pick; cf. Ter. Ad. 176 *ornatus esses ex tuis uirtutibus*; for *ex* 'according to' see on 347.

ACT V. Scene V.

998. **multa saepe**: pleonasm, cf. 44, 328.

picta: Uss. mentions the Νεκυῖαι of Polygnotus at Delphi and of Nicias at Athens.

Acherunti: locative, R. 434; so *Carthagini* (Poen. 1038), *Sicyoni* (Cist. 159), *temperi*, *ruri*; in nouns of the 3rd declension its place is usually taken by the abl.

999. **nulla...ubi**: 'no place is so fit to be called Acheron as where,' *atque* being comparative.

1000. **illic**: pronoun, with *locus*.

ibi demum 'there and there alone,' see on 105.

1002. **monerulae** is the reading of the MSS. here and in As. 694; the usual form is *monedula*. For birds as boys' pets, cf. Plin. N. H. x. 29. 44 *habebat puer...luscinias, psittacos, merulas*.

1003. **anites**, for *anates*, occurs also in Cic. Nat. D. II. 48, 124.

quicum: here plural, see on 101.

1004. **aduenienti** repeats *ubi illo adueni*.

upupa means both a hoopoe and a pick or mattock, perhaps so called from its resemblance to the curved beak of a bird.

qui is abl. fem. (see on 101).

delectem need not be an instance of the irregular sequence of tenses noticed on 28, for Tynd., not yet knowing that his work in the quarries is over, says 'a pick has been given me (perfect, not aorist) to amuse myself with'; so in Am. 195 *me a portu praemisit domum ut nuntiem...ut gesserit*, 'has sent me before,' 870 *ueni ut feram* 'I have come,' etc. On the other hand the aorist-perfect is certainly sometimes followed by the present subjunctive.

1006. **quid 'gnate mi'?** 'what do you mean by "*gnate mi*"?' cf. Bac. 114 *huc*. L. *Quid 'huc'?* 147 *caue malo*. L. *Quid 'caue malo'?* Mil. 27 *elephanto praefregisti brachium*. P. *Quid 'brachium'?* A. *Illud feminur uolui dicere*, 316 *id quod nusquam uides*. P. *Quid 'nusquam'?* 324 *illam uidi domi*. S. *Quid 'domi'?*

1008. **lucis tuendi**: *lux* is also masculine in Aul. 741 (according to Nonius), Cist. 260, Ter. Ad. 841; consequently this is not an instance of the usage noted on 852. The phrase, which Tyndarus applies to his re-appearance above ground (cf. 730 *sub terra*) is also used of being born, e.g. in Cic. Rosc. Am. 22 *ut propter quos hanc suauissimam lucem aspexerit eos indignissime luce priuarit*.

1009. **Et tu**: sc. *salue*, as in Poen. 1039 *salue*. A. *Et tu edepol, quisquis es*, Pers. 706 *uale*. S. *Et uos*. The word is often expressed, e.g. Mil. 1315 *salue*. P. *Et tu salue*, Poen. 808 *uos ualete*. A. *Et tu uale*.

aerumnam exigo: *exigere* is generally (if not always) used with words signifying a period of time, like *aetatem uitam noctem tempus*. The reading of B (and apparently of A) is *exiguo*, which suggests *exequo*=*exsequio*=*exsequor* (cf. 195 *hanc* *aerumnam exsequi*); Priscian, VIII. p. 799 mentions *sequo* as having been used in early Latin for *sequor*.

1010. **faxo uenies**: see on 801.

1011. **surpuit uendidit**: for the asyndeton cf. on 791.

1013. **Paruolum**: this older form of the diminutive termination *-ulus* is only retained after *e*, *i* or *u* (R. 856). Notice the repetition.

1014. **Illic...hunc**: referring to the same person, Stalagmus; see on 548. Sch. supposes two half-lines to have fallen out after *nam*, such as

nam *huius filium gnouit probe,*
Quom ei occurrit: ita prensum hunc

1015. **Quin**: the MSS. reading is open to three objections, (i) the repetition of the question in 1016, (ii) the difficulty of explaining the acc. *filium*, (iii) the improbability that Tynd. after hearing this wonderful news would answer only by referring to Philop., who has not yet been mentioned; (on the other hand it is quite natural that Tynd. in 1016, unable to grasp the whole situation, should ask a question on the point last mentioned, the one point he understands). The MSS. reading makes him seem to have mastered the whole situation and perceived the one point still unexplained; Phil.'s repetition in 1018 shews that this is not the case. Schoell's theory of a lacuna in which *huius filium* occurred meets the two latter objections.

eccum: see on 997; here used of persons not present, as in 169, Am. 120 *nam meus pater nunc intust eccum Iuppiter*, Aul. 781 *eccillam domi*, Bac. 568 (quoted on 997).

fratrem germanum: emphatic tautology, as in Men. 1102 *fratres germanos duos geminos, una matre natos et patre uno uno die.*

1016. **Quid tu ais?** see 289.

1018. **fur tuos** 'the man who stole you,' see R. 1315. Phil. repeats himself, as Tynd. has not yet thoroughly grasped the situation. Brix considers 1011—1017 an interpolation.

1020. **erga te**: cf. Am. 1101 *utut erga me meritast.* The words *erga te*, which Sch. inserts, might easily have been inserted before *ergo*; this would also account for the omission of TY. in BE. Other editors insert *merito* before *meritam.*

Ergo: see on 383: notice repetition and alliteration.

1021. **dic...tun es?** a quasi-dependent question, see on 207 and R. 1761.

1022 is considered by Fl. Uss. Brix and others to be a suggested variation of the next line. *Quom recogito* occurs in 51, Curc. 375, Sti. 301.

1023. **Nunc demum**: see on 105.

in memoriam regredior: the nearest parallels seem to be Pers. 640 *se in memoriam inducat* (c. gen.), Ter. Ph. 383 *redige* (*me*) *in memoriam*, Cic. Cat. M. 7 *in memoriam redeo mortuorum.*

1024. **Quasi per nebulam**: an inaccurate metaphor, as applied to hearing; cf. Ps. 463 *quae quasi per nebulam scimus atque audiuimus.*

1025. **Conpedibus**: for the abl. see R. 1212 and cf. Cic. Fam. III. 12 *leua me hoc onere*, Fin. IV. 24 *qui uirtute student, leuantur uitiis, leuantur erroribus.*

1026. **id praeuortier**: see on 460.

1027. **ut arcessatur faber ut**: cf. on 367.

1028. **peculi**: see on 20, and for the form see R. 351: Stalagmus alludes to *dem*, 'as I have no savings I ought to have something given to me.'

feceris: sc. *si quid mihi des* (Poen. 928) or *dederis*; the perf. subj. represents the fut. perf. indic.

CATERVA=*grex* 'the company of actors,' who speak the epilogue in the Cist. In the As. also the epilogue is headed GREX, in the Epid. POETA. In the Bac. there is no heading.

1029. **ad pudicos mores**: for *ad* 'in accordance with' see on 783, for *pudicos mores* cf. 55—58.

1031. **pueri suppositio**: as in the Truc.; *argenti circumductio* is a common incident.

1032. **Neque ubi**: i.e. *neque argumentum hic est, ubi* 'nor is there here a story, wherein'; the regular construction would be *neque hic...liberat*, cf. 57.

1034. **Vbi** 'whereby': for this colloquial use of *ubi* here and in 1032 see on 837.

si uobis placet: *placet* is impersonal, 's'il vous plaît'; if its subject were *comoedia*, *et si placuimus* would be mere repetition.

1035. odio: predicative dative, see on 259; here *odio esse* = 'to be a bore,' as in Ps. 1264 *nec esse odio nec sermonibus morologis utier*.

signum hoc: perhaps δεικτικῶς, with the motion of applauding, but more probably *hoc* refers to what follows, *plausum date*.

INDEX.

CAMBRIDGE: PRINTED BY JOHN CLAY, M.A. AT THE UNIVERSITY PRESS.